The Path
of
Least
Resistance

Also by Robert Fritz

A Short Course in Creating What You Always Wanted to
But Couldn't Because Nobody Ever Told You How
Because They Didn't Know Either

The Path
of
Least
Resistance

Learning to Become the
Creative Force in Your Own Life
REVISED AND EXPANDED

Robert Fritz
FOUNDER OF DMA

FAWCETT COLUMBINE

New York

For my son, Ivan

C o n t e n t s

Part Three
Transcendence

A c k n o w l e d g m e n t s

Many people have contributed greatly to this book's development: first and foremost my editor, Betsy Rapoport, who was instrumental in helping me form this new edition; Joelle Delbourgo for her vision and support of this project; and Jacques de Spoelberch, friend and agent, for his untiring work as champion of this book; Louis Savary, who was the major editor for the first edition of *The Path of Least Resistance* and a wonderful contributor to the current version; Mark Penzer for his editorial help; and Robert Hanig for his kind words in this book's preface.

I also am grateful to my assistant, Tricia Folsom, who brought materials and people together as she directed the logistics of this project; Cheryl Sylvester, for her graphics; my lovely lady, Rosalind Hanneman, who was always there to support me, read manuscripts, offer advice, and help run our household; and my son Ivan, who would often surprise me with a welcome cup of coffee, a real enthusiasm for the project, and a quick wit that always charmed the environment.

I thank Peter Senge for the years of discussion and debate about the essence of systems and structure; Charlie Kiefer for his insights and support throughout the years; all of the music and art teachers I have ever had; and all of the musicians, composers, and artists with whom I have ever worked.

In addition, my work with the DMA executive staff, Robert Hanig, Graciela Cummins, Ed Pace-Schott, Greg Murphy, as well as with the rest of the DMA staff, DMA local coordinators, and all the TECHNOLOGIES FOR CREATING® instructors throughout the world, is a continuing source of inspiration, profound friendship, and love.

P r e f a c e

In the early seventies I was privileged to be a member of a small dance company in New York City. One of my favorite aspects of this rich and exceptionally valuable experience was interacting with the other performing companies and individuals who shared the same building or were part of the then tight-knit avant-garde community. When not rehearsing or stretching, which dancers are required to do endlessly, I would observe some of the greatest names in contemporary dance, theater, music and filmmaking conducting master classes or creating their latest pieces: people like Martha Graham, Alwin Nikolais, Murray Louis, Merce Cunningham, Andre Gregory, and Ed Emshwiller to name a few. As a relative novice with little or no knowledge of who these giants were or were supposed to be, I was unfettered by any preconceived sense of awe or intimidation. In fact, I found many of them to be the most purposeful, vital, and inspiring individuals I had ever met.

I witnessed daily what appeared to be a remarkable balance of passion, critical judgment, enjoyment and enduring drive; these artists could express themselves wholly without apparent inhibition or concern for anything other than a full, accurate, and penetrating expression of their inner vision. I was almost always astonished by the final results they would produce, and the animation and enthusiasm they embodied spoke strongly to something fundamental but as yet unarticulated inside me.

I was raised in a melting-pot neighborhood in New York City, where children were generally encouraged to curb their aspiration and find some uninteresting but secure niche in our tangled society to assure themselves of a "better life." Needless to say, the experience of people doing *their own work* and exemplifying this kind of freedom and spirited brilliance came as something of a shock. After all, here were people who were doing what they cared about and wanted to do most without regard for what others would think or whether their activities fulfilled the kinds of needs our fickle society currently dictated.

I noticed that although many of my peers were good at creating what they wanted in their art, many fell far short of producing results of a similar magnitude and consistency in their lives in general. Although choreographing and performing dance pieces was the most satisfying and enriching endeavor I had yet discovered, the notion of bringing this kind of life experience of self-determination and profound satisfaction to the rest of my family, friends, and society in general, ignited an even greater flame.

What followed was a period of searching and experimenting to discover or create an approach that could help people develop and master this profound ability. I read most of the popular books, participated in many of the contemporary courses, and applied a variety of benign to extreme disciplines that promised to impart knowledge on creating. I found that although some approaches and philosophies contained many interesting and valid principles and were, for the most part, well-meaning, other elements that individuals were "encouraged" to accept were just plain absurd. This included versions of having to swallow some unbelievable fiction, becoming a practicing zealot, wearing some subtle uniform, adopting some strange vernacular or behavior, or having to manipulate yourself and others in some way to assure your continued "enlightenment."

Having acquired a taste for truth, unique human expression, and inner and outer freedom during my experience in the arts, I could not understand how these tremendous contradictions in the human potential movement could exist or be rationalized. I decided to do my best, on my own, to embody and express my deepest values and my respect for truth and individual freedom. Somehow I knew that a life built on anything less was not only impractical, but was diametrically opposed to the creative process.

I then became a manager at one of the fastest growing high-tech companies in the U.S. What attracted me to this company was its reputation for innovation, honesty, and fairness. After my interview process I was convinced that here at last were a group of people outside of the arts who understood what it took to create far-reaching results while bringing out the best in its members. Here was an opportunity too for me to be true to my values, do my best, and encourage others to do the same. The first year I was there the company grew over 400 percent and despite the extreme pressure that this type of growth produces, the company stayed true to its values. It then reorganized to prepare for its next surge of growth. Most of the values that had attracted myself and others to the company seemed now to be disregarded. This produced a pervasive yet hushed disillusionment yielding a tremendous reduction in focus and directed activity. It gave a clear message to the staff that it was not what you could do but who you knew or how you played the game that mattered. Needless to say, I was in the front ranks of the exodus this change of orientation produced.

Around that time a close friend told me about a course that helped people create the lives they wanted. I normally would not have listened but he knew me well and seemed so sure yet unobtrusive. It was as if he was telling the truth without needing my agreement or interest to bolster his ego or the value of his point of view. He also seemed to be more calm, focussed, and present than I'd ever seen him before. I decided to give it a chance and take the course. He was right. The values, dignity, and respect for the individual embodied by the technology I studied was moving, and more importantly, the results I created were fantastic and lasting. I was excited to learn that one could train to be an instructor for this course. Here was something that I could share with people that could reunite them with their natural power to create the lives they wanted without the need to resort to compromise, manipulation, or the denial of some aspects of reality.

I immediately became a teacher of TECHNOLOGIES FOR CREATING® Basic Course and met Robert Fritz, the founder of DMA, Inc., and the creator of this wonderful approach. As I might have guessed, here was a person well versed in the western artistic tradition, someone with a highly developed, intimate mastery of the creative process. Robert Fritz gained his mastery in the only way possible, through actually creating tangible results. Results like playing music with some of the most accomplished musicians in the world, successfully teaching first-year composition students to produce fourth-year results as an instructor at the New England Conservatory of Music, and being commissioned to write original music by special groups of the Boston Symphony Orchestra. Here was a man with not only the talent to create, but the ability to teach others to do the same.

I was stirred and challenged by my conversations with Robert

Fritz about TECHNOLOGIES FOR CREATING® and his vision for our civilization. Stirred because his vision focused on enabling individuals and organizations to take their destiny into their own hands and create the lives they want based on truth, freedom, health, and self-determination. Challenged because the vision included the whole of our civilization and the technology of Robert Fritz's course had the inherent qualities to make it happen. I'd heard about its successful use in situations as varied as villages in Uganda, in *Fortune* 500 companies, with Olympic athletes, in maximum-security prisions, and with the general public. I joined the organization and its founder. Their vision, focus, proven abilities, and accessible technology has aided me in my purpose of assisting others to create the life and experiences they want and to fully express their human spirit.

The Path of Least Resistance contains much of the essence of Robert Fritz's remarkable approach and perspective. Throughout the book, Fritz presents an unending wealth of dramatically original and even revolutionary ideas, concepts, and principles. His training as a composer of music and his experience as an entrepreneur become apparent in his lucid account of the part universal structure plays in human activity, from social and political movements to our daily lives. Citing seemingly opposite and antagonistic movements and points of view, he exposes the dominant structure of each and with brilliance and precision unmasks their astonishing, and at times frightening, similarity—as when he shows how those who would ban nuclear weapons and those who would build them often use the same fundamentally unworkable structure to achieve their opposing goals. With unerring insight, Fritz demonstrates how the exact same structural principles are often in play in an individual's personal life and in the lives of organizations and institutions.

The Path of Least Resistance is a thrilling and valuable adventure. It embodies the possibility that anyone can live a life of success, fulfillment, and deep satisfaction, a life in which the realization of one's highest aspirations becomes not only possible but probable.

Robert Hanig
President of DMA, Inc.
October, 1988

F o r e w o r d

When I set out to do a "little" revision of *The Path of Least Resistance*, it looked like a fairly easy job. I planned to add some new material and update about 20 percent of the book. But as I faced each old chapter, I found that I wanted to rewrite a great deal more of what I found. I ended up revising about seventy percent of the book.

Since this book is about the creative process, I wanted to share this story with you. There was no pressing need for me to change the book greatly. I was relatively happy with the first version. The book had had a wide audience, had sold exceptionally well, and had been useful to many people. But as I began to work on the revision, I found I was now able to say what I didn't have the voice to say four years before. The book itself has a vision. As I compared my original version with my new vision, I saw a discrepancy, and I wanted to write a new book that fulfilled that vision. This is the normal state in the creative process. In fact, throughout this book you will read about discrepancy as one of the most useful forces in creating.

When I first considered revising *The Path of Least Resistance*, I was unenthusiastic. Before I began to sit down with the project, doing a revision seemed like taking a step backwards, almost to a different era in my life. The day I started to work on it, however, I suddenly realized what an incredible opportunity it was to re-express and update my ideas. This illustrates another principle of the creative process. No amount of speculation about the creative process will indicate how it will actually turn out. There are joys and frustrations that are impossible to predict. This makes it all the more exciting.

The creative process is alive. It is improvisation. It is form, and style, and excitement, and drudgery. And it is one of the most powerful and intimate involvements with life I know.

Much of the work in this book has been developed over the past fifteen years through the TECHNOLOGIES FOR CREATING® (TFC) curriculum. This curriculum is taught in basic and advanced courses through one of the companies I founded, DMA, Inc.

Teaching the principles of the creative process is one of the most exciting and important methods of helping people learn to create the results they want in their lives. TFC courses have been taught throughout the world. The students come from every walk of life and every educational background. Many TFC courses are offered in some of the largest corporations in the world, others are taught in living rooms, with students from the general public. TFC courses are conducted in educational settings and even in maximum-security prisons. The standard TFC curriculum is conducted in the Third World, and specially designed TFC courses are taught in villages in rural Africa.

I can make one observation based on this experience: Most people can learn to create.

The terms *creating* and *creativity* have been used over and over until they have become banal. As a professional creator (composer, artist), I have not especially appreciated the way these terms have been misappropriated to describe noncreative acts. The *creating* and *creativity* I am writing about come from the tradition of the arts and sciences, not from psychology, the human potential movement, New Age thinking, management training, or metaphysics, which all use the terms creating and creativity in a different and often vague sense.

The participants in TFC classes learn the same creative process used by artists to paint, architects to design buildings, composers to write music, and filmmakers to create films. They learn how to apply the principles of creating used by professional creators to create what they want in their everyday lives, both personal and professional.

In TFC classes, people learn how to create by creating. The focus is not only on the specific results the participant chooses, but also on his or her life. Most people do not think of their life as a subject of the creative process, and as the TFC students apply the principles of creating to their lives, their lives begin to change.

Creating is a skill that develops over time. Like any skill, you build mastery with many experiences over weeks, months, and years. For this reason, this, or any book, can only be an opening. But openings can be profound, if they lead to real and lasting change. Experiment with the principles in this book. Apply the ideas in your own life. Begin to work with the creative process in various areas of your life.

Many of the principles you will find in this book are unique, yet many readers tell me they have an immediate intuitive recognition of them even if they have never read or heard them before. Are these principles just common sense? Yes and no. The principles in this book are easy to observe in your own life. You will recognize in your own life many of the structures and patterns I describe. In this sense you are familiar with them. But there is also another world being described in *The Path of Least Resistance*, one involving the nature of structure. Most of us have not been exposed to the subject of structure and how it can influence our lives. For many people, these insights have been eye-opening. When you begin to explore the realm of structure, some of the reoccurring patterns in your life will begin to make sense. You will begin to understand how these patterns came about, why you might not have been able to rid yourself of the unwanted patterns, and how you can build new structures that will lead to the types of circumstances you want.

Since the first publication of this book, I have received mail from all over the world from people who have been able to begin to live in the same orientation as creators. These letters have been truly inspiring to me. Lives have changed because of this work. For that, I am truly grateful.

R. F.
October, 1988

The Path
of
Least
Resistance

I n t r o d u c t i o n

In the early sixties, as a composition student at The Boston Conservatory of Music, I became aware that there was more to composing music than applying the techniques of harmony, counterpoint, form, and structure that we were being taught. The art of musical composition seemed to have a meta-musical dimension which at once attracted and mystified me. I wondered what that extra, unseen, unspoken quality was that the great works of art possessed beyond what could be taught in any conservatory.

Little by little, I began to observe connections between the creative process applied to music, painting, sculpture, dance, drama, film, poetry, and literature and how that very same creative process applied to the way people I knew lived their daily lives.

As a composer and musician, I found the creative process endlessly fascinating because in it were integrated a multitude of dimensions of human nature, from the intellectual to the spiritual, the rational to the intuitive, the subjective to the objective, the technical to the metaphysical, the scientific to the religious.

Creators are an enigma to many people, because creators seem to tolerate apparent contradictions quite easily. To creators, however, these are not contradictions but opposites that need to be balanced continually, as a bicyclist continually shifts weight from left to right to maintain balance with the least amount of effort. Creators live simultaneously in many universes. Each universe has its own set of governing principles. When a creator performs a creative act, many separate and distinct universes suddenly converge in perfect alignment.

Physicists who work with the time-space continuum tend to open themselves to transcendent and mystical experience as they explore those dimensions more and more deeply. Creators tend to experience a similar kind of opening as separate universes come together to form the single entity that is the fruit of their creation. And so it was natural for me as a composer to search beyond music, to look to all of life for principles of the creative process.

In exploring creativity, I was drawn toward two distinct but related fields: metaphysics and nature. I began to investigate various systems of metaphysics in the early sixties. I began this investigation with a healthy degree of skepticism. Much of what I found was alloyed with rigid dogma and superstition, both of which I find supremely unattractive to this day. But I also found there some principles which, when applied, release the human spirit in powerful ways. One of the fundamental principles is the relationship between your direct actions and circumstances. One way or another, the proponents of metaphysics try to understand the laws governing the universe, so that individuals can become more of the creators of the circumstances in their own lives. The general metaphysical idea is this: Find out how the universe is, then act accordingly. The hope is that these actions will lead to more of what you want, be it spiritual, material, or psychological. After years of involvement in various approaches, I lost interest.

The years I spent creating music and art were much more of a direct experience of the understandings toward which metaphysicians work. Creating, I have concluded, is the best window to the universe I know.

The second area of vital interest to me involved learning about physical nature. I spent much time in the woods observing cycles, forces in relation to each other, growth and decay, and how each element of nature affected the other elements to which it was systemically related. I was tremendously excited to find natural principles I could then use as part of the structure of the music I was composing. Because of these observations, I was able to invent new musical forms and structures and understand traditional ones, such as the sonata-allegro form, in ways I never had before.

After I received my master's degree in composition, I moved to New York City and then to Los Angeles to work as a musician. During those years, I learned more about the creative process by working with some of the most talented people in the world. Creating, as seen from inside the profession, was completely different from what I had learned at the conservatory. I saw the difference between the professionals who must create on a consistently high level and academicians who do not. The demands of professional creators generate completely different standards of measurement for use in the creative process, ones that tend to be more practical and useful in bringing into being the results a creator is creating.

In 1975, again living in Boston, I was often asked to teach people what I knew about creating. I had no notion then of forming an organization to teach people how to use the creative process, because I was still very active as a professional musician and composer. I phoned a few people I thought would be qualified and suggested to them that they meet each other and put together a course that would teach people to create the lives they wanted. I hoped my friends would develop this course so that I could recommend it to others. When I phoned them again to see what they had produced, they told me they had met and eaten a wonderful Italian dinner, but had not gotten around to discussing the kind of course I had envisioned. So, I eventually created the course myself.

After I taught the first class in 1975, I was hooked. The results the participants were able to create for themselves were, in many cases, miraculous.

One of the students was able to create a new career for herself as an "in-house" consultant for a high-tech firm. She had worked at one of the largest computer companies in New England, but the job she had was a dead-end position. She had been there for over twelve years. During the TFC course she had decided that she wanted an exciting job that included some travel, work with effective people, an opportunity to make significant contributions to any project in which she was involved, and high pay. By the fourth week of her TFC course she had begun her new job. The job she wanted did not ever exist before in her company. As part of her creative process she conceived of exactly what she wanted to do, what effect she wanted to have, and how it would benefit her company. When she first told her department head about her idea, he told her it wasn't possible. Undaunted, she continued to study her plan and the company's business direction. Four days after her first talk with her department head, she made an appointment with a senior vice-president of the firm. At first the vice-president did not see the point of forming this new position, but she had done her homework. She made such a convincing case for the new position she had wanted to create that he decided to give it to her. She did such an effective job in her new position that within a year she had a staff, a big budget, and the gratitude of the corporation.

Another TFC student was an auto mechanic. He had worked for a large chain of repair shops, but he wanted to move to the southwest and begin his own repair shop. This would be the biggest move of his life. Once he knew his goal, he began to use the techniques he was learning about translating desire into effective actions. He managed to create the resources and make the contacts he needed. Within six months he had become a partner in a busy repair shop in Santa Fe, New Mexico.

Other students have also created more and more of the results they wanted. Some of them have become involved in wonderful relationships, important projects, exciting work, enhanced career opportunities, better health, and increased financial circumstances. Even though the results the students were creating are exciting, perhaps the most profound change has not been expressed in any one result, but in a new ability. These students have been able to create almost anything that mattered to them. They have developed this skill on a conscious level. Because of this, they have been able to relate to their entire lives quite differently. Instead of being driven by the prevailing circumstances, they now know that they can create what they want in any circumstances. This is not a matter of a fictional attitude manufactured by hype and emotional fervor, but a matter of reality. The new attitudes have come from the ability to create. The students have learned the skill of the creative process by the practice of creating one result after another. Throughout the history of TFC, students learning consistently to create what mattered to them was the best result of all.

Shortly after the first TFC course I founded DMA, Inc., an organization dedicated to teaching the principles of the creative process, and I developed the TECHNOLOGIES FOR CREATING® curriculum.

I chose the letters D, M, and A, (DMA, Inc.) because of their Kabbalistic meaning. D stands for the creative force or creative intelligence, M stands for focused and free-flowing consciousness, and A stands for the life force or life breath (prana). Thus the creative force, through the vehicle of consciousness, brings forth the life force. In other, and perhaps better words, creating expresses the height of the human spirit.

During this period, I began training others to teach the DMA course, and simultaneously continued to explore what creates real and lasting growth and change in individual lives. Currently, there are more than one thousand active TECHNOLOGIES FOR CREATING® instructors teaching throughout the United States, Canada, England, Sweden, Holland, Germany, France, and several other European countries as well as Australia, Africa, and India. At this writing there are more than fifty-thousand graduates of the program.

In the late Seventies, the distinguished organizational expert Charlie Kiefer invited Peter Senge, Peter Stroh, and me to join him in starting Innovation Associates, a company dedicated to helping people build organizations using principles of the creative process. IA has become one of the most advanced firms in the field of organizational development.

In 1980, I developed a system for observing, understanding, and working with the long-range structural patterns in play in people's lives. This was an important discovery for me, since I had noticed that such patterns seem to produce dysfunctional behavior and results, habitually and predictably. I named this field of study Macrostructural Patterns.

The study of structure has always fascinated me—musical structure, visual structure, systemic structure, and especially the structure of nature and the natural order. When I began to apply structural principles to human development, I found that many of the traditional approaches to growth and human potential only reinforced limiting patterns and often created effects that were quite the opposite of what they were designed to do. This new structural discipline has now been used in psychotherapy with superb results. Many patients and clients of psychotherapists using macrostructural patterns report dramatic changes in their lives, changes that previously had seemed impossible.

In the early eighties, I founded The Institute for Human Evolution, a nonprofit, scientific, and educational organization that has the mandate to further explore, develop, and create structural approaches to human growth in the areas of psychology, psychotherapy, education, and organizational development.

Based on my work with structure and the creative process, in 1981 I made a major revision in the DMA Basic Course. Immediately, DMA instructors began reporting that their students were creating even more wonderful results and changes in their lives; vastly more important was that these changes were both more fundamental and easier for their students to create. There was something new occurring which had to do with a shift in the basic structures at play—in the ways students were approaching and living their lives.

In 1984, I created a system for consultants to use in understanding and changing the underlying structures in their clients' lives and organizations. This has led to some of the most dramatic results we have seen in helping people adopt new, effective structural patterns. This work is called *Structural Consulting*.

Through the DMA, Inc. business division, a combination of TFC trainings and structural consulting has helped companies shift to a new orientation, one of creating rather than problem-solving. This work is one of the best technologies for change available to organizations, large and small.

The work continues to develop as we delve deeper into the possibilities of the creative process. If anything could truly change the face of our civilization, it is the creative process. More and more, the TFC ideas and practices are changing lives. Once someone has mastered his or her own creative process, permanent change is the norm. Once you know how to read, you do not lose that ability, and once you know how to create what most matters to you, you do not lose that ability.

The Path of Least Resistance presents an entirely different approach to the subject of human development. This new approach has made reachable what psychotherapists, psychologists, and participants in various human potential workshops were never able to reach through their own disciplines—not only a mastery of the creative process (which by itself would be revolutionary), but the ability to make a shift in fundamental orientation to an entirely separate and unique life stance: the orientation of the creative.

Furthermore, this book is about a new understanding of structure as a dominant factor in the life of the individual and how the laws of the natural order always move according to structural principles. We all recognize the major structural principle that governs the laws of movement in nature, yet only a few apply it consciously. This principle is that energy always moves along the path of least resistance and that any change you attempt to make in your life will not work if the path of least resistance does not lead in that direction. Throughout this book you will learn to form new structures in your life that will enable you to direct the path of least resistance to where you truly want to go.

Part One

Fundamental Principles

The Path
of
Least Resistance

Forming the Path

People who come to my native Boston often ask me, "How did they ever design the layout of the roads?" There appears to be no recognizable city planning in Boston. The Boston roads were actually formed by utilizing existing cow paths.

But how did these cow paths come to be?

The cow moving through the topography tended to move where it was immediately easiest to move. When a cow saw a hill ahead, she did not say to herself, "Aha! A hill! I must navigate around it." Rather she put one foot in front of another, taking whichever step was easiest at that moment, perhaps avoiding a rock or taking the smallest incline. In other words, what determined her behavior was the structure of the land.

Each time cows passed through the same area, it became easier for them to take the same path they had taken the last time, because the path became more and more clearly defined.

Thus, the structure of the land gave rise to the cows' consistent pattern of behavior in moving from place to place. As a result, city planning in Boston gravitates around the mentality of the seventeenth-century cow.

Moving Along the Path

Once a structure exists, energy moves through that structure by the path of least resistance. In other words, *energy moves where it is easiest for it to go.*

This is true not only for cows, but for all of nature. The water in a river flows along the path of least resistance. The wind blowing through the concrete canyons of Manhattan takes the path of least resistance. Electrical currents, whether in simple devices, such as light bulbs, or in the complex circuitry found in today's sophisticated computers, flow along paths of least resistance.

If you watch the flow of pedestrian traffic in time-lapse photography, you can track the patterns of people walking on a busy street, avoiding each other on their way. Sometimes a pedestrian's path of least resistance is to walk straight ahead, sometimes to move to the right or left, sometimes to walk faster, and sometimes to slow down or wait a moment.

You got to where you are in your life right now by moving along the path of least resistance.

Three Insights

The rest of this book is built upon three important insights. The first is this:

You are like a river. *You go through life taking the path of least resistance.* We all do—all human beings and all of nature. It is important to know that. You may try to change the direction of your own flow in certain areas of your life—your eating habits, the way you work, the way you relate to others, the way you treat yourself, the attitudes you have about life. And you may even succeed for a time. But eventually you will find you return to your original behavior and attitudes. This is because your life is determined, insofar as it is a law of nature for you to take the path of least resistance.

The second insight is just as fundamental: *The underlying structure of your life determines the path of least resistance.* Just as the terrain around Boston determined the path of least resistance for the cows to follow and just as a riverbed determines the path of the water flowing through it, so the structures in your life determine your path of least resistance. Whether you are aware of these structures or not, they are there. The structure of the river remains the same whether there is water flowing through it or not.

You may barely notice the underlying structures in your life and how powerfully and naturally they determine the way you live.

Many continue to live the way they do, often feeling powerless and frustrated. They have attempted to make major changes in their relationships, their careers, their family, their health, and the quality of their lives, only to find themselves, a short time later, back in the same old familiar situation. They are following their old entrenched patterns.

They may have indeed made some superficial changes in their lives, but somehow nothing seems really to have changed. They know that there is more to life than what they have experienced, but they don't know how to create it.

If a riverbed remains unchanged, the water will continue to flow along the path it always has, since that is the most natural route for it to take. If the underlying structures of your life remain unchanged, the greatest tendency is for you to follow the same direction your life has always taken.

The third insight is this: *You can change the fundamental underlying structures of your life.* Just as engineers can change the path of a river by changing the structure of the terrain so that the river flows where they want it to go, you can change the very basic structure of your life so that you can create the life you want.

Furthermore, once a new basic structure is in place, the overall thrust of your life—like the power of the river's current— surges to form the results you truly want. And the direct path to those results becomes the path of least resistance.

In fact, with an appropriate change in the underlying structure of your life, the path of least resistance cannot lead anywhere except in the direction you really want to go.

The guiding principle that emanates from these three insights is this: *You can learn to recognize the structures at play in your life and change them so that you can create what you really want to create.*

What Is Structure?

The structure of anything refers to its fundamental parts and how those individual elements function in relation to each other and in relation to the whole. A human body's structure refers to its parts—the brain, heart, lungs, blood cells, nerves, muscles, and so on—and how these individual parts function in relation to each other and to the body as a whole organism.

Amy C. Edmondson, in her book *A Fuller Explanation,** describes the concepts of R. Buckminster Fuller's Synergectic Geometry:

> Thinking isolates events: "understanding" then interconnects them. "Understanding is structure," Fuller declares, for it means establishing the relationship between events.

Physicians and surgeons learn to think structurally about the human body. A surgeon considers not just a diseased organ but also the health and viability of the entire body. Blood pressure, brain waves, oxygen intake, presence of bacteria, and allergic reactions are considered in any surgical procedure.

You think structurally whenever you fill a glass with water. The elements of the structure are the glass, the water, the faucet controlling the flow of water, how much water you want in the glass, and how much water is already in the glass.

When you fill a glass, you have a goal: to fill the glass with the desired amount of water. You also have an awareness of the current situation: how much water is presently in the glass. If there is less water in the glass than the amount you desire, there will be a discrepancy in the system. You lessen this discrepancy by adding water, which you do by controlling the faucet. As the current amount of water approaches the desired amount of water, you close the faucet by degrees, slowing down the flow of water and stopping it entirely when the present amount of water is the same as the desired amount of water, thus ending the discrepancy.

Filling a glass with water may take only seconds, but within

* Published by Birkhauser Boston, Springer Verlag, Inc. 175 Fifth Avenue, New York, NY 10010.

that time a structural system is in play involving all the elements within that system.

Everything has an underlying unifying structure. Some structures are physical, such as bridges, buildings, tunnels, stadiums. Some structures are nonphysical, such as the plot of a novel, the form of a symphony, the dramatic movement of a film, or the structure of a sonnet. Whether physical or nonphysical, any structure is made up of parts that relate to one another. When these parts interact, they set up tendencies— *inclinations toward movement.*

All Structures Contain Movement

Every structure contains within it the inclination toward movement, that is, a tendency to change from one state into another state. But some structures tend to move, whereas others tend to remain stationary. The structures that tend to remain stationary consist of elements that hold each other in check. A wheel has a greater tendency toward movement than a brick. A car has a greater tendency toward movement than a skyscraper. A wheelchair has a greater tendency toward movement than a rocking chair. A rocking chair has a greater tendency toward movement than a couch.

What determines the tendency to move? The underlying structure.

Structure Determines Behavior

One of the most important insights of this book is in this principle: *Structure determines behavior.* The way anything is structured determines the behavior within that structure.

The next time you are in a building, notice how the structure of the building determines your path through it. Although you may move to your destination in a variety of ways within the building, your actions are still determined by the structure of the building. You do not walk through walls, you walk along corridors. You do not enter rooms through windows, you come through doors. You do not jump from floor to floor, you take the stairs, elevator, or escalator.

Similarly, there are fundamental structures in your life that determine the path of least resistance. The structures that have the most influence on your life are composed of your desires, beliefs, assumptions, aspirations, and objective reality itself.

As you consider your own life from a structural viewpoint, it is important that you do not mistake the structural perspective for a psychological perspective. Psychology is the study of the human psyche. If this were a book on psychological theory, we might be concerned with what makes you tick. Of course, there are many types of psychological theories and premises these days. The one commonality they share is the subject matter—the study of humankind.

In this book we are not studying the human mind, the human psyche, or human behavior, but rather the behavior of *structures*. We will then consider how a structure itself affects human behavior. The same structure may be applied to non-human matters and still function in the same way.

The study of structure is independent of and different from the study of psychology. But when we begin to understand how structure works and to apply structural principles to human behavior, two extraordinary principles become obvious.

One is that *human beings act in accordance with the underlying structures in their lives.*

Because humanity is part of nature, it should be no surprise that people act consistently with natural law. But for most of us, this is a new idea. In our culture we have been taught to ignore our relationship to nature, to treat nature simply as the stage or background that we use, adopt, tolerate, or oppose, as the case may be.

Some have called this too-common relationship between humanity and nature *the height of mankind's arrogance.* I do not agree. I think it is ignorance rather than arrogance that promotes the notion of the individual *against* the forces of nature. Many people see their life as a struggle against nature, a notion captured by composer Hector Berlioz's witty comment, "Time is the great teacher, but unfortunately it kills all of its students."

The second principle is: *Some structures are more useful than others in leading to desired results.*

Structure is "nothing personal." Someone in a structure that leads to pain, frustration, and hopelessness is not being designated by the universe as a victim of life. Put anyone else in that same structure and that person will have similar experiences.

On the other hand, put anyone in a structure that leads to fulfillment, accomplishment, and success, and that person will have these experiences.

People commonly believe that if they change their behavior, they can change the structures in their lives. In fact, just the opposite is true.

This is not to say that people are mechanistic. Each person is a rare and special individual. But each person is subject to the powerful influence of structure. You can't fool Mother Structure.

Some structures lead to oscillation and some structures lead to final destinations. A pendulum is structured to oscillate. A rocket is structured to lead to a final destination. A rocking chair is structured to oscillate. A car is structured to lead to final destinations chosen by the driver.

A Life of Oscillation

The structures in some people's lives lead to oscillation. These people have a general experience of moving forward and then backward, and then forward and then backward again. This pattern may repeat endlessly. Because of the structure in play, their attempts to change their life may work at first, and then not work, and then work again and then not work again. This is the experience of coming full circle. The feeling of being in a rut. Of winding up back at square one.

In fact, these people experience change, but it does not last. Progress seems to be only temporary.

All of us have been in this structure from time to time. Some people, however, live in this pattern. After a life filled with times of progress, followed by times of backsliding, a person can become discouraged. This feeling is captured in the Bruce Springsteen song, "One Step Up, Two Steps Back."

If you did not know there was a structure in play driving the action, you might wonder why your best attempts to change your life were ultimately neutralized.

This phenomenon is often inadequately explained by many psychotherapists. Words such as *sabotage, self-destructive,* and *failure complex* are proposed to give a plausible insight into chronic oscillation. Often the description of the phenomenon will be tied to the "solution" of the situation.

"If you are destructive, what do you have against yourself?" "Why do you try to defeat yourself?" "Why are you afraid of succeeding?" "What do you need to overcome?" "What is your resistance to change?"

The popular notion is that inner states of being—emotions, needs, fears, inhibitions, drives, instincts, and so on—generate your dysfunctional actions. Perhaps an "unresolved" relationship with your mother causes you to avoid romantic relationships. Perhaps a traumatic experience you had as a child causes you to fear authority figures. Perhaps you are an alcoholic because you were weaned a day too early.

The explanations and theories can be endless. All of them suggest that there is *something wrong with you.* The popular solution is to find out what causes the trouble and by correcting it restore yourself to a state of full functioning.

Often people spend years and small fortunes trying to fix the problems. After one problem is "fixed," another problem usually needs to be found to account for a continuing lack of accomplishment.

If you are in a structure that leads to oscillation, no solution will help. This is because these psychological solutions do not address the structure, but rather the behavior that comes from the structure.

This is not to say these approaches have absolutely no effect. However, usually their effect is temporary and is followed by backsliding. One step up, then one step back, and then another step back.

To attempt a psychological solution to what is really a structural phenomenon does nothing to change the underlying structure.

Oscillation can be slow or quick. The return to the norm can take place over a short or long period. A week, six months, a year, two years. When events move back to how the "problem" was originally described, the person is often shocked and discouraged at the lack of success.

If you are living in a structure that produces oscillation, you may consider this a problem to overcome. It is not. You are simply in a structure that is inadequate for creating what you want to create in life.

Structure and the Creative Process

We have been trained to think of situations that are inadequate for our aspirations as problems. When we think of them as problems, we try to solve them. When you are solving a problem, you are taking action to have something go away: *the problem.* When you are creating, you are taking action to have something come into being: *the creation.* Notice that the intentions of these actions are opposite.

When you think structurally, you ask better and more useful questions. Rather than asking, "How do I get this unwanted situation to go away?" you might ask, "What structures should I adopt to create the results I want to create?"

In the last fourteen years, through our work at DMA with the TECHNOLOGIES FOR CREATING® curriculum, we have seen tens of thousands of people make a shift in the underlying structures in their lives. This has not come from problem solving but through the creation of new structures. Because a change in structure will change the path of least resistance, these people have been able to bring into their lives what truly matters to them.

The most important developments in civilization have come through the creative process, but ironically, most people have not been taught to create. The creative process itself has a very different structure from the one most people have learned by default from our traditional educational systems and social upbringing. Creators come from a tradition entirely different from the one in which most of us have been raised.

The creative process uses a structure that does not oscillate but moves toward final resolution so that the creator brings into being the results he or she wants.

This book will give you a clear understanding of the tradition of the creative process, so that you can begin to create the results you want by learning the fundamental structure of the creative process. Then the path of least resistance will lead you in the direction you truly want to go.

This is not a book about how to solve your problems but a

book about how to create what you want to create. Many of you are already accomplished and successful. But if the structures in your life do not support your success, you will be limited. When you are able to shift to a structure that leads to resolution rather than oscillation, you will increase not only your *possibility* for further accomplishment but also your *probability* for further accomplishment.

Artists Don't Know What They Know

I recently led a special workshop in New York City for professional creators in the arts. The room was filled with filmmakers, novelists, poets, singers, jazz musicians, rock musicians, classical musicians, recording artists, sculptors, architects, composers, painters, computer artists, photographers, graphic designers, actors, and playwrights.

The idea for the workshop was to work only with accomplished professionals. It was a great privilege to work with this group of people who had already mastered their own creative process.

As the workshop progressed, one discrepancy became painfully clear. Most of these great creators did not apply the principles of the creative process they had mastered in their arts to their own careers and personal lives. The idea had simply never occurred to them.

Certainly when I attended the Boston Conservatory of Music, we were never taught how to apply what we were learning about composition and the creative process to our own lives. Years after I had graduated, it was a fantastic revelation to me that I could use my education, not only in composing but in creating what I wanted to create in my life.

If the creative process is so powerful, it would be natural to wonder why many artists have difficulties in their lives. *It is because they do not know what they know.*

Among the most appreciative participants in the TECHNOLOGIES FOR CREATING® curriculum are the professional creators, because they learn to take the mastery they have developed in their professions and apply it directly to their lives.

The rich tradition of the arts and sciences has been the best training ground for the creative process. Creators know how to form underlying structures that lead to the final creations they want. For them, the path of least resistance moves from their original concept to the completed result they envisioned.

Throughout history, almost every culture has had art, music, dance, architecture, poetry, storytelling, pottery, and sculpture. The desire to create is not limited by beliefs, nationality, creed, educational background, or era. This urge resides in all of us, but few of us have been raised in this tradition.

As you begin to understand how the path of least resistance works in your life, you will be able to share in one of the richest and most important traditions known to civilization. Your involvement in this tradition will not be limited to the arts, but can encompass all of your life, from the mundane to the profound.

The Reactive-Responsive Orientation

Your Childhood

One of the messages you are given from infancy is that there is a particular way of doing things. There is a right way of putting on your clothes, a right way of eating your food, a right way of crossing a street. When you were a child, your job was to learn about the world. You needed to know where the limits and boundaries were. You needed to know what your role was in your family, among your friends, and in your community.

If there is a "right" way to live life, then your job must be to learn that way. When you were a young child, the world was a mystery. You often didn't know why things happened as they did. Adults would tell you to take actions that often seemed unexplainable. You may have been asked to take these actions in a tone of voice that implied, "You should know exactly what I mean, and if you don't, there is something wrong with you."

At first you assumed that the big people knew what they were talking about. After all, they seemed to know how to do many things that seemed miraculous. They could drive cars and fix broken toys and cook food and run machines. They also spoke with a great deal of authority. When you did not fall in line, they could become threatening.

After a while you did not like being told what to do all the time. So you began conducting some experiments. You began to say no to the requests that were directed toward you. The results of your first experiments were both successful and un-successful. You began to receive a lot of attention. You liked that. But the type of attention directed toward you was not al-ways pleasant. You didn't like that so much. Gradually you may have found out how to get the positive attention, do what you wanted to, and not come under fire. Or you may have found that no matter what you tried, you were sometimes in trouble, and you couldn't predict what would set it off.

The major focus of your experiments was on learning about the world. By this time you had concluded that there was some-thing to know. You assumed that this was good, because when you demonstrated a working knowledge of the way the world was, you were often rewarded, or at least left alone.

As your own interests grew, you relied less and less on those who were taking care of you, and more and more on yourself and other people your own age. From several experiences you discovered that the big people didn't know all there was to know about how it is.

Maybe your mom told you that she could tell if you were lying by examining your tongue. If your tongue was blue, she knew you were telling a fib. She was always correct in her test of truth, so you developed confidence in the blue-tongue/fibbing relationship. Then one day you told the truth, but when your mom examined your tongue, she told you it was blue. Suddenly you had a crisis of faith. How could you have a blue tongue if you were not lying? It must be that tongues are not always accurate lie detectors. Or perhaps your mom made up the whole thing. If she did, she was the fibber. If that were the case, what else might she have told you that was not true? This raised some questions about the credibility of big people.

You still assumed that there was a way the world worked, but those who seemed to be the authorities on it were not neces-sarily always right. You began to find out on your own how the world worked. Those fellow explorers, your peers, were glad to tell you their ideas. You may have learned more about human sexuality from them than from your parents, even though some of the information may have turned out to be wrong.

One discovery you made early on was that big people were

unpredictable and capable of being unfair, unjust, petty, and dishonest. To guard against their wrath, you learned to try to psych the situation out. There seemed to be a balance between doing what you wanted to and doing what they wanted you to do. Over time you decided to be cooperative or uncooperative. Sometimes when you were being cooperative, the big people seemed to like you more. Since you also liked them, you adopted being cooperative as a policy. But you may have found that being cooperative didn't much matter. They might still not have seemed to like you, even when you tried your best to get along. If this was the case, you found no difference in the result when you were cooperating and when you weren't. This may have led to a policy of being uncooperative.

When you went to school, you were taught that the world was a particular way. At first you accepted the world as it was being presented. There were many viewpoints on how life is. Some of these viewpoints were optimistic. Some of them were pessimistic.

Over time you developed some of your own ideas. You changed your view of how life is, but you retained the assumption that life is constructed of concrete rules in operation. This opinion was central in developing your own ideas about how to live your life.

Some of the ideas concerned being useful to others or being good-looking or smart or strong or entertaining.

Some of the ideas concerned how dangerous the world is, so you must defend yourself and avoid trouble, or be a bigger threat than others, or control as much as you can to minimize danger.

Or perhaps your idea was that involvement with others can be problematic, so it is best to avoid involvement.

You may have concluded that the world is unfair, unjust, and will always manage to misunderstand you, no matter what you do. Therefore you developed resentment for this chronic mistreatment.

Once you formed your opinion about the world, the next step was to design a policy to use in relating to it. The policy was often formed by watching others who had gone before you. You found that their actions spoke louder than their words. You began to get a feel for the right path. You began to know what was expected of you.

You had many teachers about which conventions to adopt. Some of them were people close to you, such as parents, teachers, friends, and enemies. Some of them were heros, such as rock stars, movie stars, television stars, political stars, religious figures, and fictional characters. Some of your impressions came from books, films, television, fashion, and poetry.

The study of "how life really is" became relevant to your life. If you knew "how it is," you could find the right actions to adopt. You suspected that there were special people who truly knew "how it is." Many people were ready to assert that they knew. You had to find out who was accurate about it.

Perhaps you found a person or group of people who seemed to have the answers. Whether they were optimists or pessimists, the form was still the same. A view of the world, followed by actions consistent with that view.

What You Learn Growing Up

In one psychological study, three- and four-year-old children had tape recorders attached to them that recorded everything they were told. After analyzing the tapes, researchers discovered that 85 percent of what children were told was about either what they could not do or how bad they were because of what they were doing.

Much of what you learned growing up was what not to do and what to avoid. The majority of the behavioral rules you were taught as a child were based on avoidance or prevention of situations that may have been harmful to you or to the people around you. *"Don't play in the street." "Don't bother your father." "Don't play with matches." "Don't be late."*

Parents understandably want their children to avoid negative consequences. But the strategy of avoiding trouble is taught and reinforced until it can become an automatic lifetime habit. Your tendency toward avoidance can live long after you know how to cross the street or light a match.

What you really learned as a child is that circumstances are the dominant force in life. The message came in many forms: parental approval for the proper response to circumstances and disapproval for the improper response, rewards from teachers for the correct response and penalties for incorrect ones.

Our society is inundated with this concept. Fame, fortune,

celebrity status, good-citizenship awards, satisfying relationships, and wonderful families come from the "right" response to circumstances. Prison sentences, public embarrassment, and early death are penalties for the "wrong" response to circumstances.

One way or another, *most* people believe circumstances are the driving force in their life.

When circumstances are central to your life, you may feel you have only two types of choices: either to *respond* to the circumstances or to *react* against the circumstances. You can be either the "fair-haired boy" or the "last angry man."

Reacting or responding is more than just a policy of how to live your life. It becomes a way of life, a life orientation. I call this the *reactive-responsive orientation.* In this orientation you take action based on the circumstances in which you find yourself, or might find yourself in the future.

Unfortunately, most education systems reinforce this reactive-responsive orientation. One focus of education is to weave the child into the fabric of society. In fact, most school systems see their job as teaching their students how to respond.

Many students "adapt well" and learn how to respond "appropriately." Their actions, however, are not motivated by a love of learning or a thirst for knowledge, but by a desire to fit in and avoid trouble.

Some young people blatantly reject the imposition of what seem to them to be arbitrary values and rules for proper behavior. They react against the circumstances of their education or the authority of their parents. To reactive people, circumstances are still the driving force of their actions. "If only they could 'wake up' and respond as they should!" is a cry often heard at PTA meetings throughout this country.

Responsive Behavior

Responsive students usually receive adequate grades in school and actively adapt to the standards set by those in positions of authority.

As adults, people continue to be taught varieties of responses. Most approaches to the "development of human potential," for instance, encourage people to learn new and more sophisticated responses to the circumstances of life or "the universe."

There is nothing really *new* in the "New Age," just new forms of response. The orientation is identical to that of the "Old Age." Similar promises of a happy life are still used as a dangling carrot, as has been the case for centuries. The right response is still the ticket to heaven, nirvana, or at least to a happy and secure life.

What a trap that can be! What at first seems to free participants ultimately binds them. Such approaches—releasing repressed areas of consciousness, positive thinking, transformational experiences, accepting things exactly the way they are, "creative" problem solving, situational management, behavior modification, stress reduction, "new" styles of thinking, and even certain forms of meditation—all attempt to teach people to respond to life or to the universe as if the circumstances were dominant.

After years of practicing these various disciplines, people often still have not learned to create what they most truly want. All they have learned are textbook responses that promise, but do not deliver, success or salvation.

This is because creating and responding are completely different species.

The Reactive Orientation

Instead of responding to circumstances, some people rebelliously oppose society's version of how life is portrayed at home or in school. Their reactions can be either overt or covert.

If you are reactive, you also believe that circumstances are the driving force of life. But you believe that circumstances are not necessarily the way society presents them.

Reactive behavior may take the form of cynicism, or you may have a chronic chip on your shoulder. You may be suspicious of others or simply have a "short fuse." You may hold conspiracy theories about people in power or subscribe to a political or religious philosophy that reacts against injustice or evil.

A good test of reactiveness is this:

· Do you react against circumstances chronically?
· Are many of your actions and beliefs designed to combat negative circumstances?

· Do you see yourself in a life situation in which you must overcome the forces in play, often simply to survive?

I once visited a management group in a large high-tech corporation. Their meeting began when someone in the group made this simple and undoubtedly accurate statement: "We need to come to some agreement about the budget for this new project."

At that point an argument broke out among the entire group. They demanded reasons why the simple statement was true. The man who made the statement was forced to defend his position.

After forty minutes of arguing, with expressions of fierce hostility, the group finally decided that yes, they probably needed to agree on a budget for the new project.

They had spent so much energy establishing that simple fact that they were exhausted and shell-shocked. They avoided discussing anything else that morning. The psychological tension and anxiety in the group grew so high that if someone had introduced another topic, there would probably have been another forty-minute skirmish.

The fact is, they were out to get one another. They employed various strategies of entrapment, sometimes feigning politeness and reasonableness, at other times acting the stubborn, temperamental, explosive combatant.

I was astonished to be in the presence of this group. I was later told, "They are among the best-behaved in the company." This organization had a reputation for "hotheads" and "prima donnas." Because of their reactive behavior, their performance had suffered, and they were quickly losing the competitive edge in their industry.

Reactive people are familiar in everyone's experience. Examples of reactive behavior are found in many marriages, work situations, family relationships, bureaucratic agencies, and social interactions.

Eventually most people, even the reactive ones, learn to respond "appropriately." Society considers the educational and socializing process a success when reactive people "graduate" to being responsive ones. But the oscillation of the structures in play within the individual continues.

The Reactive-Responsive Orientation: "Nice" People and "Difficult" People

Even "nice," responsive people build up resentment over time because of their chronic position of powerlessness. When they amass enough resentment, they turn into difficult, reactive people. But because that change does nothing to enhance their power and, in fact, feels disorienting, they soon return to being nice, responsive people.

On the other hand, "difficult," reactive people create so much commotion that, over a period of time, they build up guilt as well as resentment because of their chronic destructiveness and powerlessness. When they build up enough conflict, they repent and turn into nice, responsive people. Then, usually after a brief time, they begin to experience the resentment nice, responsive people feel and then return to being difficult, reactive people.

Some people spend most of their time in the responsive mode, with temporary shifts into the reactive. Others spend most of their time in the reactive mode, with temporary shifts into the responsive. For many, life is an endless loop, moving back and forth between reactiveness and responsiveness. Oscillation begets more oscillation.

Throughout these shifts, the oscillating structure remains in place. Although people may change their behaviors, actions, policies, and even philosophies, their pattern of either responding or reacting to circumstances is still in play.

The Premise of Powerlessness

The reactive-responsive orientation contains the basic presumption that you are powerless.

If you habitually react or respond to circumstances, where does the power lie in these situations? It clearly lies outside you, in the circumstances. Therefore, because the power does not reside in you, you are powerless and the circumstances are all-powerful.

Even those who have accomplished what others might consider great success often have achieved that success in order to avoid failure. Success itself does nothing to change a presumption of powerlessness.

Other people may keep themselves from success to avoid the unwanted consequences they fear success will bring them. We all know people who stay in jobs they don't like, sometimes in circumstances that are quite painful, to avoid the insecurity and problems a new job might hold.

Whether the situation is a success or a failure, people in the reactive-responsive orientation will always feel incomplete and unsatisfied. The only difference between those who have achieved the success they seek, and those who have not is that the "successful" ones know that their success has not brought them the deep experience of satisfaction and fulfillment they really want. Their success is an empty victory.

Parents and teachers tell children what to do and what not to do in order to help children be accepted and secure in the family and in society. Children may cooperate or rebel, but it is clear to them that the adult's job is to know how life should be.

Children are really learning about power. What they learn about power is that they are powerless.

They are also learning about their purpose in life. Unfortunately, what they learn is that they are insignificant, and that they need to conform.

Under those conditions, what purpose or meaning does their life ultimately have? The epidemic of teenage suicide is one outcome of this experience of purposelessness and powerlessness.

Even a search for meaning can turn out to be nothing more than a reaction against an existential crisis. Every year young people join cults as a reaction against the lack of meaning they have experienced in their lifes.

Looking to the External

Before this time in history, human advancement was focused on sources outside the individual. Statesmen and political leaders shaped the governments that ruled us. Scientists evolved the theories that forged our industrialized society. Technicians in the giant corporations designed the tools, appliances, electronics, and vehicles that molded our daily lives. Learned professors wrote the books designed to influence our minds. Psychologists applied the therapeutic processes designed to organize our emotional lives. Medical science formulated approaches designed to restore our health. The forces that shaped our lives, then, were seen as external to ourselves. A common assumption was that, if outer circumstances were changed, the inner experience of individuals and groups would also change.

Some people believe that if we change outer circumstances so that we have adequate housing, adequate health care, a shorter work week, inexpensive rapid transportation, smaller families, and so on, individuals would be happier, healthier, more balanced, and psychologically secure.

The fact is that many people do have adequate housing, adequate health care, and the rest, yet they are still unhappy, unhealthy, unstable, and psychologically insecure.

In the early twentieth century, the American composer Charles Ives took much of his philosophical and aesthetic inspiration from Henry David Thoreau. But Ives did have one major disagreement with the philosopher. Thoreau believed that if people returned to living in the natural environment of the woods, they would automatically develop an innate transcendental spiritual orientation. Ives observed that most of the people he knew who had lived for generations under natural circumstances in the wooded hills of West Virginia and Tennessee had yet to reach this transcendental state. Instead, Ives noted, they mostly thought of themselves as hillbillies.

Thoreau had assumed that changing outward circumstances would change people's inner experiences. Charles Ives observed that it did not.

While most people's reactions and responses change radically as a result of new external circumstances such as political revolutions and technological breakthroughs, their underlying assumptions remain essentially unchanged. They continue to assume that the predominant creative force in their lives is external to them; it comes from somewhere other than themselves.

For example, while the Industrial Revolution produced great shifts of population and a reorganization of the social structure of nineteenth-century Europe, the predominant factor that determined the life and destiny of the individual was still perceived as external circumstances, just as it had been during the feudal periods and just as it has remained until our day.

Today, whether you are a farmer, a factory worker, a manager, an industrialist, or a stockbroker, you are likely to believe that the power in your life exists in all of the external circumstances to which you need to respond or against which you need to react.

Looking to the Internal-External

In the reactive-responsive orientation, there are certain internal circumstances, such as fear, anger, illness, or parts of the personality, that people treat just as if they were external circumstances. That is, people react or respond to these internal circumstances as if they were beyond their reach or control. They are seen as internally external: "I had so much anger, I had to leave the room"; or "My fear got in the way during my job interview"; or "My relationship with my father was incomplete, so I can't seem to have a good relationship with a man"; or "My mind gets in the way when I am trying to be spontaneous"; or "My ego gets me in trouble"; or "I need to overcome my sinful nature"; or "My stomach rebels against spicy food."

These are all examples of internal circumstances that people perceive as if they were external circumstances. While these circumstances are primarily inner and self-referential, they function for the reactive-responsive person as if they originated somewhere beyond the personal sphere of influence, beyond their direct control.

In talking about the reactive-responsive orientation, I call circumstantial stimuli any stimuli, external or internal, that *seem to force people to take action.*

Circumstantial Stimuli

One way to describe the reactive-responsive orientation is as a way of living in which you predominantly react or respond to circumstantial stimuli that are beyond your direct control. When things change in your circumstances, you perceive a need to react or respond to what just changed.

Some circumstantial stimuli appear friendly and welcome; others seem adversarial and unwelcome. "She smiled at me, and suddenly I felt more comfortable." "He looked away, and I began to feel insecure." "When my son dropped the dish and broke it, I couldn't stop yelling at him for five minutes." "The salesman seemed sincere, so I bought the dishwasher." "Because I ate the candy bar, I typed faster for the next twenty minutes."

While at times circumstantial stimuli evoke spontaneous re- actions, at other times they seem to call for "appropriate" re- sponses. "She had the flu, so I thought it was a good idea to bring her chicken soup." "The workmen did not do a good job, so I felt I had to sue them." "They invited me to the party so warmly that I had to say yes." "He was so bad, I had to get divorced. What would you have done?"

In each of these cases it seemed to the persons involved that the circumstantial stimuli *caused* their reaction or response. The power to influence their actions in each situation was at- tributed to the circumstances, which in some way or other forced or impelled them to take action. They did not feel they could choose what they wanted, independent of circumstances.

In the reactive-responsive orientation, it always seems that circumstances are powerful—more powerful than you are. You feel that all you can do is to react or respond to them. Even if you have developed great skill in outmaneuvering circum- stances, like a lion tamer outmaneuvering the lions, it is still the circumstances—the lions—that hold the ultimate control in how you live your life.

Avoiding the Circumstances

When Karen, a friend of mine, arrived at the party we were both attending, the room was already filled with music and guests. Our host greeted her and led her to the table where the food was spread out.

As Karen filled her plate with hors d'oeuvres and her glass with Bordeaux, she was scanning the room to see whom she wanted to avoid. Since I knew Karen well for many years, I knew this was the first thing she always did in large groups. Sometimes she and I would joke about her habit.

When Norma, a compulsive talker, began to walk toward her, Karen pretended not to see her and walked through the crowd in the opposite direction, smiling and saying hello to various people.

Just when she began to feel a sense of relief about avoiding Norma, she found herself walking directly toward an old friend, John, who had just left his third marriage. She knew that John would monopolize her time if he could, complaining about his life, as he had in the past. So before she reached him she called a quick hello to him, and took a sharp left turn.

Another old acquaintance, Greg, was just finishing telling a joke to two other people. Karen slipped in between them, in time to hear the punch line and join in the laughter. She stayed in that little group, listening to amusing stories, anecdotes, and jokes, until the group drifted apart.

Just as Karen was walking toward the kitchen, Jan, a small woman who always wore large jewelry, blocked her way. Jan involved Karen in a long and boring narrative on the benefits of fresh carrot juice. By the time she was able to extricate herself from Jan, Karen was ready for another glass of wine.

During the rest of the party, Karen avoided engaging in many conversations because she did not want to relate to the faddish people there who were talking about exotic vacation spots and esoteric metaphysics. Instead, she stayed on the edge of things and mostly remained silent. But eventually, she found herself conversing with an attractive man who showed an interest in her. When he seemed ready to extend an invitation so they could see each other again, she quickly changed the subject. This was her way of avoiding having to decide whether or not to get involved with him.

At the party, Karen was again and again using a reactive-responsive strategy designed to move around or away from unwelcome circumstances as they occurred. In the reactive-responsive orientation, avoidance strategies of this kind are common.

In these strategies, the focus is on what you want to avoid, and your usual action is to try to make sure it doesn't happen. Chronic worrying is an avoidance strategy designed to prevent or avoid the negative consequences about which you are worrying. Some people worry about getting ill, others worry about being disapproved of, others about being fired from their jobs, others about being rejected by friends, others about being made the center of attention, and so on. In each case, the focus is on what they do not want, and their strategy is designed to force them into taking preventive action.

Look at your life and notice if avoiding negative consequences has become a way of life.

There are people who stay in a relationship only to avoid the uncertainty of a new life-style without their partner.

There are people who leave a relationship only to avoid dealing with the anger, resentment, and discouragement that might come from staying within it.

For some, the decision to stay in a relationship or to leave it depends on which is the greater discomfort to avoid—the uncertainty of a new life or the resentment building up in the present one. No matter what they decide, they make their choice based on the assumption that all they can do is react or respond to the circumstances.

The Preemptive Strike

In the reactive-responsive orientation, even more common than the strategy designed to avoid immediate unwanted circumstances is a longer-range strategy designed to prevent unwanted circumstances from happening in the first place. This latter strategy is called a preemptive strike.

The preemptive strike takes many forms. Some people develop assertive personalities as a preemptive strike to avoid being manipulated by others. At meetings some people publicly criticize themselves as a preemptive strike to prevent being criticized by anyone else. Some act insecure and irresponsible in a preemptive strike to prevent having demands placed upon them. Some people act arrogant and unfriendly as a preemptive strike to prevent closeness and intimacy. Some get upset and hurt easily as a preemptive strike to prevent being confronted by anyone. Some put themselves in situations in which they appear to be victimized as a preemptive strike to prevent being taken advantage of. Some people dedicate their time and energy to selfless deeds as a preemptive strike to avoid considering their real doubts of self-worth.

A subtle preemptive strike may turn out to be a lifelong strategy. You may have learned, early on, the kinds of situations that could be threatening to you and gradually developed strategies to prevent them from recurring in your life.

Certain people may point to their life circumstances and say, "I live a charmed life," or "My life is filled with contentment," or "My life is happily normal and well-balanced." Even though these people may describe their lives as "good," a more accurate description for the lives of some of them would be "unburdened by conflict." The way their lives became conflict-free was through elaborate avoidance strategies learned along the way whenever they found themselves in unwanted situations.

Today Frank earns a six-figure annual salary and considers himself financially secure. But he grew up in a very poor family in which his parents constantly worried and fought with each other about the precarious state of their family finances. When Frank went to school, he always felt embarrassed about his hand-me-down clothes. Out of embarrassment, he never invited his friends to his house. And he often could not afford the extracurricular activities offered at school. Any money he earned in his spare time he had to contribute to the family.

Frank always thought of himself as poor. Even when he was first married, although he was already earning a good living, he budgeted the family finances carefully, even down to the smallest details, such as items on the grocery bill. Over the years he struggled to save as much money as he could to build financial security. Even after Frank became financially strong, earning more than one hundred thousand dollars a year, he carefully budgeted every dollar.

Frank steered clear of any magazine article, television program, or newspaper column on the subject of poverty. Whenever one of his high school friends invited him to a wedding or a dinner party, he never went. His circle of friends came to include only people who grew up in well-to-do families. One exception to Frank's frugality at home was the way he showered his children with presents and money. He made sure that they wore the best-quality clothes, even when they did not want to. He encouraged his children to invite their friends to the house and had a game room built for them, complete with pool table, stereo, and the latest video games.

Frank usually described his life as "comfortable" and "good."

Actually Frank's life had a continual undercurrent of insecurity. The life circumstances he had created around himself were an elaborate preemptive strategy to avoid poverty. Frank had an ulterior motive in creating his secure financial situation: never to be poor again.

Within Frank's orientation toward life, no amount of money in the world would be enough to buy him financial independence, because he carried his poverty with him in his consciousness all through life.

On the Defensive

Most of Frank's career decisions were made as a preemptive strike to prevent poverty. The way he treated his children was a preemptive strike to prevent their having the kinds of experiences he had had as a child. His obsession with the household budget was a preemptive strike to prevent any waste of money. His avoidance of hearing about poverty through the media was a preemptive strike designed to keep from reminding himself of his past circumstances, as was his refusal to see his high school friends.

Some people who enjoy better than ordinary life situations base their lives on an avoidance strategy that permeates many of their actions and attitudes. They manage to reach a certain plateau of insulation, keeping themselves "safe" and "certain."

You might be thinking, "What's wrong with that? After all, people like Frank live comfortably and safely. What's wrong with living like that?"

There is nothing inherently wrong with Frank having an affluent life, but any aspirations he may have are motivated by an avoidance of poverty. In a sense, his life spirit is chained by his preemptive strategies, and all his energy is focused on what he doesn't want.

Such people continually compromise whatever they may truly want in their lives for the sake of safety, security, and a sense of peace. However, they never experience true safety, security, or peace. Through this defensive strategy, the most they can hope to attain in their lives is complacency and mediocrity. Beneath all their pseudosecurity is an undercurrent of dissatisfaction and vulnerability to circumstances beyond their direct control.

Many of these people eventually become cynical about life. Others become stoical. Still others, like Frank, become committed to a pretense of happiness, while underneath it all they experience lack of fulfillment and dissatisfaction.

Years of avoidance strategies gradually undermine their sense of power. No matter what situations they have created to shield themselves from unwanted circumstances, they are rendered powerless. While Frank might appear to his friends to be in a position of power, mostly what he experiences is unending powerlessness, due to his constant need to assert control over his life circumstances in an effort to prevent the poverty he fears. He is never free from the circumstances—he is never free at all.

A Closed and Circular System

If your orientation is primarily in a responsive mode, the path of least resistance is to move to the reactive. But once there, the path of least resistance leads you back to the responsive.

If your orientation is primarily in a reactive mode, the path of least resistance is to move to the responsive. But once there, the path of least resistance leads you back to the reactive.

If it seems to you that this is a closed and circular system, you are right. If you attempt to solve, change, break through, transform, accept, reject, or avoid this structure, all you will do is reinforce it. As long as you try to make changes from within the reactive-responsive orientation, you will remain within that orientation.

I caution you against attempting prematurely to make a shift from the reactive-responsive orientation, because chances are you will be acting from within the reactive-responsive orientation. As a result, not only will it not work, but you will also be reinforcing that orientation.

If you cannot solve or change this reactive-responsive orientation in any way, what can you do? The answer is to do nothing to alter it until you have a deeper understanding of some of the structural mechanisms in play and how they work. In this way, you are preparing yourself for a successful shift into a new orientation in which you master the principle of the path of least resistance and truly become the predominant creative force in your own life.

Chapter 3

Creating Is No Problem— Problem Solving Is Not Creating

There is a profound difference between problem solving and creating. Problem solving is taking action to have something go away—the problem. Creating is taking action to have something come into being—the creation. Most of us have been raised in a tradition of problem solving and have had little real exposure to the creative process.

For this reason many people confuse the two. It doesn't help when some "experts" talk about "creative" problem solving. They think that the creative process and problem solving are the same. They are completely different.

The problem solvers propose elaborate schemes to define the problem, generate alternative solutions, and put the best solution into practice. If this process is successful, you might eliminate the problem. Then what you have is the absence of the problem you are solving. But what you do not have is the presence of a result you want to create.

In our society a problem mentality has become a way of life. Listen to our political candidates. What do they talk about? The problems. The problem of the deficit, the problem of international competition, the problem of acid rain, the problem of poverty, the problem of the economy, the problem of defense, the problem of the cost of defense, the problem of health care,

31

the problem of the homeless, the problem of the unemployed, the problem of crime, the problem of drug abuse, the problem of corruption, the problem of communism, the problem of inadequate education, the problem of terrorism, the problem of inadequate government, the problem of the endangered environment, the problem of welfare, the problem of AIDS, the problem of nuclear war, the problem of nuclear waste, the problem of nuclear energy, the problem of illegal immigration, the problem of pollution, the problem of traffic, the problem of prisons, the problem of elderly care, the problem of taxes, the problem of safety in the skies, the problem of safety on the highways, the problem of unfair trade practices, the problem of consumer fraud, the problem of industry, etc., etc., etc.

When a presidential candidate is on the primary trail, the local problems are the ones he or she talks about. In Iowa the candidates talk about the farm problems. Once in Michigan they suddenly forget about the farms. Now it is unemployment in the auto industry. When they reach the South, we suddenly hear about problems with the Sun Belt economy. When they reach the Northeast, we hear about our energy problems. When they get to California, we hear about the environment, drugs, and AIDS.

The assumption they seem to make is that the candidate who can best define the problems is the one we should elect. If the candidates can name a problem, does that mean they have any insight into its real causes? If they speak with great passion of the tragedy of people in pain and suffering, does it mean they can lift a finger on behalf of these people? And even if they could help, what would they then have? The alleviation of that problem. Could they predict what other problems would then arise? Could they be effective at solving them? Have they been effective in the past? If so, why do we still have problems? Why do we hear so much from the candidates about the problems and so little about the society they might want to build?

The greatest leaders and statesmen in history have not been problem solvers. They have been builders. They have been creators. Even in times of great conflict, such as war and depression, they have taken action to bring into being the society they envisioned. Two shining examples of statesmen-creators were Winston Churchill and Franklin Delano Roosevelt. They did not simply try to bring relief to their constituencies. They were able to use the times they lived in as a foundation for building a future they wanted.

Problems, Problems

An important part of the creative process is recognizing what currently exists. We do have many problems. They do need attention. But problem solving is an unsound and inadequate way of creating the civilization we want, and most often it hardly changes the difficulties that do exist. At best, problem solving can bring temporary relief from a specific situation, but it seldom leads to final success.

An example of this concerns the famine in Ethiopia. Those of us who have been interested in Third World development have seen the catastrophe coming for years. When it became a crisis of enormous magnitude, the whole world suddenly took notice. If the problem is starving people, what is the obvious solution? Food. Enormous sums of money were raised to buy and ship emergency food aid. Lives were saved. But the forces in play did not change. Ethiopia remained in political turmoil. The people who were starving still did not have the resources to produce their own food. All the food aid did was to buy precious time. But this time was not used to create food sufficiency and adequate food production for the populace. After temporary relief from the intense suffering, the tragedy continued. Was food aid the wrong solution?

No. In times of desperate emergency, as in Ethiopia, we must do what we can to address the immediate crisis. But we need to recognize that this kind of action only buys us time. If this time is not used to create a viable society, we have only postponed even more tragedy.

The Ethiopian crisis is a clear example of the deficiencies of problem solving. What was the driving force behind the actions of raising money and sending food? The intensity of the problem. Pictures of starving children flooded television. A call went out for help. People from all over the world and from all walks of life rose to the occasion. The greatest rock **stars** dedicated their talents in the biggest public event in history—Live Aid. The world was captured by the cause. Millions of dollars were raised. Relief in the form of food and medicine was rushed into Ethiopia. After distribution difficulties with the Ethiopian government were overcome, much of the food reached the people who were starving. The situation got better. The media lost interest. Fewer pictures of starving children made it to prime-time newscasts. Contributions slowed. New problems became newsworthy. The focus on Ethiopia waned. This led to less action. But today, right now, children are still starving to death in Ethiopia as in other countries in the world.

Notice that these are steps in a familiar pattern. This is movement that oscillates.

The path of least resistance in problem solving is to move from worse to better and then from better to worse again. This is because the actions taken are generated by the problem. If the intensity of the problem is lessened by the actions you took, there is less motivation to take further actions.

The structure is this: The problem leads to actions designed to reduce the problem. The problem is reduced. This leads to less need for other actions. This leads to fewer future actions. This leads to the problem remaining or intensifying anew.

The problem

LEADS TO
action to solve the problem

LEADS TO
less intensity of the problem

LEADS TO
less action to solve the problem

LEADS TO
the problem remaining

Life in the Problem Track

This pattern is not only true of world problems, it is true of personal and professional problems as well. Many people approach life as a series of problems to solve: an unhappy love relationship, a bad job, a chronic health problem, financial difficulties, a stressful family life, unsupportive co-workers, economic inadequacies, corporate politics, competition from abroad.

Many people's lives are inextricably tied to their problems. The majority of the actions they take are designed to eliminate the problems so that they can be problem-free. But with all this action they still have problems. Some of these people have the same old problems, some develop new problems.

What drives the action is the intensity of the problem. Once the intensity of the problem is lessened, people have less motivation to act. Thus problem solving as a way of life becomes self-defeating. Problem solving mostly leads to less and less action as the actions work to solve the problem!

The Business of Problems

A few months ago we were interviewing people for a senior management position at DMA. Many of the applicants boasted that they loved problem solving. "I just can't wait to get my hands on your problems!" one of them emoted.

I'm afraid he will have to wait. Someone else got the job.

Many of the men and women who applied had problem solving as a frame of reference. Why? Because the subject of problems and problem solving can capture your interest. It gives you a feeling of importance. Who but an important person could have an important problem? Managers are trained to think in terms of problems. The more senior the manager, the more senior the problems.

Ironically, problem solving can give you a false sense of security. You know just what you are supposed to do: find and solve problems. If you didn't have problems, what would you think about? How would you spend your time?

Problem solving provides an almost automatic way of organizing your focus, actions, time, and thought process. In a sense, when you have a nice juicy problem to work on, you do not have to think. You can obsess instead. You can dwell on what is wrong. You can go over it in your mind. You can worry and fret. You have something to talk about to your colleagues and friends. It can seem as if you have no choice except to cower in the face of adversity. You can experience the romance of "the individual against the elements." Problem solving can be very distracting while at the same time giving you the illusion that you are doing something important and needed.

"Creative" Problem Solving

When people talk about problem solving and creativity in the same breath, what they usually mean is finding some unusual way out of difficulties. The use of the word *creative* here is strictly about style and not substance. It has nothing to do with the real creative process as practiced for centuries in the arts and sciences.

An artist could not paint a painting using the "creative" problem-solving approach. Artists do not paint to solve problems but to bring into reality a work of art. That the painting does not exist at first is not a problem (unless you see as a problem a world filled with blank canvasses).

An example of a typical "creative" problem-solving technique is brainstorming. Brainstorming is a process in which you attempt to blitzkrieg through your preconceived "mind-set" by fanciful free association. The idea is to generate alternative solutions by overcoming your usual manner of thinking. You are encouraged to suspend your critical judgment so that you can be more inventive.

"Freeing the Wonders of Your Mind"

Much of the focus in this type of approach is in freeing the mind. This notion comes from the influence of psychologists' view of creativity. The approach itself is a problem-solving model.

The premise of the model seems to be that people limit themselves by being rigid in their thought processes. The usual style of thinking is limited by barriers of habit, barriers of belief, or psychological blocks. The solution is for the individual to overcome the barriers or blocks by breaking through them and "freeing the mind." Instead of making the usual connection between one thought and another, you are encouraged to make new associations. You must leave critical judgment out of this process, so as not to inhibit the flow of ideas.

This approach assumes that people have a wealth of creativity in them but that it is blocked. When the blocks are removed, creativity will flow like water. Even Willis Harman, an exceptional leading thinker on the evolution of human conscious-

ness, has fallen into this common trap. He writes in his book
Higher Creativity:

> Why aren't there Beethovens, Gandhis, or Ein-
> steins in everybody's family? If everyone pos-
> sesses an innate capacity for breakthrough to
> higher kinds of creativity—what is it, exactly, that
> hides the key and holds most of us back from dis-
> covering how to use these talents?

But Beethoven, for example, certainly did not think of himself as having "breakthroughs to a higher kind of creativity."
He didn't wake one morning and find that he could suddenly
compose music. Nor did he sit and meditate, waiting for a flash
of inspired brilliance to descend on his humble "lower kinds"
of creativity. He spent years studying composition. He also spent
years of hard work gaining more and more experience composing. At first his music was in the style of the Classical period
and not dissimilar from the genre of Mozart and Haydn. (The
latter was one of Beethoven's composition teachers.) Beethoven's distinctive artistic development grew over time.

The greatness of his music cannot be separated from the
greatness of the man. He was not simply a mindless channel or
a scribe somehow tapping into "higher creativity." He was a
master artist able to balance all the dimensions of his life experiences into his art, from the spiritual to the philosophical to
the sexual, and even to the ordinary and mundane. He was also
one of the greatest technical masters of his craft.

He used his life as the raw material for what he was able to
accomplish. His was more the path of continual learning rather
than that of "breakthroughs." His process was evolutionary.
And through his evolution, he was able to bring a revolution to
the history of music.

In studying Beethoven's work, the composer Roger Sessions
discussed the issue of inspiration.

> I have in my possession the last movement of his
> *"Mannerklavier Sonata"*; the sketches show him
> [Beethoven] carefully modeling, then testing in
> systematic and apparently cold-blooded fashion,

the theme of the fugue. Where, one might ask, is the inspiration here? Yet if the word has any meaning at all, it is certainly appropriate to this movement, with its irresistible and titanic energy of expression, already present in the theme.

Perhaps there are people who in their imagination can hear even greater music than Beethoven's. But creators not only can imagine or envision, *they also have the ability to bring what they imagine into reality.* Once a creation exists, an evolutionary process can take place. Each past creation builds a foundation for the next creation.

When people begin to talk about a "key" to creativity, as if the "right key" will unlock your creativity, I think it's time to head for the door.

I can imagine how approaches such as trying to "unlock" creativity were developed: by psychologists who observed that creative people often do things that are *unusual.* The originality creators seem to possess separates them from most people. If this originality could be encouraged, the theory goes, there would be more originality and creativity.

This is a little like observing that some people play the piano and some people do not. If we study the people who know how to play, we see that they push down white keys and black keys. According to the "unlocking" theory, if we could encourage the people who do not play to sit at pianos and push down white keys and black keys, eventually they would become pianists.

In some psychological tests on creativity, subjects are asked to think of as many uses as they can for a brick. The notion is that the more uses you can think of, the more creative you are. This is another variation on the theme of generating alternatives, one of the problem solver's tricks of the trade. If Frank Lloyd Wright had come up with only one use for bricks— making buildings—I suppose he would not have been considered very creative.

The Vital Question

These approaches leave out the vital question of the creative process: *"What do I want to create?"* The inventiveness of the creative process does not come from generating alternatives, but from generating a path from the original concept of what you want to create to the final creation of it in reality. A good test of any theory of creativity is: Can you write music using that theory? Can you imagine Mozart brainstorming alternatives for the overture to *The Marriage of Figaro*? If he'd used that approach, he could never have composed that music in the few hours it took him.

As Roger Sessions described, Beethoven's sketchbook is filled with themes and variations. However, these sketches represented neither free association nor generating alternatives, but rather a *focused study* of the way intervalic structures interact. "Modeling, then testing in systematic and apparently cold-blooded fashion." Beethoven's critical judgment was not suspended in his sketches, but enhanced.

The creative process is filled with a variety of styles, from highly controlled ones to very uncontrolled ones. But all these styles exist within the context of *the results the creator has in mind.*

Within this context there is a *focus of critical judgment*, not a suspension of it. As creators master their own creative processes, less and less is left to alternatives. The creator develops an economy of means. The more the mastery, the more direct the path from original concept to final creation.

Freeing the mind is a different act from *focusing the mind.* Focus needs an object of attention. To a creator, the object of focus is the final result that he or she wants to create.

Freeing the mind is a little like fishing in a pond where you hope there may be fish, without knowing what kind of fish you want or how to fish.

Creating is more like actual fishing. Before you go to the pond, you focus on the kind of fish you want to catch. If you want trout, you bring fly-casting equipment. If you want bass, you bring sinkers and bait.

There is always an unknown quality in the creative process, as there is in fishing, but when you are aware of the final result you want to create, you are able to focus the process, rather than make the process a random one.

·　　·　　·

Is This Problem Relevant?

Since they don't know how to create what they want to create, people often see problems as relevant to life and filled with important content. But upon close examination, problems are most often irrelevant. As a way of life, not much can come out of problem solving.

After years of dedicated work on the subject, psychologist Carl Jung made this astute observation:

> All the greatest and most important problems of life are fundamentally insoluble. . . . They can never be solved, but only outgrown. This "outgrowth" proved on further investigation to require a new level of consciousness. Some higher or wider interest appeared on the patient's horizon, and through this broadening of his or her outlook the insoluble problem lost its urgency. It was not solved logically in its own terms but faded when confronted with a new and stronger life urge.

The enormous amount of work that has been done on the subject of problem solving is practically useless. Little of it has had lasting value because problem solving is yet another method of finding the "proper" response to circumstances, in this case the circumstances of the problem.

From a pragmatic viewpoint, most of the people who have tried to adopt a problem-solving approach have given up. A friend of mine told me that his company had invested thousands of dollars in problem-solving approaches.

"How many of these techniques do you use in your organization?" I asked.

"None," was his answer. "We spent a lot of time generating ideas we never used. At first people were excited by doing something different. But then nothing new really happened. If the techniques had turned out to be useful, we would have used them. But all that happened was that we came up with a lot of interesting, useless stuff nobody really cared about. And with good reason. It was impractical and in many cases, just dumb."

Sigmund Freud Was a Doctor

Many of the developments in psychotherapy and psychoanalysis in the last one hundred years have been influenced by the father of psychoanalysis, Sigmund Freud. While many of the innovators in these fields may not directly subscribe to Freud's theories, they nonetheless use the same medical model.

As a physician, Freud was trained to solve problems. Observe symptoms. Diagnose causes. Prescribe solutions. He was dedicated to alleviating pain. Relief from pain was the goal of treatment.

The medical model is still the most prevalent in the world of psychotherapy. Find out what is wrong and then fix it. This model is of tremendous value in helping sick people. Problem solving has its place, and one of its best uses is in medical science. When the great film director John Houston was in his eighties, he was asked the secret of his long life. "Surgery," was his answer.

But medical science is not a method for creating health. Rather it is a discipline dedicated to eradicating disease. Newer trends in the field may consider health a goal of medical science, but so far most doctors do not make the profound distinction between alleviating disease and creating health.

A Clear Distinction

In the tradition of the arts, it is well known that creating is not problem solving. The reason that this distinction is important is that most people are truly interested in creating the lives that they want. Problem solving does not enable them to create what they want and often perpetuates what they do not want.

A marvelous example of the difference between problem solving and creating comes from comparing the reaction to the Ethiopian crisis with another development in the Third World. This second example is the ongoing work being done in Uganda by the African Food and Peace Foundation.

I was invited to participate in this project by its founders, who were excited about the idea of the creative process as a powerful foundation for world development. Instead of relief or development that depended on outside intervention of personnel and resources, this program is based on training the villagers of rural Uganda to be able to create the life they want.

The history of Uganda is one of oppression, tribal and religious prejudice, starvation, civil wars, water-borne diseases, economic inviability, exploitation, and natural disasters. Was this a good setting for the first project of this type, in which development included learning the creative process? What better place than the classic situation plaguing the Third World?

When I was approached in the early eighties by Han and Silvana Veltkamp about the project, I was captured by the idea. This was the first time development was not placed in the context of problem solving, but from a new impulse, that of vision. The Veltkamps had both worked for the United Nations in the area of development and had seen millions of dollars squandered in relief and development projects that did little to improve the lot of people in the recipient countries. Having had vast experience in development, they envisioned a project that was primarily indigenous to the population, had an emphasis on training in self-sufficiency, and would demonstrate the power of a *true* developmental approach in the nonindustrial world.

At DMA we designed a special program using the creative process as part of an integrated approach to food production, agricultural development, health, clean-water development, and education. One major strength of the project was that Ugandan leaders were able to come to the United States and train to become TECHNOLOGIES FOR CREATING® instructors. Then these young men and women went back to Uganda and moved to the villages where the project was in operation. Over the course of a few short years several changes occurred, many of them originally thought to be impossible by the villagers.

Although the political situation in Uganda fluctuated, the tribal strife continued, the economy was in trouble, and a host of other desperate problems emerged, the villages where the project was in operation told a very different story. Even in the times of unfavorable circumstances, the villagers were able to create more and more of the life they wanted for themselves.

In the area of six villages of the project, the economy changed from depressed to flourishing. This was a local phenomenon, independent of the economy of the country. The change was self-produced from the new ability of the people to create the village they wanted.

Many inspirational stories fill the history of this project. Thousands of people's lives have been changed. All of this work has been done for a fraction of the cost of the typical relief and development agency.

Mwalimu Musheshe, Jr., executive chairman of the Uganda Rural Development and Training Program, has written about the project:

> The situation in Uganda in 1981 looked grim. Idi Amin's misrule had devastated the economy, disrupted the infrastructure and, worse still, ruptured the moral fibre of Ugandans. The political and civil situation was turbulent and life was harsh for millions of Ugandans. Social services were at a minimum, and, after the "war of liberation" in 1979, witnesses to the destruction said recovery required massive foreign aid and relief.
>
> The people had lost hope and looked to the international community for intervention. That is what made the big news. That is when the African Food and Peace Foundation and the Uganda Rural Development and Training Program (formally the Uganda Project) were born.
>
> During the first community workshop in a village in western Uganda in November of 1982, it was clear that people were anxious to talk about their problems and identify community needs, which were many. The common words were, "We don't have this or that!" or "We are dying of diseases, pests, and fevers." The people wanted the Project to help them eradicate human and livestock diseases, remove unscrupulous businessmen who were cheating them, and kill the wild animals that were eating their crops. They described their children, dying of measles, diarrhea, TB, and other infectious disease because there were no drugs, hospitals were far, and bus or taxi fares were high. Others complained of the politics of the day, how repressive they were, while others talked of being underpaid for their farm produce. The people had all the evidence about the hope-

lessness of the situation and wanted solutions to their many problems.

The Uganda Project set out to work with the rural people on the premise that the people of Uganda, like all people elsewhere, are the key to their development. Another important premise was that these people have innate power and wisdom, which they could use in transforming the quality of life and that of their communities.

The team organized training workshops for the members of the communities. One significant and unique approach was that people attended voluntarily and each individual expressed him/herself fully. Through these sessions the villagers identified what the current situation was (this was termed "The situation as it is in Kahunge"). Then they reflected on how they wanted their lives, their homes, families and communities to be (these were termed their "Dreams or visions").

These people then organized themselves into groups to work on what the community wanted to create. *The major focus was on what the people wanted rather than what they didn't want.*

People focused on what they wanted in their lives and on action steps that were necessary for accomplishment. For example, when people wanted clean water, they gathered together, identified the spring to be built and protected, and created twelve new clean water sources in an area in which only two had been built over the past eight years. This was built by the villagers, and served thousands of people.

As individuals and groups shifted from a problem-solving orientation to creating visions of what they wanted—like food sufficiency, healthy children, clean environment, etc.,—local leadership emerged.

Individuals like Mr. David Abundinabo, Mrs. Margaret Ndezi, Mr. Peter Kariyo and Mr. David Wakesa articulated their visions, organized fellow villagers, shared of themselves and helped formulate village programs.

The youth of Nyakahama constructed a village school and a road; the women of Rwenkuba, in a challenge to the men, cleared a dense bush and dug a fishpond for fish farming to improve their diet and family income.

One Amos Turyahikayo of Bigldi made the following observation when comparing our program with the ones that were externally imposed. "It is now very clear to us that we have fun and love what we are doing because it is our development."

Faith Tindamanyile of Kahunge said, "We have learned new things in agriculture, health, and nutrition. But above all, we have learned to live together, and rise above our differences."

The local administrator, Paul Nyakairu, said, "The Project has shown us what we are. It is our duty to take ourselves seriously."

These examples illustrate what people can do in development when they discover who they are and take their destiny in their own hands. On the other hand, intervention by problem-solving approaches leaves the people as helpless as ever and creates dependence; people are united in a "marriage of convenience" to fight a common enemy. Energy is derived from emotions. Normally the focus is narrow. More often than not, people participate by coercion, cooption or compliance. After the activities are over, they wait until the next crisis. In the meantime, nothing happens.

What we have done in the Project is prove people can work together, live together, and create together, not by compliance, but from commitment to build the future we envision. When the people finish a building, road, well or a new garden they are excited to move to the next project. The contrast from before to now is dramatic.

No matter what your problems are, for the most part, solving them won't solve them. You will always have a new problem if you do not know how to create what you want. And creating is no problem.

C h a p t e r   4

Creating

A Lesson from the Ghetto

Recently I was traveling from New York's La Guardia Airport to Manhattan. My cabdriver chose to avoid the congested traffic on the East River Drive. His route brought me through my old neighborhood in East Harlem.

I had moved there after getting a master's degree from the Boston Conservatory of Music. What a contrast that was, cultural Boston and "culturally deprived" East Harlem. For a musician just in for the New York music scene, East 110th Street between Second and Third Avenue was just the right price in those days.

Most of us have a talent for selective memory. We remember the past as containing many more good experiences than bad ones. (My grandmother had it just the other way around.) And so, as I studied my old turf, I was flooded with wonderful memories of my ghetto days. Suddenly I was brought back to the present by an extraordinary example of ghetto art, graffiti.

This art form developed years ago. Its origin was the wanton vandalizing of property. When I lived in East Harlem, graffiti was not yet an art form. Just kids, spray cans, and walls. Mostly the kids used the walls to express their hostility by painting expletives in large, sloppy letters. Occasionally a kid would express his romantic tendencies with great declarations of love; *José loves Judy.*

Over the years the letters became more artistic and then developed into complex artistic creations. The young artists became competitive with each other. Originality and craft became the norm. The bravado of youthful energy came to be expressed in painting rather than in gang warfare. Bold designs gave way to bolder designs. The color was strong, direct, primary.

The city became the canvas. These artists would stalk at night and paint on whatever surface they found. They used up the available walls quickly and then found the perfect symbol of their art: subway cars—owned by the society the artists were separate from, vital to the movement of the populace, gray, drab, dilapidated, lifeless and institutional.

The graffiti writers would break into the railway yards and spend the night painting subway cars. Then the Transit Authority would spread their works to a mass audience throughout the city. Influenced by each other's work, the artists' creations got better. The authorities became alarmed and put armed guards around the railway yards. But by that time the highbrow art world had taken notice. Some of the best ghetto artists were sought out by art dealers. The artists switched to real canvasses. A fad rose and fell in short order.

Gallery success might have been temporary, but the artists kept on painting, growing, and developing. New artists emerged, pushing the art form further and further still. Later the city of Tokyo would invite one of the best graffiti artists to come to Japan and paint long murals on their subway cars.

What a story. Too strange to be fiction. If someone had told you twenty-five years ago that someday in New York City the "culturally deprived," undereducated children of welfare would rise up, not in violence, but in art and in dance (break dancing) and in poetry (rap), you might have asked to examine that person's sugar cube for traces of LSD.

What caught my eye and captured my imagination that day in East Harlem was a new evolutionary step in graffiti art. It was the choice of colors. *Pastels.* No longer the bright, bold, shouting colors of a few years ago, but colors that were soft, translucent, subtle, and penetrating.

Somewhere in the destructive life of the inner city, a young artist is thinking about color. Experimenting with quinacridone violet and cerulean blue. Mixing and blending opposite colors to create illusions of space and dimension. And somehow, because of this, I experience hope for our civilization.

There is a profound lesson here. It is partly about the human spirit. We have been led to believe that the circumstances of our life determine our ability to express ourselves. That for us to explore new dimensions of our being, our conditions need to be favorable. If that were true, how could such creativity, originality, and vitality come from such humble and adverse beginnings as the ghetto? How is it that it was from there, and not the sacred institutions of academia, that new thought, born of what is highest in humanity, developed and grew? Perhaps our true nature is that of creators, who can bring forth new life out of any set of circumstances.

Creating Is Not a Product of the Circumstances

Creating is completely different from reacting or responding to the circumstances you are in. The process of creating is not generated by the circumstances in which you find yourself, but by the creation itself.

It is popular to think of creativity as a product of your environment, culture, or other circumstances that foster the creative process. An example of this notion was the corporate fad, popular just a few years ago, of "engineer environments" that were supposed to be conducive for creating. But a quick survey of the history of creativity will make it obvious that people have created in a wide range of circumstances, from convenient ones to difficult ones.

As you begin to consider what you want to create in your life, it is good for you to know that the circumstances that presently exist are not the determining factor of the results you desire to create. You are not limited by them, even though it may seem you are entrenched in them.

Because creating is so essentially different from the reactive-responsive orientation to which you have been exposed, it may seem ridiculous to consider life to be any different from what you have experienced before. You may be reading these words with the suspicion that this is yet another pep talk designed to inspire you to a new way of life. Or you may think that creating is possible only for the artist, that the creative process is limited to painting, music, filmmaking, poetry, or the other arts.

Even though the most obvious expression of the creative process is found in the arts, it is in no way limited to the arts. Almost all of your life's desires can be the subject of the creative process. There need be no separation from the creative process as practiced in the arts and the same creative process as practiced in other human endeavors. In addition, the arts is a perfect arena for learning the special ability and skill of creating.

It is wise to learn about the creative process from those practitioners who know the most about it and who have used it to bring the highest fruits of the creative process into being. This is a different skill from what you have learned in school, at home, or at work, and yet it is one of the most important skills to develop in your life.

Pablo Casals, one of the greatest cellists of our century, did not limit his concept of creating to his music.

> I have always regarded manual labor as creative and looked with respect—and, yes, wonder—at people who work with their hands. It seems to me that their creativity is no less than that of a violinist or painter.

And psychologist Carl Rogers has written:

> The action of the child inventing a new game with his playmates; Einstein formulating a theory of relativity; the housewife devising a new sauce for the meat; a young author writing his first novel; all of these are, in terms of our definition, creative, and there is no attempt to set them in some order of more or less creative.

When one does not consciously know the skill of creating, it is common to suppose the creative process a product of the unconscious or subconscious, or of mysticism. Then the creative process becomes a search for the formula that will tap your hidden powers. Because your "normal" self seems not to be the possessor of such powers, you might assume they must lie somewhere else.

In the story of Dumbo the elephant, a mouse convinces Dumbo that he can fly because of a "magic" feather. Dumbo tries out the feather and finds he can fly. But one day he loses his feather and thinks he has lost the ability. The mouse confesses that the story of the magic feather was a hoax and that Dumbo's ability to fly was his own. Dumbo discovers he can fly without benefit of feather.

Many of the theories about the creative process are similar to Dumbo's magic feather. In these theories the power to create what you want depends on a magical talisman that will enable you to unlock your hidden powers once and for all.

To some jungle tribes who have not had contact with modern civilization, the jet planes they see flying overhead take on a magical meaning. These planes are seen as gods or at least vehicles of gods.

It is common to assume that the unknown is unknowable, or at least unknowable by normal means. It is our inexperience and ignorance that can make the creative process seem as if it is an outcome of magical operations, the same kind of inexperience and ignorance a jungle tribe may have about modern aviation. But, in fact, creating is a skill that can be learned and developed. Like any skill, you learn by practice and hands-on experience. You can learn to create by creating.

The Steps

The steps in the creative process are simple to describe, but they do not constitute a formula. Instead, each step represents certain types of actions. Some aspects of the creative process are active, some are more passive. Different aspects call for different skills. You may have developed some of these skills already and find that other skills are not as easy at first. Each time you create a new result, you are involved in a unique creation. While your ability will develop over time with experience, every new creation has its own individual process.

In this chapter I will outline the basic steps of creating. In later chapters I will develop these steps so that you will be able to begin to experiment with them in your own life. Think of the following as an overview of the creative process rather than as a formula to adopt.

1. Conceive of the result you want to create.

Creators start at the end. First they have an idea of what they want to create. Sometimes this idea is general, and sometimes it is specific. Before you can create what you want to create, you must know what you are after, what you want to bring into being. Your original concept may be clear, or it may be simply a rough draft. Either will work well. Some creators like to improvise as they create, so they begin with a general concept. A painter may not know exactly how the final painting may look, but he or she has enough of a concept to make adjustments during the creative process so that the painting in progress will come closer and closer to what the artist wants. Other painters know exactly what the final painting will look like before they pick up a brush. Georgia O'Keeffe said, "I don't start until I'm almost entirely clear. It is a waste of time and paint if I don't. I've wasted a lot of canvasses, so I like to be pretty clear."

Knowing what you want is itself a skill. Our traditional educational system does not encourage you to know what you want. Instead you are encouraged to choose the "correct" response from narrow choices that life seems to offer. Frequently this has little relationship to what you really want. Because of this, many people develop an ambivalence toward what they want. And why not? It is hard to be enthusiastic about the choices most people are left with. But as you develop your own creative process, conceiving of the results you want will become meaningful and interesting.

2. Know what currently exists.

If you were painting a painting, you would need to know the current state of the painting as it developed. This would be important knowledge. If you did not know what you had created so far, it would be impossible for you to add more brushstrokes or change what you had done so as to bring the painting you wanted into being.

Knowing what currently exists is another skill. While this may sound deceptively simple, in fact most of us have been encouraged to view reality with particular biases. Some people make reality seem better than it is, some make it seem worse than it is, and some minimize how good or bad it can be. One of the most important abilities creators have is the ability to be objective about their own creations. There is a notion, popular in many university philosophy departments, that you can never really view reality objectively. But in the same university, the art department teaches those students to draw portraits of models. This drawing skill helps students learn first to see, and then represent, what they are looking at. Even though each art student may have his or her own style of portraiture, anyone from the philosophy department could identify the model by looking at any of the drawings of the model.

In music conservatories students are taught to identify rhythms, harmonies, and intervals by hearing them. This skill is called ear training. This is another skill in which students are taught to identify and represent reality correctly. When they write down the music that was played, it is not a matter of "interpretation." If the student correctly identifies what was played, he or she gets an A. Students who do not correctly identify what is played get less than an A. Music students learn how concrete the perception of music can be. This is another example of training designed to enhance the ability to view reality objectively.

In a similar way, you need to develop the skill of viewing reality objectively. For many people reality is an acquired taste. At first glance you may have uncomfortable and disturbing experiences. If you were in a problem-solving mode, you would take action to restore feelings of balance and well-being. The most common way people do this is by misrepresenting reality. They may lie, rationalize, or distract themselves from what is going on. But as you learn to master your own creative process, you develop a capacity for truth. Good, bad, or indifferent, you will still want to know accurately what is going on.

3. Take action.

Once you know what you want and know what you currently have, the next step is to take action. But what kind of action do you take? Creating is a matter of *invention* rather than of *convention*. Education emphasizes convention, so you may have had little experience with inventing. Inventing is another skill that can be developed. When you take an action that is designed to bring your creation into being, the action may either work or not work. If the action works, you can continue taking it or discontinue taking it. Sometimes it will be useful to continue, sometimes it will not be useful to continue. You will know what to do by watching the changes in the current state of the result. All the actions, the ones that work and the ones that do not work, help to create the final result. This is because creating itself is a learning process, learning what works and what does not work. The stock-in-trade of a creator are the abilities to experiment and to evaluate one's experiments.

Invention is not all trial and error. As you invent actions to bring your creations into being, you begin to develop an instinct for the actions that work best. Creators are able to develop an economy of means. This generally happens over time, and the more you create, the more chance you have to develop your own instincts.

Some of the actions you take will help you move directly to the result you want, *but most will not.* The art of creating is often found in your ability to adjust or correct what you have done so far. Many people have been encouraged to "get it right the first time" or, even worse, to "be perfect." This policy can lead to profound inexperience in the adjustment process. Instead of making the most of what you have done so far, in order to bring your creation into existence, you may be tempted to give up anytime the circumstances seem against you. Sometimes people encourage others to "stay with it" and develop "determination and fortitude" in reaction to habitual quitting. But this manipulation hardly ever works. Without an ever-increasing ability to adjust the actions you take, trying to "stay with it" can seem like banging your head against a wall. After sincere attempts to "stay with it" fail and fail again, the path of least resistance is to quit. You may have thought your habitual giving up was a serious character flaw. But this is probably not the case. It is not fortitude, willpower, or determination that enables you to continue the creative process, but learning as you go.

4. Learn the rhythms of the creative process.

There are three distinct phases of the creative process: germination, assimilation, and completion. Each phase has its own energy and class of actions.

Germination begins with excitement and newness. Partly this germinational energy comes from the unusualness of the new activity.

Assimilation is often the least obvious phase of the process. In this phase the initial "thrill is gone." This phase moves from a focus on internal action to a focus on external action. In this phase you live with your concept of what you want to create and internalize it. It becomes part of you. Because of this, you are able to generate energy to use in your experiments and learning. The drama of the first blush of germination is over, but this new, quiet energy of assimilation helps you form the result.

Completion is the third stage of creation. This stage has a similar energy to germination, but now it is applied to a creation that is more and more tangible. In this phase you use the energy not only to bring to final completion the result you are creating but also to position yourself for your next creation. In other words, this stage leads also to the germination of your next creation.

5. Creating momentum.

Many of the theories describing creativity these days have a tone of "beginners luck." For professional creators there is a different tone, that of ever-increasing momentum. Not only is the creative process a reliable method for producing the results you want, it also contains seeds of its own development. Who do you think has a greater chance for successfully creating the results they want: those who have done it for years, or those who are novices? It is true that some first-time novelists write masterpieces, but this is the exception, not the rule. Even Mozart, perhaps the most gifted composer in history, developed and grew in his art. The music he wrote in his thirties was far more advanced than what he wrote in his twenties or in his teens. The more music he wrote, the more he was able to write. His increasing experience gave him the momentum typical of the creative process. If you begin to create the results you want today, you are more prepared to create the results you want ten years from now. Each new creation gives you added experience and knowledge of your own creative process. You will naturally increase your ability to envision what you want and your ability to bring those results into being.

The Orientation of the Creative

The Structure of the Creative Process

The creative process has a structure different from that of reacting or responding to circumstances, one that resolves rather than oscillates.

Just as reacting or responding to circumstances can be an orientation, so creating can be an orientation. People in the reactive-responsive orientation sometimes create, and people in the creative orientation sometimes react or respond to circumstances. What determines your orientation is where you spend most of your time. For many people, much of their life is organized around the circumstances in their lives. For others, much of their lives are organized around creating what they want to create.

There is a dramatic difference between the two orientations. In the first, you are always subject to the whims of circumstances. In the other, you are the predominant creative force in your own life, and circumstances are one of the forces you use in the creative process.

The shift from the reactive-responsive orientation to the orientation of the creative is both simple and complex. It is easy to live in the realm of the creative, but it is so unusual that

56

many people find it hard to leave their past learnings behind. The shift can be aided by experiences of the creative process, but it is not a gradual manifestation. When you are in the reactive-responsive orientation, it seems difficult to make this shift, but when you are in the orientation of the creative, it is clear and obvious.

The Orientation

Living your life as a creator is truly a special existence. It is hard to describe to a person in the reactive-responsive orientation quite what it is like. Not only are the same events understood differently, but the possibilities and actualities of life are completely different. The orientation of the creative is not simply a different context, as it sometimes has been inadequately described by people not in that orientation. It is living in a different universe.

A person in the reactive-responsive orientation is in a kind of maze. The circumstances are the walls. The person's life consists of negotiating through the maze. Some people have found safety in traveling the same route, and some are consistently surprised when confronted with a new dead end, but either way there is always a limitation of choice, often between the lesser of two evils.

When you are in the orientation of the creative, life is often interesting, exciting, and special. This is not because creators try to be interested in whatever they are doing, but because they are involved in life on a level where there is always the possibility of something new and wonderful happening that has never existed before.

The orientation of the creative is not a perpetual state of euphoria, however. Creators experience frustration, pain, sadness, depression, hopelessness, and fatigue, as well as hope, joy, ecstasy, fun, and exaltation.

People in the reactive-responsive orientation often avoid both very negative and very positive emotions, and yet, ironically, they often make their emotions the centerpiece of their existence. They use their emotions as a barometer to measure their reactions or responses to the circumstances they are in. Because of this, they often have an unfounded hope that new circumstances will come along and "free" them from their conflicts. After all, if some circumstances make you sad, other circumstances can "make" you happy. If you take this notion seriously, life becomes a search for the "right" circumstances: the "right" job, the "right" relationship, the "right" financial situation, the "right" neighborhood, the "right" method or doctrine to believe in, the "right" purpose in life, the "right" friends, the "right" opportunities.

Creators understand that their emotions are not necessarily a sign of the circumstances. They understand that in desperate circumstances they may experience joy, and in jubilant circumstances they may feel regret. They have the wisdom to understand that their feelings change from good to bad and back to good. They know that any emotion will change. But because emotions are not the centerpiece of their lives, they do not pander to them. They create what they create, not in reaction to their emotions but *independent* of them. On days filled with the depths of despair, they can create. On days filled with the heights of joy, they can create.

The Spirit of Creating

People in the reactive-responsive orientation often give each other advice designed to motivate the "right" response. Some of this advice is a reaction against other responses they have. If you seem to be rigid—*"loosen up"*; if you seem to be in a rut—*"take risks"*; if you seem to fear the unknown—*"have courage"*; if you seem unenthusiastic—force yourself to *"be committed"*; if you experience hopelessness—convince yourself that *"you can have it all!"*

What motivates a creator? *The desire for the creation to exist.* A creator creates in order to bring the creation into being. People in the reactive-responsive orientation often have trouble understanding this sensibility: to create for the sake of the creation itself. Not for the praise, not for the "return on investment," not for what it may say about you, *but for its own sake.*

Poet Robert Frost captured the spirit of the orientation of the creative when he said:

"All the great things are done for their own sake."

Those of us who have children may already understand this principle. You love your child for *who the child is*, not as an extension of your identity or as an example of your good parenting or even as a companion. The child has a life of his or her own. The child is a separate being. The parent loves the child enough to bring the child into being and nurture the child until adulthood.

This is similar to the experience of creators. Their creations are like their children. They bring the creations into maturity so that the creations can live. They do not confuse their creations with their own identity. You are *not* what you create. Even though your creations come from and through you, your creations are separate from you.

When you separate yourself from your creations, you can experience one of the most profound understandings of creativity—love. *The reason you would create anything is because you love it enough to see it exist.* This is not as corny as it may seem, because this love is real. It is not manufactured in some workshop in which you are told to "love what you do, unconditionally!" Why would you create anything you did not love enough to see exist?

When I was an undergraduate at the Boston Conservatory, I joined the Newman Club. I was not a Catholic, but I liked the priest who led the discussions. In those student days I prided myself on my agnostic leanings, and I really went to argue about the existence of a Divine Being. The priest was well versed in the writings of Saint Thomas Aquinas and made a good case for a "Prime Mover." But one day he made what I thought was a leap of logic. "And God created the world because of love," he said.

"Wait a minute," I interrupted. "How did you get there?"

After a good twenty-minute impasse he finally said, "It is a matter of faith."

This answer was not good enough for me. Faith was the excuse you used if you didn't have a good argument. But somehow the idea—God created the world because of love—stayed with me through the years.

Then one day, in the middle of composing some music, I suddenly understood what the priest was talking about. I was creating this music because I loved it enough to see it exist. And I could imagine God—the Creator—creating the world for no other reason than love.

Had my priest friend better understood the creative process, he could have easily shared with me the profundity of his point of view. Here I was, a composer studying at a conservatory, already engaged in the creative process. If he had asked me this simple question, "Why do you compose?" I could have made *his* point. My priest friend had been taught to enact "proper" responses to life. For him the proper response was his religious doctrine of faith, learned from scholarship rather than direct experience.

I do not fault him in the least. Creating was neither in his experience nor in his orientation. He was doing the best he could within his orientation. And his words stayed with me until I could better understand them. For this I am truly grateful.

I share this story with you not as a inducement to believe in any particular religious or spiritual doctrine, but as a fascinating example of an inability to explain the orientation of the creative from the viewpoint of the reactive-responsive.

In fact, people from divergent religious, philosophical, spiritual, and political beliefs have been masters of the creative process. From atheists to Born-Again Christians. From Jews to Muslims. From Buddhists to Hindus. From capitalists to communists. From the political left to the political right. Creating is not the property of any special creed, nationality, race, religion, political leaning, or any other definition people give themselves.

If, like most of us, you have been raised in the reactive-responsive orientation, you probably have had little experience in doing what you do out of love of the thing being done. Most people do not spend their lives doing what they love. To them, doing what they love is a luxury, not a usual way of life. And often they confuse distraction with love. Hobbies, entertainment, and vacations can be such distractions. Yes, you can love your hobby, but is your hobby your life's work or just a respite from what you do not like? For too many, life is filled with unpleasant necessities that do not feed the human spirit, even though they may feed the human body.

Many people develop degrees of cynicism because there is nothing they love. This does not mean they have no capacity for love. Rather, they have not had the experience of creating. The caring they might have had was discouraged. They have developed a life policy of avoiding being a "sucker." They do not trust people who deeply care about life in ways that are unimaginable in their experience. They cannot invest their life spirit in anything, because nothing seems that important.

They can have a "lacklust" for life. Their lives go on, as in Robert Frost's poem, *The Death of the Hired Man*, "And nothing to look backward to with pride, and nothing to look forward to with hope / So now and never any different."

If you advised such a person to find something to love, he or she would not be able to take your advice. It is only when you begin to create for the sake of the creation itself that you can begin to understand the orientation of the creative. There are no tricks, no right responses, no ulterior motives. Just the love of the thing.

Obligation

In the orientation of the creative you have no obligation to create what you love enough to create. You do not need the creations you create. Artists truly understand this point, because there is no real need for art.

Actually, you need very little. With enough food, water, and warmth you can live for years.

In the reactive-responsive orientation, however, circumstances seem to demand actions. You may have characterized your desire to fulfill these demands as needs.

People often translate what they *want* into what they think they *need*. Partly this translation is designed to justify what they want. If they can make their desires seem like needs, they believe they have "no choice" except to work to fulfill them.

When needs become your nomenclature, you can never be sure which desires are authentic and which are not. If you make it seem as if you "need" what you want, how could you know what you love enough to bring into existence?

This kind of thought process is, after all, a form of self-manipulation. To the reactive-responsive person it is not acceptable to spend your life on what you love, because what you love is not tied to the circumstances.

Reactive-responsive people suspect that doing what they want would be selfish. This suspicion comes from a lack of self-knowledge. They may also believe that they do what they do in order to control their selfish interests. They often manufacture visions of misbehavior from doing what they want. They create the illusion of an inner conflict between blatant and destructive self-indulgence and sublimation of desire for the sake of others. When they make these assumptions, they can only perpetuate the myth that nothing they do is by free choice, but fulfills the "need" to reconcile competing opposites.

Mother Theresa does not do what she does because she needs to do it. She does what she does out of the kind of love I have been describing. If she were merely trying to bring relief to the suffering people she serves, she would become overwhelmed. She understands the depth of the capacity of human beings toward *both* good and evil. Because she understands this, she is able to make a conscious choice for good. Not out of a premise of obligation, but out of love for good.

One of the most important lessons I have learned in the past fifteen years of teaching the creative process concerns the true nature of people. When people are united with their real power—the power to create what they want to create—they always choose what is highest in humanity. They choose good health, exceptional relationships, and love, and relevant life purpose, and peace, and challenges worthy of the human spirit. People, I have come to discover, are profoundly good. But, you might well think, what about our destructive tendencies? What about all the examples of wars, inhumanity, and needless cruelty?

Those who spend their lives destructively are not in touch with their power to create. Instead, the manifestation of evil throughout history has come in reaction to the *inability*, not the ability, to create. Power-wielding, manipulation, terrorism, militarism, and lust for power do not come from having power, but from not having power.

If you thought you could not create what you wanted to create, it might seem to you that what you want is inconsequential. After all, if you can't have it anyway, why consider what you want?

In the DMA TECHNOLOGIES FOR CREATING® courses, participants

learn the important skill of conceiving of what they want. At first they may not know what they want, but when they begin to consider the question, they have a basis for new experiences. Perhaps they cannot name what they really want at first. Experimenting with what they choose brings what they truly want into sharper focus. Most often, they are able to create the results they want by learning how the creative process works. Then they can better conceive of future results they want to create. After the direct experience of creating what they have chosen, these people know that what they want is not arbitrary. It is one of the most important factors in their lives as creators.

The TECHNOLOGIES FOR CREATING® course is occasionally conducted experimentally in high schools. Students are asked to list what they want. Usually they want results, such as jobs after school, boyfriends or girlfriends, guitars, motorcycles, cars, and even better grades and better relationships with their parents and teachers.

Before they had taken this course, these students had been taught by parents and teachers that they cannot create what they want. They have had ample direct experiences of their inability to create. If you come into their classroom and try to convince them that they can create what they want in life, they're more than eager to prove how wrong you are. No amount of propaganda would change their attitudes or their perception.

Their perception is well-founded. If they have not had the experience of creating what they really want, why should they believe they can do this? In addition, they do not see many adults in their lives creating what they want. Often these are the same adults who are ready to give a pep talk at the drop of a moan.

By the end of the TECHNOLOGIES FOR CREATING® course, these students know they have the ability to create because they have done it. There is absolutely no hype given to them. They are more than capable of making their own conclusions:

"Did you create the job?"

"Yes."

"Did you create the relationship?"

"Yes."

"Did you create the car?"

"Yes."

"Did you create the motorcycle?"

"Yes."

"Did you create a good relationship with your parents?"

"Yes."

"Did your grades go up?"

"Yes."

After this kind of experience, these students have made two important discoveries: that they can create what they choose and that what they want is not inconsequential.

If, at first, they want goals that are not ranked as among the highest in the history of the human race, so what? What they create is important to them—they love the creation enough to bring it into being. It is one thing to speculate about what someone else should want; it is quite another to bring into existence what you actually do want.

The experience of creating has changed these students' lives. If the specific result created was "insignificant" by the world's standards, what was significant is the reality and power of the creative process. No longer do these young people have to spend their life in a compromise because they know no better. In fact, their real altruism is now more able to be expressed. Not by a sense of obligation to do good in the world, but out of an authentic desire—simply the love of the thing.

Creation Expressing Itself

There was a time when automobiles, telephones, television sets, solar reflectors, and space shuttles did not exist and were not even envisioned.

There was a time when rock music, atonal music, or even classical music did not exist and were not even thought of.

Two hundred years ago the fields of sociology, anthropology, biochemistry, paleontology, and nuclear physics did not exist. Today they do.

During this last decade a technological revolution has changed the world in ways that were unimaginable twenty years ago.

When composers create, they begin with a blank sheet of music manuscript paper. When artists paint, they begin with an empty canvas. It is sometimes difficult for us to think that something new can actually be created, something that did not exist before.

I often hear people assert, "There is really nothing new" or "Everything that is now created has been done before." I usually ask them if anything like Beethoven's Grosse Fugue, Op. 133, existed before he wrote it.

Certainly the string quartet for whom Beethoven composed the fugue had never seen anything like it. In fact, they said that it was unplayable and impossible to listen to, with all of its "random dissonances" and extreme voice-crossings. So Beethoven withdrew the piece and, in place of it, provided the musicians with a tamer work.

When the musicians first saw the *Grosse Fugue*, they thought old Beethoven had lost his stability, but Beethoven viewed his composition from a different perspective. "I write this music for a future time," he said. Today, most string quartets include the *Grosse Fugue* in their standard repertoire.

The arts and sciences are filled with example after example of new creations, works that never existed before they were created.

However, many people still prefer to think there is really nothing new under the sun. Writer D. H. Lawrence believed this until, at the age of forty, he discovered how wrong he had been.

> I remember I used to assert, perhaps I even wrote it: Everything that can possibly be painted has been painted, every brushstroke that can possibly be laid on canvas has been laid on. The visual arts are at a dead end. Then suddenly, at the age of forty, I begin painting myself and am fascinated.
>
> By having a blank canvas, I discovered I could make a picture myself. That is the point, to make a picture on a blank canvas. And I was forty before I had the real courage to try. Then it became an orgy, making pictures.

The discovery D. H. Lawrence describes is common in the orientation of the creative. What may have seemed dead suddenly has life.

The Secret of the Creative Process

A common mistake people make when first entering the orientation of the creative is to seek to "find out" what they want as if it were a deeply hidden treasure to be discovered and revealed.

They are looking in the wrong direction. Creating what you want is not a revelatory process, nor is what you want something to be discovered.

If not by revelation or discovery, then how do you derive the *what* in the question What do I want?

The answer to this question is known, either rationally or intuitively, by those who are actively involved in creating.

The answer to this question permeates all creative acts, from creating your life the way you want it to be to designing the latest technological advances in computer science.

Our educational tradition unfortunately has had a tendency to belittle the power and significance of this answer. And yet, once you begin to use it, new creative power and flexibility are available to you.

How do you create the *what* in "What do I want?"

YOU MAKE IT UP!

Please do not miss the point. This is truly a remarkable insight into the deeper nature of the creative orientation. If not by need, and not by the demands of the circumstances, and not by revelation, then how do you conceive of what you want? Simply by "making up" the results.

Years ago I consulted with an engineering group in a high-tech organization. When I mentioned to the engineers this insight about the creative process, they looked at each other with knowing grins. Then one engineer after another said, "That's exactly what we do. We make up what we create." One of them added, "But then we have to write technical articles explaining how we made it up in such a way that it doesn't seem made up!"

•　　•　　•

Making Things Up

Creative people know they make up what they create. But there is a strange prejudice in society about the notion of people making things up. One reason is that making things up is not characteristic of the reactive-responsive orientation upon which so much of our society is based. Since the reactive-responsive orientation relies so heavily on rationale and justification, to simply say "I made it up" seems almost heretical.

When creators are interviewed by the media, they are almost always asked to tell how they got the idea for their creation. Often, after a few attempts to explain that they "just made it up" leave the interviewer dissatisfied, they make up a story of how they "did it."

But the fact is that Albert Einstein made up the theory of relativity, Marie Curie made up the theory of radiation, Thomas Edison made up the light bulb, Mary Cassatt made up the painting *The Bath*, Anton Webern made up the *Six Bagatelles for String Quartet*, Emily Dickinson made up the poem "Because I Could Not Stop for Death," Ilya Prigogine made up the theory of dissipative structures, Joni Mitchell made up the song "Court and Spark," Harriet Tubman made up the "underground railway," and the founders of the nation made up the United States of America.

Even though it is common to focus only on the story of how a creation came to pass, it is important to realize that, no matter what these stories may be, the creator conceives of the creation at the moment of making things up. Composer Arnold Schoenberg was asked if he ever heard his music perfectly performed. He replied, "Yes, when I first conceived it."

As we view Hollywood's movie version of how the great creators "made up" their creations, we may receive a false impression. In the film versions there is drama. There are high strings, tremolo, súl ponticello, in the background music. All the signs point to a mystery taking place. The protagonist, whether a young Tom Edison, as played by a young Mickey Rooney, or old Thomas Edison, played by a middle-aged Spencer Tracy, is facing an inner struggle. The tension mounts. The camera moves to close-up as the stationary figure thinks and thinks. Eureka! Inspiration strikes. Suddenly all is action. The figure is in motion. The music is animated. The audience has been privileged to witness the awe-inspiring moment as the dramatic tension reaches its climax. Oh, if life were only like the movies! Especially black-and-white movies from the forties.

In real life, making it up is often less than dramatic. Many of the most inspired inventions were conceived without fanfare, drama, or inspiration (let alone background music). Drama is the exception, not the rule.

Even the scriptwriters of Thomas Edison's film bios were working on their script between bites of corned beef sandwiches and sips of Coca-Cola. They were fabricating a fantasy world of which they were not a part.

The creative process can look many different ways. Some of your best creations may come from the most normal experiences, and some of your worst may be the product of what seemed to be "divine inspiration." There seems to be no relationship between the final worth of a result and the experiences the creator has while in the process of creating.

Focus on the Result

In the creative orientation the most powerful question you can ask yourself is, "What do I want?" At any time and in any situation—regardless of the circumstances—you can always ask and answer that question.

The question, "What do I want?" is really a question about results. Perhaps a more precise way of asking that question is, "What *result* do I want to create?"

The question, "How do I get what I want?" is a question about process, not result. As an initial question, it is quite limiting. If you ask the question, "How do I get what I want?" before you ask, "What result do I want to create?" you are limited to results that are directly related to what you already know how to do or can conceive of doing.

In 1878, when Thomas Edison decided to create the electric light, it was already well known that electricity could produce light. The task before Edison was to find a material that would not burn out and instantly consume itself. He began by reading everything that had been written on the subject, and it is reported that he filled two hundred notebooks with jottings and diagrams.

All the scientists before him had followed a certain process:

They looked for substances that would reduce resistance to the electric current, but they had found none that would produce an electric light. Instead of following the same process and limiting himself to producing results he already knew about, Edison tried the opposite: He looked for substances that would increase resistance to the electric current. After testing countless resistant materials, he settled on a carbonized element and placed it in a vacuum bulb, thereby creating the familiar incandescent light bulb.

By keeping his focus on the result he wanted to create—an electric light—Edison was able to focus the process toward a successful result.

Frank Lloyd Wright was the creator of "organic architecture." In designing a house, Wright first conceived of the result he wanted to create: for him, it was a sense of interior space for living.

In his view a house was not simply a set of boxes within boxes, with rooms sealed off and connected to other rooms only by doors in partitions and dark halls, but primarily an entire space in which to live.

With his focus on living space as the result he wanted, Wright was open to new possibilities in design, ones that had never occurred to most of his fellow architects, who were still designing houses by rearranging sets of boxes, the traditional process of architecture.

In Wright's house, for the first time, the kitchen became an attractive feature; living and dining area became unified; floor spaces became living spaces; terraces, balconies, and windows allowed the outside and inside of the house to flow into each other so that the outside was brought in and the inside was brought out. His floor-to-ceiling windows invited daylight to flood the interior, and low-pitched roofs with wide overhangs created a sense of spaciousness and organic interaction with nature.

As Wright stayed focused on the results he wanted to create, the "how" of obtaining those results developed organically. He did not limit his concept or his process to standard procedures. Because he knew the result he wanted, he could invent processes that were uncommon and different from those of his contemporaries.

If you ask the "how" question before the "what" question, all you can ever hope to create are variations of what you already have.

Artists have a clear sense of this need to focus on the result they want. Speaking to young writers, Gertrude Stein once said, "You have to know what you want to get. But when you know that, let it take you. And if it seems to take you off the track, don't hold back, because perhaps that is instinctively where you want to be. And if you hold back and try to be always where you have been before, you will go dry."

When the process comes first, the process itself will limit the actions you will be able to take and thereby limit the possibilities of what you can create.

As the artist Chuck Close has said, "You can give the same recipe to ten cooks, and some make it come alive, and some make a flat soufflé. A system doesn't guarantee anything."

Pablo Picasso, as a mature artist speaking to young painters, encouraged them to conceive of new paintings rather than ones that followed the processes of the past.

> With the exception of some painters who are opening new horizons to painting, the youth of today do not know anymore where to go. Instead of taking up our researches in order to react sharply against us, they apply themselves to reanimating the past. Yet the world is open before us, everything is still to be done, and not to be done over again. Why hang on hopelessly to everything that has fulfilled its promise? There are kilometers of paintings in the manner of; but it is rare to see a young man working in his own way.
>
> Is there some notion abroad that man must repeat himself? To repeat is to go against the laws of the spirit, its forward motion.

The Premature Process

Premature focus on the process will limit and inhibit your effectiveness.

Our educational system does not focus on the results you as a student want in your life. Instead it promotes the notion that what you should learn is process. You should learn how to do mathematics and construct grammatical sentences. You should learn how to write research papers and do laboratory experiments in biology. You should learn how to draw, to speak in public, to read musical notation, perhaps even to write a poem or two. You should learn how to run a computer and a word processor, and you should learn some crafts skills in shop courses or some household skills in home economics courses.

The assumption is that as you become fluent in these processes, the results you want in your life will take care of themselves. Consequently few educators ask students the question, "What do you want in your life?"

True, for their first ten or twelve years, children are asked, "What do you want to be when you grow up?" But the children's answers are usually discounted unless they happen to follow in the footsteps of one of the parents. Similarly, people often ask adolescents, "What do you want to do when you get out of school?"

Usually, even though that question is asked, the young people have had no educational experience of the creative process. From their vantage point, the game of life appears to involve choosing from among uninteresting alternatives proposed by adults.

In the educational system, aptitude is often substituted for vision. For many people, their doing well on certain aptitude tests in secondary school was a great tragedy, because traditional guidance counseling helps students find out what they might be good at and helps them design careers around their aptitude.

Many people have mindlessly followed advice coming out of that mentality and become physicians, lawyers, engineers, accountants, nurses, and chemists, only to discover to their dismay, twenty or thirty years later, that they never really cared about what may now be the only field or profession they know. A major part of their life was spent developing what they happened to have an aptitude for at age fifteen.

I know several members of the Boston Symphony Orchestra who are bored being symphony musicians, yet their whole life revolves around the investment they have in staying where they are. One very great musician said to me, "I don't like playing in the symphony, but it's all I know how to do."

Organically Formed Processes

In the creative orientation, when you answer the question "What do I want to create?" it is not clear whether what you want is possible. Yet throughout the history of the world many results have been created that seemed impossible at the time they were conceived.

Before the creation of anesthesia, physicians were convinced that painless surgery was impossible. In 1839 Dr. Alfred Velpeau said, "The abolishment of pain in surgery is a chimera. It is absurd to go on seeking it today. 'Knife' and 'pain' are two words in surgery that must forever be associated in the consciousness of the patient. To this compulsory combination we shall have to adjust ourselves."

Before the creation of the airplane, many scientists were convinced that flight was impossible. Simon Newcomb, a well-known astronomer, was convinced that he had logically proven this impossibility. He wrote, "The demonstration that no possible combination of known substances, known forms of machinery, and known forms of force can be united in a practical machine by which man shall fly long distances through the air, seems to the writer as complete as it is possible for the demonstration of any physical fact to be." Ironically, Newcomb made this statement in 1903—the year the Wright brothers made their first flights at Kitty Hawk.

Many scientists were convinced that the atom could not be split or an atomic bomb created. In speaking to President Truman in 1945, Admiral William D. Leahy commented on the United States' atomic bomb program. "That is the biggest fool thing we have ever done," he said. "That bomb will never go off, and I speak as an expert in explosives."

Napoleon was convinced that the idea of a steam engine was impossible and told its inventor so in no uncertain terms. "What, sir!" exclaimed Napoleon to Robert Fulton, "you would make a ship sail against the wind and currents by lighting a bonfire under her decks? I pray you excuse me. I have no time to listen to such nonsense."

Once a vision is clear, processes organically form that lead to the accomplishment of that vision. This means that, in the creative orientation, process is invented along the way.

What Is the Formula?

A common rule of thumb in life is to have a formula about how things should work, so that if you learn the formula, you will always know what to do. From a reactive-responsive orientation, this notion is very appealing, because with such a formula you would hypothetically be prepared to respond appropriately to any situation. Unfortunately, at best this would prepare you for situations that are predictable and familiar. Your mastery of those situations would be similar to that of a well-trained mouse in a maze.

From the orientation of the creative, on the other hand, the only rule of thumb about process is not to have a rule of thumb. *The process should always serve the result.* And because a new result might require a completely original process, limiting yourself to preconceived notions of what processes are available can be fatal to spontaneity.

As painter Jack Beal put it,

> I have purposely tried to keep myself relatively ignorant on the subject of color. . . . I have tried to keep my color on an intuitive level . . . I have tried not to learn what warm and cool means or what the primary colors are. . . . I know some of these principles because you can't help but learn, but I try to let my color be as spontaneous as possible to the subject I'm painting.

It was said of Frank Lloyd Wright that he was never a slave to patterns, not even to those he himself developed. The history of twentieth-century art is filled with examples of artists radically changing the processes they had used. Some artists gained "followers" in a specific process they employed and then shocked the "true believers" later by inventing or adopting a completely different process.

In the first part of this century the two most dominant influences in music were Arnold Schoenberg and Igor Stravinsky. Schoenberg was the first to compose atonal music. Stravinsky wrote tonal music and was described as a neoclassicist.

Two schools of thought developed around these two towering giants. "Disciples" wrote dogmatic manifestos about the "real" future of music. Composers who wrote in one school of thought were considered invalid by the devotees of the other school. Because of this, friendships broke down, enemies were made, and the opposing camps became entrenched. There are even famous stories about people refusing to talk to each other because of their differing points of view. But none of these goings-on seems to have had any effect on the truly great composers working in this era.

Schoenberg and Stravinsky were not dogmatists. Stravinsky eventually shocked his followers by composing atonal music using the twelve-tone technique invented by Schoenberg. And Schoenberg shocked his followers by composing tonal music in C major.

For both men, the point of composing music was never the celebration of process but the artistic expression of their musical vision.

In her book *A Fuller Explanation*, Amy C. Edmondson describes R. Buckminster Fuller's Invention of the Octet Truss:

> Our familiarity with the IVM enables us to visualize and appreciate Fuller's "Octet Truss." Awarded U.S. Patent 2,986,241 in 1961, this structural framework is so widespread in modern architecture that one might assume buildings have always been constructed that way. Again, as the story goes, the invention can be traced to 1899 when Bucky was given toothpicks and half-dried peas in kindergarten. So extremely farsighted and cross-eyed that he was effectively blind (until he received his first pair of eyeglasses a year later), Bucky Fuller did not share the visual experience of his classmates and therefore lacked the preformed assumption that structures were supposed to be cubical. Thus, as other children quickly constructed little cubes, young Bucky groped with the materials until he was satisfied that his structures were sturdy. The result, much to the surprise of his teachers (one of whom lived a long, long life, and periodically wrote to Fuller recalling the event) was a complex of alternating octahedra and tetrahedra. He had built his first Octet Truss—also the first example of what was to become a lifetime

habit of approaching structural tasks in revolutionary ways.

Buckminster Fuller was four years old when he built the first Octet Truss.

Process, Process Everywhere, but Not a Vision in Sight

Learning processes has become the socially acceptable response. There is an abundance of processes for losing weight, growing hair, building muscles, vitalizing energy, having successful romantic relationships, quitting smoking, dressing successfully (and with the right colors!), reducing stress, overcoming psychological barriers, finding enlightenment, becoming self-actualized, learning to love yourself, contacting "higher intelligence," finding peace of mind, enhancing your sexual prowess, analyzing your dreams, integrating your mind, body, and soul, opening your heart, closing your past, being more "left" brain, being more "right" brain, becoming more affluent, etc., etc., etc., etc.

This is a wonderful age we live in. So much is available. But often the criteria people use to determine which direction they should take are dictated by notions about process rather than concepts about results.

In a conversation I had with a friend recently, she talked about "the sacredness of process," and "transcendental appreciation of one's process." I could almost hear a choir of angels softly singing as she rhapsodized.

This is such a foreign notion to a creator. When you create, process is functional. There is no dogma to adopt, no romance to maintain, no philosophy to uphold. Process is invented and designed to serve the result you desire. This is its only purpose.

It is best to allow processes to form organically from within the vision of the result. It is unwise to limit the way a result can happen by any given process. At the time you conceive the result you want, the actual way you will bring it about is always unknown to you, even if you have a hunch about it.

C h a p t e r   6

Tension Seeks Resolution

The path of least resistance oscillates in some structures and resolves in others. If you are in an oscillating structure, you will experience a recurring pattern. This is a pattern that moves toward what you want, and then away from what you want, and then toward what you want, and then away from what you want, and so on.

If you are in a structure that resolves, the path of least resistance moves toward final resolution of the structure. One major skill of the creative process is forming structures that resolve in favor of the creation. These structures are the most useful because they support movement in the direction of your final result.

In this chapter we will begin to consider how this movement is generated from the structure. In later chapters I will describe how to form structures that support you in creating what you want to create.

Tension-Resolution Systems

One basic principle found throughout nature is this: *Tension seeks resolution*. From the spiderweb to the human body, from the formation of galaxies to the shifts of continents, from the swing of pendulums to the movement of wind-up toys, tension-resolution systems are in play.

We can observe in nature and in our lives both simple and complex tension-resolution systems that influence not only the changes that occur but *how* those changes will occur.

The simplest tension-resolution system is a structure that contains a single tension. The tendency of the structure is to resolve the tension. If you stretch a rubber band, the tendency of the rubber band is to pull back to resolve the tension in the structure. A compressed coiled spring has a tendency to release the tension by springing back toward its original state.

In tonal music, because of the acoustical phenomenon of the overtone series, certain harmonic structures tend to move to other very specific harmonic structures. In tonality, the dominant seventh chord has a structural tendency to resolve to the tonic chord. In the popular musical phrase to which we associate the words *"Shave and a haircut, two bits,"* if we hear the melody played or sung only as far as *"Shave and a haircut, two—,"* we have tendency to resolve the tension generated by that musical phrase by adding the final note (associated with the word *bits*).

Tension-resolution systems are found throughout ordinary conversation. If I ask you a question such as, *"How are you?"* the structural tendency is to answer the question. This is because the question sets up a tension, and the answer to the question resolves that tension. This is known as an antecedent-consequential phrase; it is the most natural phrasing found in language and thought processes that depend on language. These phrases may be either question-answer, or statement-comment or question-on-statement:

"Did Martha go with you to the dinner?" (Tension)
"Yes." (Resolution)

"I think that their offer is unacceptable." (Tension)
"So do I." (Resolution)

Sometimes the resolution sets up a new tension that strives for new resolution. This is still a system composed of simple forms of tension-resolution:

"Yesterday we had three guests." (Tension)
"Who were they?" (Resolution and new tension)
"John, Irene, and Butch." (Resolution and new tension)
"Who is Butch?" (Tension)
"John and Irene's dog." (Resolution)

Once a tension exists, the path of least resistance leads toward resolution. The examples above are easily resolvable. Even if the answer to a question is "I don't know," the tension in the structure is resolved.

A simple tension-resolution system is in play in your own life when you are hungry. Hunger creates a tension. That tension is resolved when you eat. Similarly, thirst creates a tension. That tension is resolved when you drink.

Conflict of Tendencies

When tension-resolution systems are connected to other tension-resolution systems, they may compete with each other. In that kind of structure you have a conflict of tendencies. As one tension-resolution system moves toward resolution, the other tension-resolution system moves toward even more tension. Once the tension in the second system is higher than the tension in the first, the structure moves toward resolving the second system. But this will increase the tension in the first system. This structure will lead to oscillation because of the competing tension-resolution systems. Since this conflict is created by the structure, I call it *structural conflict.*

Structural Conflict

Structural conflict comes from two simple tension-resolution systems that compete. If you were hungry (tension), you would naturally tend to resolve this tension by eating (resolution).

TENSION   RESOLUTION

hungry   ———————————▶   eat

However, if you are sufficiently overweight, you may choose to go on a diet designed to bring you to a desirable weight. This sets up a separate system of tension resolution. If you are over-weight (tension), the tendency is for you to take action designed to resolve the tension, namely, not to eat (resolution):

TENSION	RESOLUTION
overweight	not eat

The simple tension-resolution system of "hungry-eat" and the simple tension-resolution system of "overweight–not-eat" are tied together, but they are in conflict. You cannot simultaneously resolve both tensions; that is, you cannot eat and not eat at the same time:

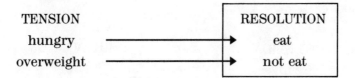

TENSION	RESOLUTION
hungry	eat
overweight	not eat

As you attempt to resolve one system, you deny the other and increase the tension in it. If you don't eat, you grow more and more hungry, which increases the tension in the hungry-eat system. The path of least resistance in this system is to eat. If you eat, you gain weight, which increases the tension in the overweight–not-eat system. Then your natural tendency is to diet. But when you do—you become hungry. Then you shift back to the hungry-eat system.

Together, these two simple tension-resolution systems form a complex relationship. The two points of resolution cannot both exist at once—you cannot simultaneously eat and not eat.

You also cannot resolve the tension in these two systems sequentially, since the resolution of one tension increases the tension of the other system.

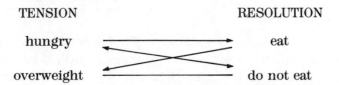

TENSION	RESOLUTION
hungry	eat
overweight	do not eat

On the level of *appearance*, many dieters seem to be taking action to achieve what they ultimately want—to lose weight. On the level of *structure*, however, their actions are designed to resolve a structural conflict. Because of the structure in play, while they may temporarily lose weight, the path of least resistance will eventually lead them to regain the weight they lost. But once they become overweight again, the path of least resistance will be to return to their diet.

Another common example of a structural conflict occurs in many large corporations that need to invest in research, building new factories, or opening new markets. These investments are designed for long-term growth. When corporations spend money for these types of investments, the profits are lower at first, but the hope is that the investments will lead eventually to higher profits. The immediate effect, however, is quite the opposite.

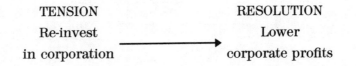

TENSION   RESOLUTION

Re-invest   Lower

in corporation   corporate profits

The capital to invest comes from shareholders who buy stock with the hope of a high return on investment (ROI). The corporation is concerned with the expansion of its capacity, which may yield long-term higher profits, but the immediate result is a reduction of the return on investment for shareholders.

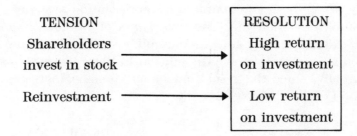

TENSION   RESOLUTION

Shareholders   High return

invest in stock   on investment

Reinvestment   Low return

on investment

Again the behavior is oscillation. First investors buy shares of the company because they're interested in ROI. Money comes into the company. The money is used to invest in long-term growth. Profits are reduced. Fewer investors are attracted to the stock. Less money is available for recapitalization. The company changes its focus to raising new capital. In order to be attractive to investors, the corporation reduces reinvestment in the company so it can show higher profitability.

This pattern of oscillation has made it difficult for many multinational corporations to make effective long-range plans. Hostile takeovers, a lag in research and development, and competition from companies who are not in this structural conflict have become a reality for many organizations.

Appearance

In this structure there is a shift from one tension-resolution system dictating the action to the other tension-resolution system dictating the action. This may be called a *shift of dominance*. These shifts of dominance form the behavior of oscillation. The forces in play may not be obvious. In fact, the dieter may wonder why it is sometimes easier to diet than other times. If you did not know that structural conflict was driving the action, you might become confused about just what is going on. On the level of appearance, the dieter tries to lose weight, tries to control his or her eating habits, and eventually fails. What is the problem? Too little self-control, not enough self-discipline, emotional complexes, self-hate, self-destructive tendencies, lack of willpower, lack of determination, an unfulfilled sex life, the economy?

The structure in play leads to oscillation. This is all it can do. Someone who takes actions to resolve a structural conflict often bases those actions on the appearance of the behavior—for example, the failure to diet successfully. That person is unaware that he or she is in an oscillating structure and that any actions he or she takes can only reinforce the underlying structure, ultimately leading to an experience of powerlessness.

One reason dieting is often unsuccessful is that the actions themselves are merely a strategy designed to overpower the structural tendencies in place. What happens, however, is that as one part of the structure is manipulated or stretched by the strategy of dieting, the other system (the desire to eat because of hunger) compensates by increasing its dominance. As you put pressure on one part of a structure, the rest of the structure pushes back. In system dynamics this is called *compensating feedback*.

A Classic Conflict Structure

The structural conflict most common is everyone's life is formed by two competing tension-resolution systems. One is based on your desire. The other is based on an incompatible dominant belief that you are not able to fulfill your desires.

This may not be intuitively obvious to you. Why might you have a belief that you cannot have what you want? Because there are certain limitations to the physical world. When you are growing up, you need to learn about those limitations. Some of these limitations are formed by *actual impossibilities*. Time, for example, only moves in one direction: forward. Time does not move backward. You do not grow younger and younger and eventually reenter the womb. This impossibility is part of the nature of the physical world you need to master. If you did not know this property of time, it would be difficult to negotiate the world. You may desire to have time go backward, and having such a desire would be consistent with the nature of the universe, but the accomplishment of that desire would be inconsistent with the nature of the universe, and therefore impossible.

Another limitation of the physical world is that everything that has a beginning will eventually have an ending. This is true of planets and people. This is true of our individual lives. Within the physical universe, some events have a dimension of *inevitability*, such as the birth-death cycle. Once anything is born, it is inevitable that it will eventually die.

As children we learn what our limitations are. Children are rightfully taught limitations essential to their survival. But too often this learning is generalized. We are constantly told we can't have or do certain things, and we may come to assume that we have an inability to have what we want. When we do manage to get what we want sometimes, we may not see it as a direct result of our efforts. We let our failure to achieve something reinforce our feeling that we cannot have it or don't deserve it. This assumption can become an invisible policy that goes unexamined throughout our lives.

Within inevitability there are events that are not inevitable.

Even though time only moves forward, much of what can happen within that movement is not fixed and determined. Many of the choices you make, the creations you create, and the circumstances of your life are not predetermined. Some of the choices you make are better than other choices you make. The choices you make have consequences. Part of the creative process is learning how to make choices that lead to consequences you favor. When you create, you are taking action in a realm that is noninevitable, nonfixed, open, and subject to your actions.

It is also our structural tendency to generate desires. We desire to breathe. We desire warmth and sustenance. Life itself is a desire. We also have desires that are beyond simple human needs. We desire to build, explore, develop, and create.

People both want to create what most deeply matters to them and simultaneously believe deep down that they cannot have what they want. This very human dilemma is actually a structural conflict.

Desire creates a tension, which is resolved by having what you want:

TENSION   RESOLUTION
desire ———————————————→   have the
                                           desired result

The belief that you are unable to have what you want creates a tension that is resolved by not having what you want:

TENSION   RESOLUTION
belief ————————————————→   do not have the
                                           desired result

Together these two tension-resolution systems create structural conflict, since the two points of resolution are mutually exclusive:

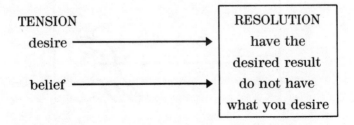

TENSION   RESOLUTION
desire ————————————————→   have the
                                           desired result
belief ————————————————→   do not have
                                           what you desire

Here is an analogy of how this structure plays itself out over time. Imagine yourself in a room. Imagine yourself midway between the front and back wall of the room. Imagine that the result you desire is written on the wall in front of you. Imagine as you move toward that wall that you are moving toward what you want.

Imagine the belief "I cannot have what I want" written on the wall behind you. As you move toward the back wall, you are moving away from what you want.

Imagine that around your waist are two gigantic rubber bands. One rubber band stretches from your waist to the wall in front of you. This represents the "desire" tension-resolution system.

The second rubber band stretches from your waist to the wall behind you. This represents the "inability to have what you want" belief tension-resolution system.

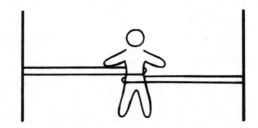

Now, imagine what happens as you begin to move toward having what you want. As you approach the front wall, what happens to the rubber bands? The front one, of course, relaxes, and at the same time, the one behind you stretches further. As you approach the front wall, where is it easiest for you to go? Where is the greater tension? Where does the path of least resistance lead?

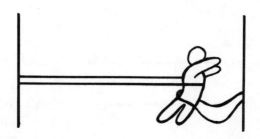

Clearly the path of least resistance leads toward the back wall. As you move toward creating what you want, it becomes harder and harder to take the next steps toward creating it. If you have reached the wall and have created the result, it becomes harder and harder to hold on to that result. It becomes easier and easier to lose ground and move back toward not having what you want. In nature, energy moves where it is easiest for it to go, and you are part of nature. So, one way or another, sooner or later, you will move back the other way. You will do so *not* because you have some deep-seated self-destructive urge or because you actually want to fail, but because you are moving along the path of least resistance formed by the structure in play.

Now, imagine what happens as you begin to resolve that tension by moving toward the back wall. As you move away from the result you want, there is a shift of dominance. The rubber band that had the most tension is now resolving, but the rubber band that was resolved is now increasing its tension:

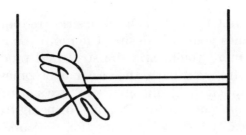

Obviously the path of least resistance now leads back *toward* the front wall, toward the result you desire. Over time you will tend to continue to move back and forth, back and forth, first toward one wall and then toward the other as the path of least resistance changes. These shifts may take minutes or years.

Most often the oscillation occurs over a longer period of time, and the phenomenon can be difficult to observe at first.

Though the specific actions taken might differ, anyone in this structure would behave in fundamentally the same way no matter what his or her desire. Any desire can be substituted for any other desire, and yet you will still see oscillation.

"Solving" Structural Conflict

At first sight it would seem easy to "solve" stuctural conflict by breaking either of the two component tension-resolution systems. One "solution" is to change the dominant belief from "I can't have what I want" to "I can have what I want." There are many methods for attempting to change your beliefs, *but all of them fail in this structure*. If you place the new "positive" belief—"I can have what I want" (or some variation)—on the front wall, changing your belief becomes your new desire. As you progressively adopt your new belief (as you move toward the front wall), the "can't have what I want" tension-resolution system becomes dominant. Ironically, it then becomes easier for you to believe you cannot have what you want than to believe you can have what you want, no matter how sincere you are or how diligently you try to brainwash yourself.

The other obvious "solution" to structural conflict is to give up your desires. This is often a misrepresentation of Eastern philosophy. "You suffer because of your attachment to your desires. If you were to give up your desires, you would no longer suffer."

If you attempt to relinquish all desires, relinquishing your desires becomes your new desire. The more you approach "no desire," the more you'll have the structural tendency to fail. The less "desire" you have, the easier it becomes to have desires. Also implicit in "giving up desire" are spiritual goals such as enlightenment or reaching Nirvana or being freed from the "illusion of reality." These goals function the same as any other goals in this structure. They still are connected with the "I can't have what I want" tension-resolution system.

Desire is tendency—the tendency of change, formation, and re-formation. The idea of "giving up desire" is consistent with the nature of the universe in which we live, because it is yet another desire. There are some desires we may never be able to achieve in this time-space universe. The desire to have no desire is on this level. It is consistent with the universe to have it, inconsistent to achieve it.

·   ·   ·

Structural Conflict Is Not Resolvable

Structural conflict may be defined as two or more tension-resolution systems in which the points of resolution are mutually exclusive.

Mutually exclusive points of resolution are not resolvable, either simultaneously or sequentially. Structural conflict operates at a completely different level from that which is colloquially thought of as emotional conflict. Emotional conflict operates primarily at the level of feelings and is experienced in such forms as anxiety, confusion, frustration, or contradictory emotions, such as love and hate for the same person. Structural conflict operates at the deeper, life-orientation level; it may give rise to these emotions or to a wide range of other emotions, from inner peace, lightness, and overwhelming joy, to apathy, heaviness, depression, and great sorrow. Your emotions often are generated by the structure you are in. The actions you take to avoid unwanted emotions or to foster wanted emotions do nothing to change the structure causing the emotions. Therefore, these actions do not succeed.

You also have a structural tendency to attempt to resolve a structural conflict. It is natural to continue trying to resolve a structural conflict even though the conflict is not resolvable. Designs do not always accomplish what they are intended to accomplish.

In the early days of aviation, many machines were designed to fly that never got off the ground. You may have seen old newsreels of one such machine with its many layers of wings, swiftly moving down the runway only to collapse before takeoff. Another such device had wings that flapped mechanically like a bird's. While the machine may have amused the designer's friends who had come to watch, it never amazed them as it sat stationary on the runway furiously bouncing and flapping its wings, forever earthbound.

Although those machines were designed to fly, there was something in the structural makeup of their design that made flight impossible.

People often attempt to circumvent the effects of structural conflict with great hope and optimism, which is usually followed by great disillusionment. It is inherent in this structure that any actions you take to solve structural conflict only reinforce the experience of limitation and hence the structure itself.

Since the nature of this conflict is structural, it is only by changing the underlying structure of your life that you can make any real and lasting change. However, any attempt you make to change the structure from within this structure will not work. Because of the structure in play, the path of least resistance will lead you to futile actions, actions designed to relieve the conflict, but that ironically will only entrench the conflict further. In fact, if you are in a structural conflict, you will develop strategies to compensate for the inability of the structure to support final resolution.

The nature of creating generates a completely different structure. But creating is *not* a solution to structural conflict. It is independent and unrelated to structural conflict. *It does not oscillate.* As we begin to explore the creative process, you will learn how to form structures that resolve and support your creations.

Before we can explore the structure of the creative orientation, however, we need to examine more thoroughly the compensating strategies people use to attempt to resolve unresolvable structural conflicts. Because these strategies are so firmly entrenched in our lives, we need to understand more about what they are and why they are inadequate for creating desired results. Then the distinction between the oscillating structures of structural conflict and the resolving structures central to the creative process will become more obvious.

Compensating Strategies

As we have discussed, structural conflicts lead to oscillation and not to final desired results. Consequently, people have a tendency to develop compensating strategies to deal with the inadequacies of the structure. How do these compensating strategies develop? Usually gradually. Your own compensating strategies develop so subtly that they are probably not obvious to you.

If your car's front wheels were out of balance and pulled slightly to the left, you might develop a compensating strategy of steering to the right when you wanted to move straight ahead. If the car's tendency to pull to the left developed gradually, your compensating action would also develop gradually. You might not even realize that you were steering to the right to compensate for the car's structure.

Once you had the wheels balanced and aligned, however, your compensating strategy of steering to the right would no longer be useful. You would no longer need to take compensating action, *because the structure had changed.* A shift in the structure leads to changes in your behavior.

In a similar way, when you move from a structure that oscillates to one that resolves, you may automatically change some of your behavior.

If you try to change your behavior without first changing the underlying structure causing that behavior, you will not succeed. This is because structure determines behavior, not the other way around.

Imagine that a friend of yours was riding with you in the car one day and noticed that you tended to turn the steering wheel to the right. If your friend knew nothing about wheel alignment, he might point to your behavior and suggest a change. "Don't steer to the right, steer straight ahead."

If you took his advice, you might change your actions temporarily, but in a short time—in order to stay on the road—you would return to steering to the right.

Much of the advice people give each other will not work, because it is designed to change compensating strategies without any notion of the underlying structures that are causing them.

Our human tendency is to propose theories of why people take the actions they take. Let's invent an almost plausible-sounding explanation for your action of steering to the right:

> "You steer to the right because of your overly developed left-brain functioning. You are too mental and have not developed your intuitive side. What you should do is focus on your receptive nature through meditation and change of diet. Your diet should have many more grains and vegetables. This will balance out your high protein intake and help you become more yin."

There are three major strategies designed to compensate for the fundamental unresolvability of structural conflict. They are: *staying within an area of tolerable conflict, conflict manipulation,* and *willpower manipulation.*

If you are in a structural conflict, you may temporarily reach your desire, but it will become harder and harder to hold on to it. The great love affair turns into a painful relationship, the fantastic job opportunity turns into a disappointment, the corporate triumph turns into disaster.

Because the path of least resistance moves toward and then away from your desired results, you may develop one or more of these three strategies to deal with future desires. All of them inhibit true creating. All of them reinforce the existing structural conflict and lead to oscillation. But all of them are prevalent throughout our society and throughout our lives.

Area of Tolerable Conflict

A common strategy is to attempt to minimize the amplitude of the oscillation produced by structural conflict. The structure in structural conflict has a goal. This is not the goal of defeating you, as some might guess. This is not the goal of forcing you to suffer hardship by trials of your sincerity, as others might guess. In fact, the goal of the structure *has nothing to do with you.* This goal is purely one that arises out of the makeup of the structure itself. The goal is equilibrium. Using our analogy of rubber bands and walls from the previous chapter, the goal of the structure is to have both rubber bands contain the *same amount of tension.* Oscillation occurs because there is a difference in the amount of tension in each part of the structure.

There is a point between both rubber bands at which both tension-resolution systems are exactly equal. But it is impossible to maintain this equality of tension, because of the natural shifts in the tension-resolution systems. Sometimes your desire causes differences in the system, sometimes your belief that you cannot have what you want causes differences in the system.

The more difference in one tension-resolution system over the other, the wider the oscillation. If you could limit the oscillation, it would not be as pronounced or uncomfortable.

Oscillation of structure creates oscillation of emotional experiences. With wide oscillation you can experience an emotional roller coaster. Many people do not like being on an emotional seesaw, so they adopt a strategy of minimizing the oscillation. This is done by remaining within an area in which they can easily tolerate the feelings generated by the system. Within this area of tolerable conflict, the pattern of oscillation continues to occur, but with decreased amplitude.

• • •

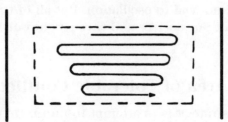

All of us know people who seem to continually "keep the lid on." Others try to "maintain an even level." An entire generation in the fifties grew up with the message, "Don't rock the boat." A person in this strategy avoids change. When confronted with a challenge, such a person attempts to minimize change by moving away from any potential experience of conflict.

What determines the point at which a shift in direction will take place? For different people there are different points, because different people have different degrees of tolerance for discomfort. The point at which you shift direction marks the outer limit of your area of tolerance of conflict. Were you to take even a single step beyond this area, you would feel pronounced discomfort. Often, therefore, the shift actually occurs before you reach the outer limit of your tolerance.

The behaviors found in this strategy are designed to limit aspiration and to minimize loss. This is the strategy encouraged by most institutions and organizations, including public education, government bureaucracies, and corporate life. The larger the organization, the greater the likelihood of this strategy becoming the norm. When people join organizations that have this strategy, they are brought into the fold by the message, delivered either subtly or overtly, "Don't make waves."

These organizations are not consciously or maliciously designed to thwart creativity and aspiration; they just do. The structural conflict begets the strategy of maintaining an area of tolerable conflict, which begets the behavior of reaching for only that which is "realistic" and minimizes risks. Predictability and certainty are highly valued, to the detriment of creativity and greater accomplishment.

This strategy is not only found in large organizations but also in the personal lives of vast numbers of people who have learned to minimize risk, limit their aspirations, and fit into a prevailing mediocrity that society seems to encourage. Life, to these people, can seem like the food you may sometimes have in your refrigerator—not old enough yet to throw out, but not good enough to eat.

Conflict Manipulation

Given the fundamental unresolvability of structural conflict, people often gravitate toward taking less and less action in favor of what they actually want. A common result is that people find they *only* take action when there is pressure on them. They then develop a strategy of mobilizing themselves into action by building up the pressure. Often they apply this strategy to other people as well. In this strategy you try to "motivate" yourself or someone else into taking action by presenting a vision of the negative consequences that will ensue if action is not taken.

Conflict manipulation always has these two steps:

1. *Intensify the conflict*—usually by presenting a "negative vision" or unwanted consequences if action is not taken.

2. *Take action designed to reduce the pressure*—usually by preventing the unwanted consequences from happening.

CONFLICT

ACTION

A person adopting this strategy does not take action to create what he or she wants. He or she takes action only to reduce the pressure that is synthetically manufactured by visions of negative consequences.

A corporation may launch a new program to avoid a potential loss in market share to a threatening competitor. An employee may show a burst of energy following a performance review at which his continued employment was called into question. A smoker may decide to give up cigarettes after hearing the latest statistics linking smoking and lung cancer.

Within the conflict structure, conflict manipulation produces movement first toward a vision of negative consequences and outside the area of tolerable conflict:

Movement in this direction continues as the internal experience of conflict increases to a critical point. Worry increases, concern intensifies, disaster seems imminent. The focus is on problems that exist and potential problems arising out of inaction. Structurally the desire tension-resolution system is more and more dominant.

Then the structure compensates, catapulting the person in the opposite direction, into action toward what is desired:

At this point the strategy of conflict manipulation seems to be working. The person takes action in the desired direction and may even succeed in producing short-term results. The structure has had a shift of dominance. As the movement continues toward the desired result, that tension-resolution system relaxes the tension. But then, the "I cannot have what I want" tension-resolution system increases its tension. The path of least resistance will soon shift away from the desired results.

The person originally used pressure to mobilize himself or herself into action, then took actions to reduce the pressure. The more this action is successful, the less pressure there is. Less pressure creates less motivation toward action. Over time, the extreme movement in the oscillation is reduced. The actions are neutralized. Movement returns to the area of tolerable conflict.

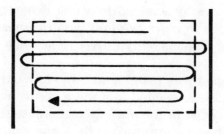

The long-term effect of this strategy reinforces the general experience of powerlessness in two ways. First, the strategy itself emphasizes that the power resides in the circumstances you wish to avoid. Second, the strategy confirms that despite your "best efforts," you have achieved nothing lasting.

If you worry chronically, you use conflict manipulation. If you are driven by your concerns, you use conflict manipulation. If you react to your negative emotions, you use conflict manipulation.

As we saw in chapter 3 on problem solving, the actions you take to reduce the intensity of the problem lead to less intensity and then to fewer future actions. Problem solving is an example of conflict manipulation.

I once spoke at a conference entitled "Creating Peace." Helen Caldicott, founder of Physicians for Social Responsibility, was one of the other speakers. I had never heard her speak before. She was very effective at creating an atmosphere of fear, doom, and trauma in the room. She explicitly described how your skin would look after the nuclear bomb fell. She explicitly described holocaust, famine, radiation poisoning, change in the earth's atmosphere, and final destruction of the planet. As she spoke in a monotonous Australian accent, people began to cry. The room got hot. Fear and then more fear took root. By the end of her talk the audience was ready to explode into action. The event was supposed to be a call to "sanity" against the insanity of impending nuclear war. Instead it was insanity against insanity. The more intense the horrific vision, the more powerless these people felt.

The synthetic raising of emotions is not new. This has always been one of the manipulations used to rally people into action. In fact, I believe Helen Caldicott is sincere, even though she is using the same kind of conflict manipulation that has been used for centuries by some of the worst demagogues. But this approach has led to more fear and powerlessness in the devotees of "social responsibility." Over time they are less able to act.

Nuclear weaponry is real. Should we close our eyes to this? No. But how has fear added to a more secure world? Why do these weapons exist in the first place? Because the military on both sides of the Iron Curtain use the same strategy of conflict manipulation. The conflict they attempt to increase is based on a terrifying vision of the world dominated by the other. They fund their armament policies by creating horrific visions of being conquered by an enemy that has superior strength in bombs. To these people, the fear is just as real as it might be for Helen Caldicott. It is just a different fear. The actions they take lead to more powerlessness and more bombs.

Can more of the same kind of thinking save the world? Is there really a difference in structure, form, or pattern between the antinukes and the pronukes?

After years of conflict manipulation, the people who use this strategy often feel less and less powerful and less and less able to act. When this conflict acts as the driving force, actions taken to reduce it can never build long-term creations. If we try to build our civilization's future based on conflict, we will end up with much of what we have today.

The more extreme the conflict, the more extreme the actions. The terrorist is an extreme practitioner of conflict manipulation, someone who creates as much conflict based on terror as he or she can so that others will take the actions the terrorist hopes for. This is usually done in the name of higher values.

Often an extreme conflict will lead to counterinstinctive behavior, such as mothers having lots of children—so that they can die for the "cause." A mother's natural instinct is to have babies so that they can live, not die. But her natural instinct can be defeated if the conflict is high enough. This tragic pattern has filled many pages of modern world history.

Some groups begin with an honorable cause and then degenerate into conflict manipulation. Greenpeace, for example, has adopted this strategy in recent years. Allegations of secret operations, sabotage, and extreme propaganda have plagued what was once an effective and credible organization. Does Greenpeace live in a different world than Jacques Cousteau? His institute addresses many of the same issues concerning the environment, but with much greater effectiveness. Cousteau's work is not based on conflict, but on true love of the beauty of the planet.

Many people mix conflict manipulation in with otherwise good works. Futurist Jean Houston slips into conflict manipulation when she writes in *Life-force: The Psycho-Historical Recovery of the Self*:

> It is significant that the current crisis in consciousness, the loss of a sense of reality felt by so many, the rising tides of alienation, occur concomitantly with the ecological destruction of the planet by technological means. We are forced into the awareness that we are not encapsulated bags of skin dragging around a dreary ego. Rather, a human being is an organism-environment, symbiotic with many fields of life.
>
> This brings us to the momentous point in human history where, if we are to survive, we have no choice but to reverse the ecological and technological plunder; and that will mean discovering or rediscovering forms of consciousness and fulfillment, forms of human energy apart from those of consumption, control, aggrandizement, and manipulation. It is time to take off the human shelf all those potentials lying dormant there that were not immediately necessary to man in his role as *Homo laborans* or as Promethean man-over-nature.

Here is an example of some interesting thoughts mixed with conflict manipulation. A relationship between the environment and consciousness? Interesting. The development of greater potentials lying dormant? Interesting. But if we do not take the actions, according to Houston, we are doomed. The tone of urgency, crisis, plunder, and a potential lost moment in this "momentous point in human history" is the conflict. The action designed to reduce this conflict is: "we have no choice but to reverse the ecological and technological plunder." What if we don't? We will not survive.

The message is clear. Do the rights things or get creamed. If you took this seriously, you would take action in the name of preventing dire consequences, but its real goal would be to reduce the conflict produced by contemplating the dire consequences. Your actions would reduce some of your experience of conflict, even though the situation might remain the same or even get worse. Less conflict would lead to less action. This is the path of least resistance. The structure compensates for the manipulation. Extreme oscillation to one side leads to extreme oscillation to the other, and over time, the swing of the oscillation is again reduced. The effects are short-term at best.

As Robert Frost so aptly put it:

"I never tried to worry anybody into intelligence."

Many of the attempts at visionary altruism have exactly the opposite notion: *Worry people into intelligence.* The approach can be attention getting, but can lead to little more than an increase and then a decrease of the driving conflict. The changes of intensity of the conflict often have nothing to do with any change of circumstance. The conflict and the actions related to them do not contribute to creating a new and better world.

And how about a good dose of guilt? Guilt is often used as the conflict designed to manipulate you into better actions. Psychologist Rollo May has written:

> If you do not express your own original ideas, if
> you do not listen to your own being, you will have
> betrayed yourself.

Betrayal for not listening to yourself? Betrayal for not expressing your originality? Whatever happened to free will? Why must you be obligated to express yourself? How true can you be to yourself when you have "guilt-tripped" yourself into it? This is not choice, but coercion.

Similarly, Helen Luke has written in *Woman, Earth and Spirit*:

> Commitment to our unique way in life is our task
> today and every day. It is not to be undertaken for
> our self-improvement, nor for the salvation of the
> world or society, but simply because we can do no
> other if we are to be true to the individual *hypoth-
> esis* of our lives.

How is it commitment if you can do no other? I thought commitment was a choice, not an obligation. This type of thinking
is common in this day and age. We live in an era of platitudes
and mottos. Many of them are designed to manipulate people
into action:

> If you're not part of the solution, you're part of
> the problem.

This one, popular in the late sixties and early seventies, was
clever. No matter what you did, you were involved with the
conflict. And if you happened not to be directly involved, you
were the cause of the conflict.

Silvano Arieti has written in his book *Creativity*:

> Creativity is one of the major means by which the
> human being liberates himself from the fetters not
> only of his conditioned responses, but also of his
> usual choices.

Here creativity becomes the action designed to reduce the
conflict of fetters of conditioned responses and usual choices.
Again, the action addresses conflict. The notion of creating as
therapy has been tried and perhaps is as useful as any other
type of therapy, but you would find it difficult to create what
most mattered to you based on a strategy of defeating the conflict of usual choice and conditioned response.

So many of the notions of human growth are filled with these
kinds of conflict manipulation. I suppose it is considered good
marketing. Create a perceived need in the prospective client.
Encourage a sense of urgency. Make it seem as if there is no
choice. But conflict manipulation has a structure that cannot
lead to growth, just more extreme oscillation. Thus many of the
people who attempt to cause change, often with real sincerity,

do not change and do not grow. The structure of conflict manipulation does not support change.

Negative Visions: Fear, Guilt, and Pity

Conflict manipulation has become a popular strategy in promoting and fundraising for a number of community causes—social, health, political, religious and so on. At one time or another many of them employ the same formula, though some manipulate through fear while others use guilt and pity.

Organizations fighting cancer attempt to scare you into quitting smoking or eating certain foods by threatening you with a vision of cancer.

The heart societies try to get you to follow low-cholesterol, salt-free diets by threatening you with a vision of a heart attack.

Every day hundreds of radio and television evangelists promote a vision of evil in an attempt to scare you into being good. A lot of good it has done some of them.

While environmentalists attempt to scare you into supporting environmental regulation by promoting dire visions of acid rain and polluted waters, at the same time, using the same strategy, some business and political leaders attempt to scare you into supporting environmental deregulation by promoting a dire vision of a ruined economy and widespread high unemployment.

The "moral majority" attempts to scare you into voting for their candidates by promoting a vision of amoral and unpatriotic officeholders.

Using the emotions of guilt and pity, certain hunger-relief organizations attempt to gain your support by promoting visions of starving children. Certain disaster-relief organizations attempt to gain your support by promoting visions of human misery.

Equal rights and civil rights organizations attempt to enlist your support, often through guilt, by promoting visions of injustice, racism, hate, sexism, and prejudice.

Groups organized to protect endangered species induce a combination of guilt and pity by promoting a vision of the slaughter of whales, seals, and other forms of wildlife so that you will send money and support their causes.

The great irony is that each one of these groups, by using conflict manipulation, promotes a vision that is, in most cases, the *opposite* of what they really want to see created on the planet. One tragedy of our times is that well-meaning people often lend enormous amounts of energy to visions they really do not want to see happen.

Breaking Habits Through Conflict Manipulation

A popular approach in trying to change destructive habits, such as overeating, alcohol or drug abuse, gambling, smoking, and so on, is to use variations of conflict manipulations. The two basic steps, however, remain the same.

Step one of conflict manipulation is to intensify or exacerbate the conflict. When you attempt to break bad habits, this step is usually carried out by envisioning the terrible negative consequences of your bad habit, the one you are trying to break.

Step two is to take action designed to relieve the emotional conflict that was set up in step one. When you're trying to break a habit, the action you'll take at this point is to stop or reduce the unwanted habit. Stop drinking, stop excessive eating, stop taking drugs.

As many experts on addiction know, the first few attempts to overcome abuse usually end up with the addicted person returning to the unwanted habit. What they do not know is that they are using conflict manipulation, which will not lead to success because of the inadequacies of the structure. When the addict lessens the conflict set up in step one by temporarily stopping the habit in step two, the path of least resistance leads him or her back to the original habit.

CONFLICT

STEP 2   STEP 1

ACTION

Eventually, in response to such "failures," those using conflict manipulation often move to the strategy of never letting the conflict reduce in intensity. Thus, step one is always being applied. Alcoholics continue to tell each other that they will always be alcoholics and that at any moment they may revert to drinking, no matter how many years they have been on the wagon. Similarly, in some programs designed to help people stop overeating, participants are trained to warn themselves continually that they are powerless and uncontrollable and, therefore, must at all costs keep a close watch on themselves. If they do not, they are told, they will overeat.

In the reactive-responsive orientation, since the power in life is assumed to be in the circumstances, it seems as if the only alternatives addicted people have are either to remain addicted or to engage continuously in conflict manipulation, in which case they continually exacerbate emotional conflict in order to keep from drinking, gambling, overeating, and so on.

If those were the only choices for addicted persons, then certainly in most cases conflict manipulation would be the better of the two alternatives, since most addictions have direct detrimental physical and emotional consequences.

However, whether or not a person drinks or does not drink, uses drugs or doesn't, overeats or does not overeat, no real change happens in the basic underlying structure in the addicted person's life through the use of strategies based on conflict manipulation. Why do you suppose addicted persons drink or overeat or take drugs or smoke in the first place? Structurally, these habitual actions themselves are attempts to reduce various kinds of emotional conflicts that the addicted person experiences. Such conflicts may involve deep loss, grief, fear, and guilt. The strategy to break an addictive habit is generally to make the conflict about having the habit more dominant than the distress that it is an attempt to resolve.

In *Positive Addiction*, William Glasser describes certain nondisruptive habits such as meditation, jogging, yoga, and other forms of exercise as useful substitutes for negative addictions.

A man who had been an alcoholic for many years was able to

substitute an hour of daily meditation for his drinking habit. For him, meditation became a positive addiction. When asked what happens to him on days when he doesn't meditate, he described physiological symptoms similar to those he previously experienced when attempting to withdraw from alcohol, except that his present symptoms were due to withdrawal from meditation.

The underlying structure of positive addiction is the same as that of negative addiction. While a positive addiction is much healthier than a negative one, it still produces an undermining effect. The addiction itself, whether positive or negative, is a strategy to avoid the negative, unwanted consequences of the withdrawal symptoms. In one way or another, the addicted person is in a state of manipulation. This is not always necessary.

Stanton Peele, a well-respected expert on addictions, contends that the best way to stop an unwanted habit or an addiction is simply to stop. He believes that is what most people actually do. He cites case studies that contradict the common notion that addictions are very difficult to stop.

For example, according to the studies quoted by Peele, 95 percent of the soldiers who were addicted to heroin in Vietnam were able to end their use when they returned to the United States. Furthermore, 85 percent of those who were classified as seriously addicted were able to quit when they returned home. Based on common notions about drug addiction, experts had predicted epidemics of heroin addiction when these servicemen returned to the United States. But the epidemics never materialized. Why not?

Peele proposes that these servicemen—and people in general—have much more capacity for self-reliance than they are given credit for. He further suggests that many of the experts dealing with addiction use approaches that undermine the individual's self-reliance, thus making it more difficult rather than less difficult for the clients to change unwanted habits.

When a real change in the underlying structure occurs, it is possible for the path of least resistance to lead directly toward what you want. A natural effect of following that path may be a change in unwanted habits, habits that might interfere with what you really want. Self-sufficiency is not based on willpower, but on strategic choice.

Dr. Janice Keller Phelps, M.D., coauthor of *The Hidden Addiction—And How to Get Free*, has said:

> Many traditional approaches toward addiction distract the patient from chronic depression, but biochemical imbalance still remains. The creative process is a door that allows for a new biochemical balance to be formed and maintained.

Conflict Manipulation and Powerlessness

Reality does include cancer, addiction, and other serious health problems, such as hunger and starvation, excessive armaments and wars, cruelty and misery, environmental imbalance and endangered species, sexism and other prejudice, terrorism and fanaticism.

Many of these situations are fundamentally caused by people's chronic experience of powerless; others, while not the direct results of such powerlessness, are aggravated by it. Attempting to change situations that have their roots in powerlessness through a strategy that reinforces powerlessness is folly.

That conflict manipulation is used in personal relationships, business and legal negotiations, politics, education, advertising, fundraising, and throughout society is not a "problem" that needs to be "solved" and should not become the subject for new conflict. The structure itself has built-in limitations that cannot lead to desired results. As you begin to work with the concept of structure, notice the degree of conflict manipulation in your own life, both that coming to you and that coming from you. When you begin to look, it becomes obvious that many of the interactions people have with each other are products of conflict manipulation.

Willpower Manipulation

Many people find that they take little or no action unless they motivate themselves through heightened volition, "positive attitudes," or inspiration. The use of willpower is another strategy designed to overpower structural conflict by forcing oneself into action. If you succeed, you may be considered "strong-willed"; if you fail, you may be considered "weak-willed." Most people feel that they never have enough willpower to accomplish anything of significance, but they nonetheless believe that willpower or positive attitudes are essential to success.

The Powerlessness of Positive Thinking

A familiar strategy in this mode is to fortify willpower through positive thinking, exaggerated affirmations, motivational resolve, and inspirational fervor. Some of the theories suggest that it is necessary to "program" the mind with positive propaganda so that you can enlist the cooperation of your subconscious, which is presumed to control the course of your life. The assumption is that if you can change the "program" of your subconscious, you will live happily ever after.

Every year thousands of books and magazine articles encourage people to develop their willpower this way. Dozens of cable television programs are dedicated to these approaches. Subliminal message tapes, affirmations, self-hypnosis, positive reinforcements, motivational meetings, slogans and mottoes taped to the bathroom mirror, and cheerleading of all kinds are attempts to overpower structural conflict through exaggerated determination and the "power of positive thinking."

If you assume that you can influence and direct your subconscious, what messages do you give it by using many of these programming techniques? *It is very hard to communicate with the subconscious. It takes special and extraordinary means. Old "programs" have enormous power. The subconscious is stupid and unruly. It must be treated like a child.*

If you thought that programming the subconscious was the key to your life, why would you want to influence it with that kind of message? When you try to force-feed the subconscious with positive thoughts, the actions of manipulation speak louder than the propagandistic positive words.

Affirmations

A popular technique for force-feeding the subconscious is the use of affirmations. This is the practice of repeating "positive" thoughts to yourself. Sometimes you are encouraged to repeat these phrases like a mantra, other times to write them over and over, a little like a naughty student writing "I will not make fun of the teacher anymore" over and over again on the blackboard.

The following is an actual list of affirmations used by the proponents of this approach:

> The Universe supports me.
> The more I love myself the more others love me.
> Money is my friend.
> It is now okay for me to approve of my parents.
> I love myself now, today, and always.
> Everything I give is returned to me one-hundred fold.
> I deserve to be wealthy.
> Where I am and what I am doing right now is meant to be and I am loving every moment of it.
> I am in the right place at the right time doing the right thing successfully.
> Since people treat me the way I treat myself, I now treat myself fabulously.
> All my relationships are loving, lasting, and harmonious.
> I forgive my parents for their ignorant behavior toward me.
> I survived my birth, therefore I love life more than death because I chose to survive.
> I am highly pleasing to myself.
> My heart is full of love and I generate love to all I meet.
> It is safe for me to ask questions when I don't understand.
> I am willing to surrender to my life just the way it is.
> I have the right to say no to people without losing their love.
> I love and approve of myself and I always will.
> Love is letting go of fear.
> My parents love me whether they know it or not.
> Love heals everything.
> I can have it all.
> I know it will happen.

Some of these ideas seem like nice, friendly thoughts. Innocent and sweet. Others sound like pop-psychology anthems designed to combat deep inner self-destructive urges. Let's look at the implications of a few of these phrases:

· *The Universe supports me.* The word *support* here refers to your growth, life sustenance, and well-being. If the Universe really supported you, why would you need to mention it repeatedly? To repeat this phrase over and over again suggests that you don't really believe it, because who but someone who does not believe the Universe supports him or her must attempt to force the mind to accept this thought? You are actually affirming that the Universe does not support you but that you would like it to and that the Universe better get on the stick.

Some people do experience that the Universe supports them, but people who have that experience usually do not feel they have to make a repeated point of declaring it. If you thought something was true, why would you need to repeat it to yourself, trying to brainwash yourself with the idea? Let's change the phrase "The Universe supports me" to "My heart beats." Can you imagine saying this phrase over and over?

My heart beats.
My heart beats.
My heart beats.
My heart beats.
My heart beats.
My heart beats.

· *All my relationships are loving, lasting, and harmonious.* If this were true, then it would be accurate to report it. But usually the person who is affirming this has the opposite experience. Saying something that isn't true is called lying. Why would you need to lie to yourself? Can't you take the truth? What you are actually affirming here is that you need to lie to yourself. This phrase belies a disrespect for the other people you may be in a relationship with; it implies that they "need" to be loving, harmonious, and they better stick around, or they'll be nothing more than "fair-weather friends." God forbid that you have moments of conflict or that these people leave your life or you leave theirs. This affirmation is designed as a reaction to reality, which is that not all relationships are smooth, permanent, and free of conflict.

· *I am highly pleasing to myself.* If so, why mention it and mention it and mention it? What happens on days that you are not highly pleasing to yourself? Do you have to be highly pleasing to yourself all the time? Aren't you allowed a bad day? If you were not particularly pleased with yourself, what's wrong with that? The affirmation implies that there is something wrong with you if you are not pleased, and it also implies that you are not pleased. So the real message is . . . "There is something wrong with you."

· *I am willing to surrender to my life just the way it is.* Many people who advocate "surrender" appear to be using the opposite of willpower manipulation. But "surrender" is simply another form of willpower. The thought here is, "I will not interfere with the Universe in its wisdom. I will not try to control the circumstances. I will give in and let go." But why do people adopt this policy? Because the active approach did not work well, so now they want to overcome their conflicts by using the passive approach. What is it that you are surrendering—your desires, your will, your personal opinions? Now you *will* that you will *not will*. Toward what end? So you can be one with the Universe? Then this becomes your new desire, and your will is expressed as an openness to the circumstances from which you will take your cues. This is another reactive strategy—reaction against the inability to create desired results, reaction against the experience of failure.

The theme of surrender results from a conclusion about the nature of the Universe: You are powerless to effect your own destiny. Any attempts to change this situation will end in failure or even disaster. You had better see the light and cooperate or be creamed. This is the message the universe is trying to get through our thick heads: "Go with the flow." Often this thinking is accompanied with platitudes of respect for "how life is." But the platitudes do not hide a disrespect for all of the forces in play in life. The nature of structure leads to various degrees of action—sometimes extreme action, sometimes extreme inaction, and degrees between these points. In white-water rafting, if you simply "go with the flow," you end up on the rocks.

Surrender has the connotation of "I give up, I give in." The tone here is not one of working with the forces in play, but that of acquiescence. To place this thought in the context of an affirmation becomes almost absurd. Affirming that you surrender is actually willing yourself to surrender. Forcing yourself to "let go" is hardly letting go, but imposing. The policy of surrender itself is an expression of willpower, imposing on yourself the behavior and attitude of surrender. Often, surrender of this type implies a battle between your ego and the will of the Universe, with the further implication that they are at odds, so to consider what you might want is a form of arrogance. I once met a woman who said, "I only want to do God's will."

"Whose will is it to do God's will?" I asked her.

After a long pause she said, "Mine."

· *I know it will happen.* Often this phrase is used to foster belief in yourself and to build self-confidence. In fact, you don't know if "it" will happen, you only know if it seems probable. Even the most predictable events may not happen. If you suddenly die, for example, you could not do many of the things that are now very predictable. But beyond that, this affirmation is a prime example of positive thinking's lack of respect for the truth. Only when something is completely done can you say with full confidence and veracity, "It can be done."

The Disempowerment of Positive Thinking

What is wrong with positive thinking? In a word—*truth.* One of the skills of the creative process is to assess the current state of the creation in progress. This is difficult if you have a bias. If you try to impose a positive view on reality, you will not easily be able to adjust your actions in the creative process.

For years advocates of positive thinking have claimed that your attitudes will shape your destiny and that if you think positive thoughts, positive results will occur. The strategy you use is to force yourself into thinking the "best" of any situation.

If you wake up in the morning and you feel sick, tired, and headachy, one school of positive thinking would have you force yourself to think something like, "Boy, I feel great today. Isn't it fabulous to be alive?"

A second school of positive thinking would have you say to yourself something like, "I really feel sick. I think it's just wonderful that I feel sick, because good things always come from these kinds of situations. What a wonderful learning opportunity."

Positive thinking is a willpower strategy designed to help people exert their will over themselves as a kind of self-manipulation.

There are two assumptions, generally unexpressed and unexamined, at the roots of both schools of positive thinking. The first is that you need to control yourself by overpowering your habitual negativity. The second is that the objective truth about reality is somehow dangerous to you and that you must therefore impose upon the truth a beneficent interpretation.

The radical difference between positive thinking and the creative orientation can be seen in parallel assumptions about the creative process.

First, in the orientation of the creative, there is no need to control yourself. Instead, the orientation assumes that whether you are habitually negative or not, you have a natural inclination toward creating what you most truly want. Furthermore, there are no inner forces you must overcome, only inner forces that might be aligned organically as part of the creative process. This is not programming yourself, but rather working with all of the forces in play—including the forces you may not especially like.

Second, in the orientation of the creative, it is essential to report to yourself what reality truly is, no matter what the conditions and circumstances may be. A clear description of reality is necessary input in the creative process. Were you to impose any "rose-colored" or otherwise synthetic views on your reality, you would obscure it.

In the orientation of the creative, if you woke up feeling sick, tired, and headachy, you would report the truth to yourself, exactly as you observed it. Furthermore, there would be no need to interpret the ultimate meaning of your situation ("Good things always come from these kinds of situations"). Reality may, of course, include your opinion of the situation, for example, "I feel sick, and I don't like feeling this way."

Let's examine what happens schematically when you try to overpower structural conflict through willpower. At first, your exaggerated determination may drive you in the direction of what you desire and out of the area of tolerable conflict.

·   ·   ·

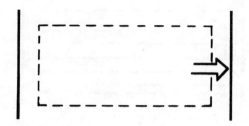

In the short run, you may achieve a successful "break-through." Willpower manipulation, like conflict manipulation, often does work in the short run, but it has detrimental long-term consequences. Once again, even if you reach the front wall, the structure compensates for the exaggeration in the oscillation and you move backward. The structure does not support your willful determination. "Holding it together" and "getting yourself up" for each new event and each new day becomes exhausting. Eventually the compensation leads you away from what you want. This "failure" is not a sign of the weakness of your "intention," nor is it some kind of "inner resistance," but simply the natural movement of this structure. The path of least resistance, determined by the structure, cannot lead in any other direction than away from your desired result, no matter how hard you try to "keep the faith."

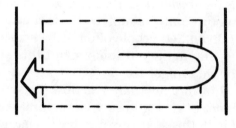

Over time, as the structure continues to compensate, the oscillation will continue. You will eventually gravitate back to the area of tolerable conflict:

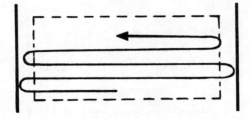

Like conflict manipulation, willpower manipulation will re-inforce your experience of powerlessness over time. It does so first through the message implicit in the very attempt to in-spire and motivate: that you require outside prodding to control your powerful inertia and "resistance" and negative thoughts. Second, you experience powerlessness because once again you have tried something, and despite your best efforts and deter-mination, it has not worked. No lasting change has occurred.

Some Words of Advice

As you may imagine, if you are in structural conflict, your best compensating strategies will not work. Throughout the years, when I have described this structural phenomenon, the natural tendency of most people is to ask, "How the hell do I get out of this!"

I can understand. The experience of clearly seeing how your actions fail to lead you to eventual success may not seem like good news. You may feel frustrated when you realize that struc-tural conflict is *nonresolvable*, that any action you take from within this structure only reinforces it. Because of the nature of this structural conflict, people often feel a sense of hopeless-ness and doom. The more you understand this structure, the more frustration you might feel.

But you can shift into another structure. This, however, can-not be the product of trying to solve structural conflict. If you are dissatisfied with this structure and try to change to another, more useful structure based on your dissatisfaction, *it will not work*. This is just another form of conflict manipulation. Your action, trying to get out of structural conflict, will be motivated by the intensity of the conflict you feel. I have seen thousands of people go slightly crazy with this. Yes, you can shift to another structure that will support you in creating the results you want, but never from the motivation of ridding yourself of structural conflict. Why? Because creating is different from solving or eliminating. As we progress through this book, I will guide you through this shift in structure. "Help is on the way." As you learn more and more about your own creative process and about the skill of creating, you will be able to form structures that will lead you to real and lasting success. This change will not be in reaction to anything. The creative process is not a "solution" to your problems in life. It is just the best method of creating the results you want to create in your life.

In the next chapter we will begin to explore the structure creators use to create. This is an entirely separate structure from structural conflict. This new structure is not a solution to the phenomenon of oscillation. Rather it is independent of it. This new structure is called *structural tension.*

C h a p t e r   8

Structural Tension

A Change of Structure

It is possible to change the structures in our lives, but as we have seen, most attempts at change are strategies that operate within structural conflict. Since structural conflict is not solvable or resolvable, actions taken within that structure can lead only to compensation and oscillation. When this structure is dominant, we waste energy trying to change our patterns of behavior.

To change this structure there must be another structure in play, and this structure must take precedence over the old structure, so that the path of least resistance will change and energy may move easily along that new path.

The structure that is senior to structural conflict has the following properties:

· It incorporates structural conflict into itself.
· It transposes a complex structure into a simple structure.

This senior structure can become more important and more dominant only if structural conflict *is part* of the new structure. Oscillation may still occur in some of the movement, but

114

that oscillation is simply a characteristic of normal fluctuations while the senior structure *moves toward resolution.*

This senior structure must be a simple tension-resolution system, one that resolves. The structure that is best will contain one major tension whose tendency is to *resolve completely.* Creators know how to form this kind of structure in the creative process and orchestrate the structural tendencies so the resolution is in favor of the *results they are creating.* Within a structure such as this, the forces in play work together to enhance the processes used to create the result, focus energy toward that result, and create momentum as tension moves toward resolution.

I call this senior structure *structural tension.*

Structural Tension

Structural tension is formed by two major components:

1. A vision of the result you want to create.
2. A clear view of the reality you now have.

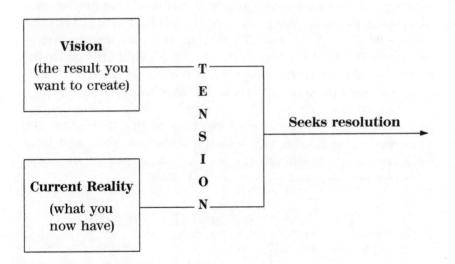

In the beginning of the creative process, there will be a discrepancy between what you want to create and what you currently have in relation to the creation. When you begin to create, your creation does not yet exist, except as a concept. Part of the skill of the creative process is bringing what you conceive into being.

The discrepancy between what you want and what you have increases or decreases during the creative process. As you move closer to final completion of the creation, there will be less discrepancy. As you move farther away from the final completion of the creation, there will be more discrepancy.

Creators have a higher ability to tolerate discrepancy than most others. This is because discrepancy is the stock-in-trade of the creator. When you create, you become a player of forces such as contrasts, opposites, similarities, differences, time, balance, and so on. When you create, one of the important forces you can use is discrepancy.

Those who do not understand discrepancy often feel discouraged when there is more discrepancy between what they want and what they have and encouraged when there is less. But to the creator, all of the forces in play are useful. If there is more discrepancy, there is more force to work with. If there is less discrepancy, there is more momentum as you move toward the final creation of the result.

People sometimes have the peculiar notion that discrepancy is not a good thing. They may even turn discrepancy into emotional conflict. They want life tied up into nice neat packages. They don't like loose ends. But in life, and therefore in the creative process, there are forces moving in different directions. There are pieces that do not fit, and there is discrepancy.

Creators not only tolerate discrepancy, they appreciate and encourage it. Discrepancy contains the energy that enables you to create. The discrepancy between what you want and what you currently have forms the most important structure in the creative process, that of *structural tension*.

The Armature and the Engine

Structural tension is the armature of the creative process. It is the bones. It is also the engine of the creative process and the energy source for that engine.

Tension strives for resolution. The structural tendency of a stretched rubber band is to relax, or resolve the tension. You, as a creator, establish tension, use tension, play with tension, orchestrate tension, and resolve tension in the direction you choose.

The way you form structural tension is by first conceiving of a result you want to create and then by observing the relevant current state of the reality you have in relation to that result.

This is simple to describe, but not as easy to accomplish as it may at first sound. The elegance of the structure should not be confused with a simplistic concept. Most people do not easily fall into this skill. Structural tension can be both a developed skill and an acquired taste.

When you form structural tension, it can be resolved one of two ways: toward the fulfillment of your vision as a reality, or toward the continuation of the reality you now have.

If you have an intolerance for discrepancy, you will tend to quickly resolve the tension in favor of continuing your present circumstances rather than working toward your vision.

Being "Realistic"

You weaken structural tension when you lower your vision. If you compromise what you want, you do not create the true discrepancy that forms the tension. It is all too common in our society to misrepresent what we really want. We have been encouraged to "be realistic," "be practical," and "want only what you can have." The irony is that you want what you want, whether or not you misrepresent that to yourself.

You do not know what you can accomplish. Is it "realistic" to give up before you start? Is it practical to lie to yourself? History is filled with examples of individuals creating results that were previously thought to be impossible.

In the beginning of the creative process, you know only what seems probable. You do not know what may or may not be possible. The likelihood of creating a certain result may seem probable, and yet you may not be able to create it. It may seem impossible to create a particular result, and yet you may be able to create it.

The only time you know for sure whether creating a result is possible or not is when you have done it. All other thoughts on the matter are simply speculation.

There are those who are convinced that circumstances determine what you can and cannot create. This view is most often held by people who do not create results they want. Yet for nearly every person in a given set of circumstances that seemed to prevent him or her from creating a desired result, someone in the same set of circumstances has done it.

What are our limits? The truth is we do not know. The fact is that so many individuals have created what they wanted in the face of presumed limitations, that it seems *unrealistic* to impose limitations on ourselves before testing the waters, experimenting with, and engaging in the creative process.

This is not to say you must believe everything is possible. One of the sillier mottoes of the New Age movement is "You can have it all." Creators do not make slogans the centerpiece of their creative life. Creators understand that you cannot have it all. You cannot be physically in two places at once; for example, you cannot physically be in London and Mexico City at the same time. You cannot reverse time; you cannot hold on to anything forever, because anything that has a beginning will eventually have an ending.

If you cannot have it all, the relevant question is, what matters enough to you to create? Creators create hierarchies. Creators assign relative importance to what they create. It is not relevant to "have it all." It is relevant to have what most matters to you.

"I Don't See What I See"

Another way of weakening structural tension is to misrepresent current reality. This strategy is often employed by people who "hold the vision" while ignoring what is going on around them. These are the idle dreamers who give real visionaries a bad name. Do not confuse a creator with a dreamer. Dreamers only dream, but creators bring their dreams into reality. Only an accurate awareness of reality and an accurate awareness of your vision will enable you to form structural tension as an important part of the creative process.

When you form and hold structural tension, resolution moves toward the vision you want to create. Holding structural tension is not the same as evoking a magical incantation, but rather organizing forces in play. The energy generated by the discrepancy you establish is directly useful in the actions you take on behalf of the vision. Movement leads to more movement. Even if you are moving in the wrong direction, it will be easier to change course and move toward your final result than not to move at all. If you are moving away from your vision, you increase structural tension. This leads to more energy and more pull in the direction you want to go. If you move toward what you want, you build momentum, and it becomes even easier to move toward your vision.

Once you establish structural tension, your natural tendency will be to generate actions in order to resolve the tension. From the inception of the creative process to its conclusion, the actions you take will be supported by the structure. All of the actions you take to create your vision will help you move toward the result you want, including the ones that are not directly successful.

The more experience you have with the creative process, the more you will be able to master structural tension.

At first you may have only moments of structural tension. These are focused times when you are clear about what you want and where you presently are. These are marvelous first steps in your own development. These moments are like those of a t'ai chi master holding a perfect balance of yin and yang energy so that the intrinsic energy is one force emanating from two poles.

As you work with your own creative process, these moments will become extended. Eventually you will live in a state of structural tension. You will consistently and automatically have an awareness of where you are and what you want to create.

As in any learning process, mastery does not come at once. It comes over time and with experience. The more you practice creating, the more you will master your own creative process. As you practice conceiving of what you want to create and form that concept into vision and current reality, you begin to work with the natural forces of the creative process.

As you work with your own creative process, you may discover that it is harder to clearly see either your current reality, your vision of the result, or both. You will develop this skill over time. Learn what you have to learn. If your ability to conceive of what you want to create needs work, practice conception. If your ability to objectively and accurately observe reality is limited, practice observing reality.

If part of current reality includes structural conflict, you will experience a degree of oscillation. But this oscillation will not prevent you from creating the results you want. If structural tension is the dominant structure, the major movement will be to resolve this simple tension-resolution system.

The compensating strategies arising from structural conflict do not help create structural tension. This is because if you compensate for structural conflict through conflict manipulation, you will tend to define reality as worse than it is. If you use willpower manipulation, you will tend to define reality as better than it is. And if you use the strategy of staying within the area of tolerable conflict, you will define reality within narrow limits of how good or bad it might be. Any biased view of reality makes structural tension hard to form or maintain.

Also, if you compensate for structural conflict by misrepresenting what you want to create, that would weaken structural tension.

Charlie Kiefer, a graduate of TECHNOLOGIES FOR CREATING,® founder of Innovation Associates, and a distinguished expert on organizational development, has commented on this issue:

> Unfortunately, organizational life enables us to easily collude with both ourselves and others in not looking at the truth. We develop certain unspoken rules which everyone observes, and norms which make it virtually impossible to talk about the truth. In most business organizations, for example, political realities, personal comfort, and bad habits are all senior to the truth.
>
> Organizations committed to the creative orientation reverse these priorities. Knowing how things really are is senior to politics, personal comfort, and bad habits. In fact, truth is recognized as essential for the development of structural tension. Moreover, truth is necessary to establish trust and develop a culture based on learning, both critical elements for organizations established in the creative orientation.

Michael Greata, cofounder and vice president of engineering of Apollo Computer, commented on the creative process that brought Apollo from a small start-up company in 1980 to an over-half-billion-dollar corporation today:

We coalesced around a vision that was going to happen because we said it would. People believed both in the vision and in themselves.

Our vision crystallized quickly, and has stood the test of time. All start-ups have this question in the beginning: "Will it work?" When you have something that is truly new, you don't have any of the established norms to meet.

One way to heighten the tension is to *set the amount of time between the vision and current reality.* It's like raising the stakes in a poker game.

Creators know how to orchestrate structural tension. As you begin to learn more about your own creative process you will begin to develop a "feel" for it. In the next chapters we will examine in depth the two elements of structural tension: *vision* and *current reality.*

Vision

The best place to begin the creative process is at the end. What is the final result you want? This way of thinking helps you conceive the result you want to create independently from how you will create it. This is probably the opposite of what you learned in school. Our educational system teaches us how to enact procedures. Students are taught the *how* long before they are taught to consider *what* they want.

Learning how to do anything before you have any notion of what you will use this knowledge for can give you a false sense of purposelessness. Some of the best education relates what the student is learning with what can result from its mastery.

Start with Nothing

When you first set out to conceive of a result you want, start with a clean sheet, a blank canvas, a fresh beginning. Preconceived ideas are just that, ideas you have already thought of. When you are conceiving of a new creation, it is best to begin without considering what you have thought before, or done before, or even what others have done before. With each new creation, begin anew in your mind. This technique can make quite a difference in your effectiveness.

When I conceive of a result I want to create, I always begin as if nothing existed before. I do not consider the past at all. I focus on what I want to see exist. I start from nothing.

Form It in Pictures

Usually I think visually. I tend to think in pictures. Often I picture nothing at first, and then gradually I picture the result as I would like to see it in its completed form. Even when I compose music, I often have a strong visual image in mind.

There is a pop-psychology theory, slightly in vogue these days, that some people are by nature visual, others aural, others kinesthetic, and so on. If you find it difficult to think visually, you may consider yourself forever limited. Some people have a tendency toward one or another style of perception, but this is only their starting point, not their ending point. Some people are more natural readers than others, but most people are capable of becoming literate. The artist Agwam is of the opinion that people are visually illiterate. He has created a course that teaches visual literacy to children. His theory checks out. Most people can learn to be visually competent.

Being able to picture what you want to create has great benefits. First, as you envision your creation, you are able to assimilate an enormous amount of data at once. The Chinese saying that a picture is worth ten thousand words is often true. A visual image gives you information that is not available in words. Relationships among the different elements of the structure become clear. The shape, contour, design, function, impression, feel, and life of your creation form and crystallize from even a simple picture.

The marvelous ability to form a picture of your final creation enables you to work from knowledge rather than from speculation. This is the reason many professional creators are often so sure of themselves. Even the most insecure artist can have tremendous confidence in his or her vision.

Learn to form pictures of what you want. This may take practice. As you experiment with picture forming, you will be able to clarify what the result you want will be.

Look at your result from many angles in your imagination. Try adding new elements. Try taking out elements. Look at the image from inside, outside, above, below, close, and distant. As you practice changing frames of reference, you will get to know more and more about what you want to create.

Sometimes you will be surprised. Often you will not. But you will always learn more about your concept.

How Clear Must the Concept Be?

How clear do you need to be about the result you want? *Clear enough that you would recognize the result if you had it.* Some people think that there is a relationship between the clarity of the original concept and the ability to produce it. This notion is mostly found in self-help books that do not really deal with the creative process but rather approaches to programming the mind. There is a profound difference between the two.

Approaches to programming the mind assume that creativity and the ability to manifest results are products of the way you control or unleash your "vast mental powers." Techniques to force-feed the subconscious attempt to focus the mind's abilities toward the desired results. Since the guiding principles of these approaches are that you are a product of your thinking and that your mind will determine what results you get, the degree of clarity of the result you want is considered a tool in the mental programmer's arsenal. According to this approach, the clearer the desired result is, the stronger the message to your mind. But in the creative process, *degree of clarity* is *not* the standard of measurement to use. As long as you would recognize the result if you created it, it is adequately clear.

Consider for a moment how some artists create their art. Some painters are not at all clear about how the final painting will actually look. They improvise and experiment. They watch the progress on the canvas as it develops. They may not know what colors the final result will have. They may even be surprised at the final form of the painting. Is this "playing around until something worthwhile shows up"?

Not at all. If it were, the artist would not know how to develop the painting in his or her desired direction. Adjustments would be random rather than purposeful.

An experiment with monkeys in the sixties is an example of a random approach. Monkeys were given paints, brushes, and canvasses. They played with them and produced a series of pictures. The researchers framed, signed, and presented some of the pictures to the art world as a new artistic discovery. The fact that they were produced by monkeys was strategically hidden at first. The pictures received critical acclaim. After the monkeys were revealed as the artists, some detractors of modern art were overjoyed to use this episode as proof positive that abstract painting was invalid. The public loves a good scandal, and this had the makings of the best. After all, the ivory-tower experts had been caught with their pants down. We have the human tendency to enjoy seeing the "experts" bewildered by their own "expertise," especially experts who have no sense of humor about themselves.

But wait. Let us revisit the artistic monkey story. There are some lessons that are relevant to the creative process, ridicule notwithstanding. First of all, it was a concept that brought monkey and paint together. It was a concept that chose the colors they were to use. It was a human decision to determine which paintings to sign and frame and which ones to reject. This decision was based on a concept of worth and aesthetic values. The random action of the monkeys (I am assuming they were random, apologies to any monkeys as needed) were only part of an entire process that produced these paintings. Much of the process was not random. Many of the final results were the direct product of human concept, decision, and standards of measurement that were used to produce the results.

Some of the standards of measurement that determine the nature of a desired result are general, others are specific. If you want to create a house, you may have a general concept of how much space there should be, how many rooms, what kind of location, what the price range should be, what the neighbors should be like, what the quality of the local school system should be, the size of the property, and how much direct sunlight should shine into the rooms, yet have no idea of what the house with these qualities would look like. The result you have in mind would be easy to recognize, even though the actual physical appearance of the house may not be clear to you at all. In fact, there may be several types of houses that fit the bill.

The artist who experiments with an improvisatory process may be unclear about how the final painting may look, but extremely clear of what he or she wants to express. In this sense the painting itself is part of a process; *the final result is the power of the expression.*

Jackson Pollock was famous for the "action" school of painting. He often used the technique of spilling paint on his canvasses. Certainly he could not know how the paint would splash at any given moment. How clear must he have been about the result he wanted if he left so much to chance?

In fact, he was very clear. His sketchbooks were filled with carefully constructed drawings and watercolors that are similar in style to his "action" paintings. As you view these chronologically, you can see him working out his ideas. The progression of his concepts developed over time. What he accomplished by "splashing paint" becomes completely understandable.

Pollock adopted a process called creative ritual. His concept of great painting included complex structural relationships. Before he painted, he sometimes spent hours working out algebraic equations. Part of his creative process included preparing himself with very intense mathematical work on structure. Then he would burst into improvisation with paint. This may be one reason his paintings contain a powerful expression of both structure and fire, mind and soul, head and heart perfectly balanced together.

I was once discussing Pollock with an artist friend of mine. My friend said, "Of course his work would be powerful, he was a good painter, and he knew what he wanted." This was a telling remark. Pollock had a clear vision and the ability to bring his vision into being. What more could you ask of the creative process?

In an interview in 1952, Pollock was asked about his process of painting. Was his process essential to his art? "The process is only a means to an end—creating the painting I want," Pollock answered, "It doesn't mean anything itself. It's only a way of creating the result."

As you begin your own creative process, realize that there is no "right" way of doing it. There is no "right" way of painting a painting, no "right" way of composing music, and no "right" way of creating your life. Much of what you will do will be based on personal style, preference, values, and desires. As you experiment with your own path, you will become an expert on your own creative process, and that is the only one that is directly relevant in your life.

From Concept to Vision

There is a difference between a concept and a vision. Concept comes before vision. Concept is general, vision is specific. In the conceptual period you are experimenting with ideas. You are mentally trying out various possibilities. This is a formative period. You may meditate, think, walk, look at the sky, watch television, take a warm bath (one of my favorites), sleep, dream, talk with friends, and so on. In a way the conception period has the feel of play to it. Playing around with concepts. Trying it this way and that way. Living with it in your imagination for a period of time. Getting to know it well enough that you know what you like and what you don't like about it.

Once you have formed the concept, the next step is to crystallize it. This is an act of focusing. *Given the various ways in which the concept might manifest itself, how do you want to see it manifested?* The same principle of the conceptual stage applies to the vision stage. The vision need only be clear enough that you would recognize it if you created it. But what is the essential difference between conception and vision? *The difference is in focus, and focus is made possible by limitation.* When you focus a concept into a vision, *you are limiting many ways into a single way.* All vision is concept, but not all concepts are vision.

While in the conceptual stage you are trying out many possibilities, in the vision stage you have decided on one and only one.

Once you have formed your vision, you have achieved an evolutionary step in the creative process, from the general to the specific. This step is exemplified throughout the arts and sciences. General principles of electronics are used in the specific form of the microchip or the semiconductor. General principles of architecture take the specific form of New York's World Trade Center. General principles of blending spices become a specific coq au vin. General principles of aerodynamics become a specific 747 jet airliner.

Imagine for a moment that you are an architect and you can build any kind of house. First you need a general concept about the house. How big is it? What materials will you use? What will the location be like? What is the budget? These are very general questions that help to form a general concept, but answering these questions does not give you a vision of the house. However, once you have your general concept, you can easily begin to get specific. What style is the house? What is the feel of the place? How many rooms are there and where are the rooms located? Where is the kitchen? Is it modern, Art Nouveau, traditional, space-age?

As the concept gets clearer and clearer, a very specific house begins to form in your mind. You become the final authority on what you want.

In the first class of the TECHNOLOGIES FOR CREATING® course, students work with this principle. First they conceive of a result they want. They form several pictures of it in their minds. Then, they write a description of what they pictured. After this is accomplished, they experiment with their concept. They rethink it. They form new pictures of it. As they work, the concept becomes clearer and more detailed. They begin to have a "feel" for it. In a short time, they begin to have a specific vision of the result they want to create. A man in one class began with the general concept of a vacation house. As he pictured the result he filled in more and more details. He added a water setting. Then he decided he also wanted woods. He tried out a warm climate. Then he tried out a mountain setting. He liked that better. He added accessibility to stores, shops, and services. He started with a log cabin. Then he decided he wanted more room. The house became two stories. He added more and more details. By the end of the exercise he had a vision of just what he wanted, and by the time the course ended, he had bought a house that completely fit his vision. In the past he had daydreamed about a vacation house, but this was just wishful thinking. Then, his concept was unformed. But when he began to form a general concept into a specific vision, he was focusing his own creative process. He was more and more able to see exactly what he wanted, and this, along with other TFC techniques, helped him create the result he wanted.

A woman in another class had a general concept of having her own business. She began to form pictures of a business she might want. At first she had a little difficulty in forming a general concept, because she kept matching businesses she already knew about with what she might want. It is a common beginner's mistake, to attempt to match what already exists with what you might want instead of forming the concept from scratch. After a few false starts, she began without a preconceived idea. She began to picture herself being fascinated with the work she would be doing. Then she imagined co-workers. Then she imagined her life as an independent businesswoman. Little by little she filled in the concept and tried out different aspects of the business she was picturing. The more she conceptualized the business, the more tangible it became. At first she pictured a service business, then she tried out a products business. Later, she pictured her own shop. She then decided she preferred a service business. She began playing around with the concept of travel. After a few minutes, she had a very definite vision for her business, a travel agency. This was a new idea for her. As she moved her concept into a specific vision, she was able to take her first steps in building what is now a very successful, and unique, travel agency.

A Transition Period

As you form your vision, you simultaneously teach it to yourself. There is a transition from concept to vision during this period. At first you are trying ideas out for size. You are playing the field of ideas. You are learning more and more about what you like and what you don't like. You may fall in love with a certain idea for three or four days and find that by the end of the week you are completely bored with it. You may think little of an idea at first, only to find that it grows on you and you eventually like it. As you conceptualize, you learn. And what you learn is directly useful in creating your vision.

Some people become fixated in any of the many stages of the creative process, and in this stage it is possible to play around with ideas and never form concept into vision. Learning during this process must lead to choices if you are to move from the general to the specific. When you limit, you must include and exclude. This is one of the very important acts of a creator. The greatest creators know just what to include and what to leave out. A writer friend of mine once said, "In order to get some of my books to work, I need to throw out some of my best lines!"

During the transition period between concept and vision, you begin to have an instinct for what and what not to include.

The Vision Becomes an Entity

There is a point in the transition period when the vision takes on an identity all its own. It becomes a separate entity from you. It may be your vision, but it has a separate life.

Many fiction writers report that the characters they themselves have conceived begin to take on a unique identity. They are often surprised to discover what these characters seem to want to do in the plot. Sometimes the originality of a plot comes from the mixture of many strong characters having their own personalities, values, and motivations. The writer shepherds their development in the story, yet is sometimes as surprised about their behavior as the reader is.

As you form your vision, there is often a moment when it becomes concrete. This is a crystallization process. I can imagine Walt Disney playing around with the concept of a mouse. He begins to form an idea around this mouse. The mouse begins to have a personality. Disney gives the mouse a name. It is Steam Boat Willy. He casts his mouse in a cartoon. He likes the little character, but his name is somehow not suited to his personality. Disney changes his name to Mickey, and an empire is built.

Mickey changes form and matures. In his first role as Steam Boat Willy, he is skinny and has a long nose. From the thirties to the forties his nose becomes shorter and more buttonlike. His tummy grows. His voice changes. He becomes cuter. He looks less and less like a real mouse. His animated world changes from black and white to color, and from simple animation to elaborate animation, as in Disney's *The Sorcerer's Apprentice*.

His relationships change. He obtains a pet dog, a girlfriend, and some charmingly dopey friends. In the fifties he has a daily television program with talented children disciples. Later gigantic theme parks are created in which he plays a central role. People all over the world grow to love the little mouse.

Mickey's maturation is not unlike the development of a human from childhood to adolescence to adulthood. He even outlives his creator.

When your vision becomes an entity on its own, you can develop a complex relationship with it. You are the parent and it is your child. You are its champion and also its critic. You are both passionate and dispassionate about it.

Your Life as a Creation

It is not common for people to think of their own lives as creations. You are not encouraged to have with your own life the kind of relationship a creator has with his or her vision. But your life can be a creation. What a difference that is from reacting or responding to the circumstances. Your own life can become a separate entity, and when it does, you can form it, mold it, and change it the way you want. When you are able to do this, you are free to develop your life as independent of your identity. You can succeed or fail without the added burden of an identity crisis.

When your vision begins to take on its own identity, it may seem unusual at first. But this is a process similar to becoming involved with another human being. You have first impressions. You learn more about the other person over time. Even after years of knowing your vision, you may be surprised to discover new traits.

The Vision Is About What You Want

Too often people do not ask themselves what results they want, but instead substitute questions about process or questions about problems and their solutions. When I consult with organizations, the question What result do you want? presents many managers with great difficulties. Often they will give vague, indirect answers that do not capture what they really want. Sometimes they name what they think is a solution to a problem they haven't even named, or a process they think they need. For example:

> We want a system to develop evaluation methods in assessing what the client might find helpful.

> We want marketing that supports users with new approaches in nontraditional media and provides test cases for further engagement.

> We want to create strategy objectives so that we
> can reorganize the department and be competitive
> in the marketplace.

Today these types of statements are common in companies
from the largest to the smallest. One of the trends in management technique is to define the purpose or mission of the organization. The description is often nebulous. But many groups
within organizations continue to write such mission statements just because it has become corporate practice to do so.
From the mission statement, objectives are created, tactics are
designed, roles are assigned, meetings are scheduled, and not
much happens. Why? Because these people *still do not know
what they want.* I have often spent many hours with corporate
executives helping them describe what results they want.

Is this because it is so hard? No. It is because many executives
are not in the habit of separating what they want from what
they think is possible. They also have the added burden of management training that uses obscure language, unclear concepts,
psychological management dogma, and the reactive-responsive
orientation.

Charlie Kiefer described the situation in organizations this
way:

> The unfortunate fact of the matter is that most
> planning in modern American business is done
> from the reactive-responsive orientation. Through
> elaborate methodologies the organization seeks to
> determine the current state of affairs it faces. It
> plots its current financial situation, the capacities
> of its people, and the products it is currently ca-
> pable of creating. It examines the competitors' ca-
> pacities and likely responses, as well as probable
> legislative actions, and so on.
>
> Having done a thorough and complete analysis
> of these factors, the organization then takes the
> almost tragic step of charting a course to *optimize*
> performance in light of these current circum-
> stances. In essence, the organization says, *"Given
> these circumstances, what is the best we can hope
> to do?"*

Imagine instead people in an organization operating from a creative mode. They approach planning, first by determining what they truly want to create, thus in essence becoming true to themselves. And then they analyze current reality (perhaps in exactly the same manner as before). Now, however, it is only to use that analysis as a foundation to build a bridge to what they truly want. Such an organization is on the road to greatness.

Knowing What You Want

The following principles will help you experiment with conceiving of what you want to create.

1. Ask yourself the question, What do I want?

It is amazing how often people do not ask themselves this obvious question. You can ask and answer this question at any time. However, when you are not trying to solve a problem or determine a process, you are in a much better position to ask and answer this question.

Practice asking yourself this question in many types of situations. Do not save it only for those times of great importance. If you are in the habit of working with this question, you will develop an instinct for knowing what you want. Even if you have been indecisive in the past, you will become decisive by building up experience over time.

Knowing what you want has two important advantages. You are able to focus your attention quickly, and you are accurately describing the truth to yourself.

Whenever you are confused, you can become clear by asking and answering this question. Confusion usually comes from focusing on process, or solution, and not being able to see where you are going. When you are considering what you want, your ability to focus your attention toward desired results eliminates this confusion. When you are confused, it is usually not about where you want to go but how to get there. If you try to find a way to get there before you know where you want to go, naturally you can expect confusion to accompany your quest.

When you are overwhelmed, you have more input than you can handle at once. This is the experience of being pulled in different directions. This is the experience of powerlessness in creating your own future. This is the experience of not being able to keep up with events. When you focus on the results you want, the input that seems to be bombarding you will organize itself into useful order.

There is a profound difference between fact and speculation. When you determine what results you want, it becomes a fact that you want that result. Sometimes people choose processes, assuming they have determined what they want. This is a false assumption. Often process is used to speculate about what you want, rather than to serve creating what you want.

When you ask and answer the question What do I want? you are creating a fact, not just some vague speculation.

2. Consider what you want independently of considerations of process.

When you try to determine what you want by considering process, you limit your ability to conceive of the result you want to what you already know how to do. But the creative process is filled with discovering what you *do not know*. Those who attempt to make results dependent on process are severely limiting themselves. This is a good way of repeating history, but not a good way of bringing something new into being.

You will need to consider process when you create. But this should happen only after you know what result you want. In fact, you will probably be surprised at the clever ways in which you will invent the path between your current reality and your vision.

Sometimes a result you want is actually only a step in a process. Money, for many people, is not a result, but a process toward other results they want. For some people, personal relationships are not results, but steps toward fulfillment or satisfaction. If you discover that a result you want turns out to be only a step toward some other final result, find out where the step is supposed to lead. What would you do with the money? What would you derive out of the relationship? A final result is something that exists by itself. Its purpose is not to lead you to other results, even though it may.

3. *Separate what you want from questions of possibility.*

In order to conceive of what you truly want to create, you must separate what you want from what you think is possible. In 1903, when Orville and Wilbur Wright were building their first airplane, the rest of the scientific and technical world were asserting the impossibility of a heavier-than-air machine sustaining itself in flight. What the Wright brothers wanted was certainly not based on what seemed possible. But they knew what their vision was.

If you find yourself limiting what you want based on what seems possible to you, you are censoring and inhibiting your vision. If you don't admit to yourself what you want simply because it does not seem possible for you to have it, you are actually misrepresenting the truth to yourself.

Lie detectors measure physiological stress. When you lie to yourself or misrepresent the truth in any way, you increase the stress on your body. After years of misrepresenting your true wants, the increasing stress can lead to health problems. Lying to yourself always breaks down your relationship with yourself, creates stress, and represents the truth as potentially dangerous and threatening.

Once I was leading a workshop for the Easter Seal Foundation. The people with whom I was working were all suffering from lung ailments such as emphysema, lung cancer, and asthma. In one section of the workshop, the objective was for participants to practice separating what they really wanted from what they thought was possible.

One elderly woman was having particular trouble with the exercise.

"Remember, the exercise is to separate what you want from what you think is possible," I said to her. "So, what do you want?"

"I can't say," she replied. "It really isn't possible."

"Well," I said, "for the moment, don't consider whether or not what you want is possible. What do you want?"

"I can't say what I want because I can never have it."

"I can tell you what you want," I said.

"You can?"

"Sure," I replied. "What you want is good health."

"But I can never have it."

"But isn't that what you want?"

"But I can never have it," she repeated.

"Well," I asked, "If I were a magic genie and could wave a wand and give you perfect health, would you take it?"

She paused for a moment, and quietly said, "Yes."

"If you would take it," I added, "you must want it. Furthermore, even if it doesn't seem at all possible to you—even if it's NOT possible—the real truth is that you want perfect health."

"Yes," she said. "That's so."

"So, now tell yourself the truth about what you want," I said. "It's never wrong to tell yourself the truth about what you want, even though you think it's not possible to have it."

She paused. Then, looking down at the floor, she said quietly, "The truth is I want to be healthy."

"What just happened to you when you said that?" I asked.

"I don't understand this," she replied, looking very different than she had looked up to that point. "I feel physically lighter, as if a weight has been lifted off my shoulders. I feel clearer. It's almost as if there is an energy flowing through me now."

Whether or not her illness persisted, she no longer had to bear the additional burden of feeling obligated to misrepresent to herself the truth about her desire for health. Certainly the additional stress she was placing on herself by denying what she wanted was not helpful.

There are enough well-known instances of people being able to overcome great health obstacles, partly by holding a clear vision of the result they wanted, that it would be presumptuous to say that miraculous cures are impossible. "Babe" Didrikson Zaharias, an Olympic sports figure and professional golfer crippled by sickness, was told she would never walk or play golf again; she created a vision of herself playing professional golf and lived to play tournament golf for many years. Expert physicians held no hope that Helen Keller, left blind and deaf by an illness in infancy, could ever take her place as a contributing member of society. But her teacher, Anne Sullivan, held the vision of a Helen who could communicate, be responsible, acquire an education, and serve society in unique ways.

Extraordinary changes like these are far less likely to happen as long as you lie to yourself or misrepresent the truth about what you really want.

The phenomenon that the woman described of being physically lighter and feeling energy flowing through her is a very common experience when you begin to tell yourself the truth about what you want.

A TECHNOLOGIES FOR CREATING® student in New York City had been working for nine years as an assistant to a theatrical agent. She had been promised equity in the business but she had not received it. She became pregnant and could no longer do her job. During her TFC course, she heard of a job opportunity as an assistant theatrical agent. Although she doubted she could handle the job with a baby, she interviewed anyway. The agent, it turned out, loved the idea of her working at home and offered her the job. In addition, the agent provided her with an office to work in part time and offered her three times her previous salary. After a few months in this job, she was offered a full partnership in the business. Had she not separated what she wanted from what she thought was possible, she never would have accomplished these results.

During his TFC class, an Atlanta cabinetmaker decided he wanted to expand his shop, update his tooling, and work with other people. This seemed impossible for him to accomplish, but he wanted it anyway. Within five months of completing the TFC course, he won a major contract of nearly a million dollars. He totally retooled his operation and expanded his work force. This occurred after years of struggling. Had he simply governed his aspirations by what seemed possible, he never would have been able to create what he did.

The art of accurately naming the result you want begins with separating what you want from questions of possibility.

The Vision Is an Organizing Principle

In a conversation with artists, Picasso described how the original vision of a painting affects the final result.

> It would be very interesting to record photographically, not the stages of a painting, but its metamorphoses. One would see perhaps by what course a mind finds its way toward the crystallization of its dream. But what is really very serious is to see

> that the picture does not change basically, that the
> initial vision remains almost intact in spite of ap-
> pearance.

Vision has power, for through vision you can easily reach beyond the ordinary to the extraordinary. Vision can help you organize your actions, focus your values, and clearly see what is relevant in current reality.

Roger Sessions, describing how Beethoven's musical vision affected his compositional process, wrote, "When this perfect realization was attained, there could have been no hesitation— rather a flash of recognition that this was exactly what he wanted."

"This vision of the whole," Sessions went on to say, "assumes an ever more preponderant role, and appears more and more to be the essential act of creation."

Vision also has a magic quality. I define magic as seeing the results without seeing the entire process leading to those results. Roger Sessions observes that the composer is not so much conscious of the ideas and processes as he or she creates but is led on by the vision. "Very often," Sessions explains, "he is unaware of his exact processes of thought till he is through with them; extremely often the completed work is incomprehensible to him immediately after it is finished."

It is as if the composer had been led to the result by the inner eye of vision. Many creators express this sense of surprise and awe at their own creations.

The inner eye of vision can see what isn't there yet, can reach beyond present circumstances, and can see what, up to that point, has never been there. It is truly an incredible human faculty that is able to see beyond the present and the past and, from the unknown, to conceive something not hitherto in existence.

The great twentieth-century composer Karlheinz Stockhausen wrote, "We need to close our eyes for a while and listen. There is always something unheard of in the air."

Current Reality

Reality Is Not the Enemy

There was a man who woke one day convinced that he was a zombie. When he told his wife he was a zombie, she tried to talk him out of this outrageous opinion.

"You are not a zombie!" she said.

"I am a zombie," he answered.

"What makes you think you are a zombie?" she asked rhetorically.

"Don't you think zombies know they are zombies?" he answered with great sincerity.

His wife realized she was not getting anywhere, so she called his mother and told her what was going on. His mother tried to help.

"I'm your mother, wouldn't I know if I gave birth to a zombie?"

"You didn't," he explained, "I became a zombie later."

"I didn't raise my son to be a zombie, or especially to think he is a zombie," his mother pleaded.

"Nonetheless, I am a zombie," he said, unmoved by his mother's appeal to his identity and sense of guilt.

Later that day his wife called in their minister to talk to her husband.

"You are not a zombie, you are probably going through a midlife crisis," the minister said, trying to be the psychologist he always wanted to be.

"Zombies don't have midlife crises," was all the man replied.

The minister recommended a psychiatrist. The wife got an emergency appointment, and within the hour the husband was in the psychiatrist's office.

"So, you think you are a zombie?" the psychiatrist asked.

"I know I am a zombie," the man said.

"Tell me, do zombies bleed?" the psychiatrist asked.

"Of course not," said the man, "zombies are the living dead. They don't bleed." The man was a little annoyed at the psychiatrist's patronizing question.

"Well, watch this," said the psychiatrist as he picked up a pin. He took the man's finger and made a tiny pin prick. The man looked at his finger with great amazement and said nothing for three or four minutes.

"What do you know," the man finally said, "zombies *do* bleed!"

There once was a lion who came upon a monkey. The lion thought this was a good chance to confirm his position of prominence in the jungle.

"Hey, monkey!" the lion growled.

"Yes, sire," the monkey answered in a shaky voice.

"Who is the king of the jungle?!" the lion growled even louder.

"Why, you are, sire, you are!"

"And don't you forget it!" the lion said, very pleased with himself.

A little later the lion came upon a zebra.

"Hey you . . . zebra!" the lion roared.

"Yes, sire," the zebra answered in a nasal voice.

"Who's the king of the jungle?!" the lion roared some more.

"You are, sire, you are!" the zebra said with a timid and forced enthusiasm.

"And don't you forget it!" the lion roared.

A little later the lion came upon an elephant. "Hey you, elephant! Who's the king of the jungle?!'' the lion roared and growled with his most ferocious roar and growl.

Without saying a word, the elephant picked up the lion with his trunk and threw the lion against a tree. Then he walked over to the lion and stepped on his tail. Then the elephant picked the lion up again and slammed him down on the ground.

As the elephant walked away, the battered lion lifted his head and yelled, "Hey, don't get mad just because you don't know the answer!"

Some people have a lot of trouble with reality. It seems as if it should be simple enough: See the obvious. But as children we have all had the experience of saying something that was undeniably accurate, only to be shushed up by an adult.

> "Grandma's house has a funny smell."
> "Quiet. Don't say that!"

Children learn to lie because that is one of their only defenses against authority figures, who are often many times their size and weight.

> "Were you in my closet?!"
> "Uh, no."
> "Then why is your gum wrapper in my closet?"
> "Uh, er . . . I don't know."

> "Did you do your homework?"
> "Uh, yes I did it, but I left it on the bus."
> "This is the third time this week you didn't have
>   your homework, and you always have some
>   flimsy excuse."
> "Uh . . . well, a lot of weird things happen to my
>   homework. I can't help it."

> "What time did you get in last night?"
> "Not too late."
> "Well, I happen to know it was two-thirty in the
>   morning!"
> "Gee, it didn't seem that late. Anyway, we had a
>   flat tire. And if you knew what time it was,
>   why did you ask me?"

"I was just wondering if you knew!"
"Well, I . . . ah . . . didn't think it was that late . . .
     because my watch broke."
"Let me see your watch."
"I, ah . . . can't find it."
"What is that on your wrist?"
"Oh . . . that's a . . . different watch."

And as adults:
"Do you know how fast you were driving?"
"No, was I going faster than the speed limit?"
"The radar clocked you at seventy-five."
"Really, it didn't seem that fast. Maybe my speed-
     ometer is broken."

Give Me a Good Reason

Not describing reality accurately often becomes self-propaganda. You may be late for an appointment and on your way
over think up the most plausible excuse. By the time you arrive,
not only are you ready to recite it, but you almost believe it
yourself. Avoiding describing reality accurately is often a strategy to overcome the negative consequences of your actions.

Our society puts a high premium on reasons and excuses.
Most people learn that if they have a good reason for not succeeding, they can sometimes avoid negative consequences.
Many people misrepresent reality though a smoke screen of
plausible-sounding reasons that are designed to distract themselves and others from the truth.

Some people learn that others put less pressure on them
when they are sick. So they often get sick to have a legitimate
excuse not to live up to expectations.

Some people use being in a state of emotional upheaval as an
excuse: "If I'm upset, do not ask me to be responsible."

Being a "victim of circumstances" is a common reason some
people use to explain their actions. "Look, I tried to be at Sara's
birthday party, but my boss called just as I was leaving the
house. You know how much he loves to talk. So I was stuck on
the phone with him. What do you want me to do, lose my job?"

The defense of Dan White, who shot San Francisco council-
man Harvey Milk and Mayor George Moscone, was that his blood
sugar was off that day. This became known as the "Twinkie"

defense. The defense was taken seriously. White got off with a light sentence.

A society that fosters reasons and excuses for irresponsible or destructive behavior has little chance of reaching its potential greatness. Since the tradition of the arts does have a standard of reaching for what is highest in humanity, are excuses seen as valid or needed? The "I had a good reason" excuse is seldom found in the arts as an attempt to explain a bad performance, a bad film, a bad painting, a bad record, a bad play, a bad novel, or a bad poem.

Some people seem to enjoy concocting a dramatic explanation for why they can't have what they want. The love of reasons for why you "can't" can supersede the pursuit of what you want.

Reasons

Sometimes knowing the reasons for failure can help you adjust the actions you take to shape your final creation. But this is quite different from using reasons to justify failure. Discovering the effect of the actions you take is designed to be a learning experience, rather than a justification for not succeeding.

For example, it is important to know the causes of the explosion of the *Challenger* space shuttle that cost the lives of the crew. Knowing has at least two functions. One is to correct the error in the future, to enable those who next venture into space to be as safe as we can possibly manage.

Knowing what happened also helps ease the pain sometimes evoked by reality. It is hard to accept that those very special people, the crew of the *Challenger*, are gone from our midst, especially since just moments before the explosion they were waving to us on network television. It is hard to witness some of the best of our generation taken so quickly and so dramatically.

When we have an explanation, it helps us to accept the truth—that they are gone, that we will not see them again in this life, that the full promise of what their lives could have been in the future is now impossible.

It is common for people to fill themselves with details when they lose a loved one. What did he do in his last days? What did he do or say in his last hours? Who was with him when he died? What was the medical explanation for the death? Was there anything that could have saved him?

What real difference do the answers to these questions make? None in reality. No amount of detail about the circumstances of someone's death brings that person back. Then what is the purpose of wanting to know?

Knowing the details of "how it happened" helps you learn a reality that is hard to accept. The period of grieving is a time to teach yourself the reality that someone or something is gone. Often people who are grieving over the death of a loved one experience phases of emotional upheaval, followed by phases of resolution and peace. Then, as if from nowhere, their emotional upheaval begins again. Each time this happens, the grieving person confronts a different aspect of the reality of loss.

Until he or she accepts all of reality, the grieving person is not able to move on fully in life. That person can become fixated on the past, trying to hold on to the time when his or her loved one was still alive.

When my father died, my mother was not able to accept the reality that he was gone. She left his belongings exactly as they were on the day he died. She would not let anyone move or change his closet, dresser, or night table. She kept the workbench at which my father practiced his hobby of making stained glass just as it was on the day he died. I think she thought that she was being true to him by preserving these objects just as he had them. As if, somehow, that would bring him back.

Her family and friends tried to help her through her grief, but she was inconsolable. She tried to keep my father alive in her mind, and by doing so she rejected a part of reality in her life. Becoming fixated on the past and not accepting the present reality does not diminish suffering, it prolongs it.

Whenever my mother saw others celebrating an anniversary, she would find a way of telling how many years she and my father had been married and what anniversary this would have been. She would spend hours reminiscing about their past together, as if old arguments were still going on, as if he were still there to be mad at or to laugh with or to plan with.

My mother did try to continue to live without my father, but without fully accepting the reality that he was gone, she could only partially live her life. And as time went on, the gap between the part of her moving into each new present moment and the part of her that held onto the past widened.

My mother died three years after my father. I don't think she had a true moment of joy during those three years. Because she had not accepted his death, she could not accept her life. She died as suddenly as he did, without warning.

Those who learn to know reality, without holding on to the past, are in the best position to truly live their lives. This is anything but amnesia. This is not forgetting the past, but remembering that the past is over. The past is not the present. Whether the past has been filled with loss and failure or filled with success and victory, the past is not the present. And the present is not the past.

Two Tendencies

There is a difference between passively learning reality because life forces you to and actively teaching yourself reality. When you seek to know reality and learn what there is to learn, you can best create what really matters to you. Like art for art's sake, this is truth for truth's sake—the desire to know reality because it is real, and for no other reason.

The foundation of reality is the only place you can start the creative process. There are no tricks to this. Learning reality is an ability that is important to master and yet human to avoid.

There is a conflict of tendencies here. One tendency is to view reality selectively. Our natural aversion to pain and suffering leads us to avoid new experiences of pain and suffering. We develop a strategy of avoiding looking at reality for fear of what we might find. We would rather not receive bad news.

A second tendency is the human longing to create. As we move in time and space, we live in a constant state of change, and we have a natural tendency to want to determine what this change will be. Will it be positive or negative? Smooth or abrupt?

Furthermore, we have deep aspirations. We are natural builders. We build civilizations. We desire to build our own lives.

To fulfill this tendency, we need to know what reality is. Whether we like what we find or not. Whether it makes us feel good or bad. Whether we are frustrated by it or satisfied.

These two tendencies lead to different actions. One is to avoid knowing reality, the other is to know reality. The conflict between the two is usually not pronounced, but sometimes it is. When you are creating and also trying to avoid pain, you will come to a crossroads of decision. When push comes to shove, what do you do? Do you avoid the potential pain and misrepresent reality, or do you accurately represent reality to enable yourself to create your vision and feel whatever there is to feel?

This is a matter of values. That which you hold to be more valuable will guide your actions. If the avoidance of pain is a higher value than the creation of what you want, your actions will be to avoid the parts of reality that seem problematic. If your creation is a higher value, you will pursue an accurate representation of reality and let your emotional chips fall where they may.

Your Concept of Reality May Not Be Reality

The artist and teacher Arthur Stern once took several of his students to Riverside Park in New York City. He pointed to three architectural structures across the Hudson River: an apartment house, a storage tank, and a factory. Stern asked his students to name the color of the buildings. His students were in agreement that the apartments were red, the storage tank was white, and the factory was orange. Stern then handed the students some small gray cards, each with a small hole punched through it. (Stern calls this card a spot screen.) He then asked each student to hold the card at arm's length and look through the hole at each of the three structures. Again he asked his students what colors they saw. The students were silent for quite a while, until one finally spoke. "They're all blue, like the rest of the scenery over there when you look through the hole in the card." The other students agreed, the "red" apartment building was blue, the "white" storage tank was blue, as was the "orange" factory. Stern's students had made a remarkable discovery. What they saw first was not reality, but their concept of reality.

One of the traditional discoveries of art students is that they are not seeing what is before their eyes but rather what is in their minds. Artists learn the skill of seeing what they are looking at rather than seeing a concept of what they are looking at. This is a necessary skill in order to render a likeness of a tree or a human face. If the artist cannot draw or paint what he is looking at, he will not be able to represent it accurately.

Arthur Stern writes in *How to See Color and Paint It*:

> Students expect water to be blue, so they paint a lake blue. But this lake may actually appear red, orange, yellow, and brown, because it's filled with the reflections of the autumn trees on the shore. Or students paint clouds white because they expect them to be white—though clouds can actually be yellow, red, or violet, since the color of the sunlight shining on them changes throughout the day, and they also reflect the colors of the land below.
>
> The purpose of the spot screen, like many other devices invented by artists over the centuries, is to turn off that mental filter so that you don't paint what you expect to see. Thus, looking through the hole in the spot screen, the students were able to ignore the fact that they were looking at red, white and orange buildings in a late afternoon shade. They now saw that the buildings were bathed in blue light reflected from the sky and the surface of the river.

Reality Is Not a Concept

When it comes to observing reality, people often do not see what is before their eyes. Instead, people see their concept of what reality should be. They are not seeing what is before their eyes, but what they expect to see.

Concept is useful when you are constructing a vision of your creation, but a concept of reality can get in the way of seeing current reality.

We have learned to rely on our concepts of reality more than on our observations of reality. We do this for convenience. It is more convenient to assume that reality is similar to our preconceived ideas than to freshly observe what we have before our eyes. We have the marvelous ability to generalize. This is helpful in many ways. Learning patterns of behavior, knowing trends, knowing the tendencies of actions, make simple what would otherwise be complex.

But just as art students need to learn to see what is there, creators need to learn to see reality without the filter of concepts of reality.

Similarities and Differences

One of the ways we identify reality is to compare what we see with what we already know. We classify into types. If we did not have this ability, we would not be able to learn from our experiences. If you had never seen or heard of a taxicab before, your first experience with a cab would mean forming a new classification: cab. Then the next time you saw a cab, you would recognize it. You would observe the ways the second cab was like the first. Perhaps they were both yellow. Perhaps they both had writing on the side. Maybe both had meters inside the vehicle near the driver. The similarities would help you classify the second vehicle as being in the same category as the first.

What this process enables you to do is to utilize all of your previous experiences of cabs. If you were unable to create such classes of identity, you would need to learn what each new cab was from scratch. How inefficient it would be always to start over again! Building a base of knowledge enables you to navigate easily through everyday life. This is a remarkable human ability. By identifying similarities, we can grow in our experiences. We can learn about the world and use that knowledge to walk down a street, order food in a restaurant, or make a phone call.

I have had the experience in a foreign country of being confronted with a phone system that is completely different from any I was used to. I love the experience of moving from a world I know to a world I don't know. How marvelous it is to no longer know how to get a dial tone, how much money to put in the phone box, or how to get the operator. And when I finally get the operator, to realize she doesn't speak my language, nor I hers. In times like these we can come to appreciate the multitude of learnings we take for granted. But imagine if you had to go through your life without ever knowing how the phone system worked or how to use the television or how to open a door. The charm of the occasional disorientation would soon be over, and real disorientation would take its place.

Language is made possible by our ability to identify individual objects and ideas and to organize them into classes. When we use the word *tree*, we identify a type of vegetation. No one tree is identical to any other tree. But we can classify trees as members of a group, and by so doing we can bring all we know about trees in general to any specific tree under consideration.

Once we have identified similarities and classified them into types, a next step is to observe differences: from the general characteristics of the type to the differences of the item in question.

If we are talking about the tree in the front yard of the Joneses' house, at 331 Pleasant Street, in Lake Mills, Wisconsin, we have a general idea of the way this tree is similar to other trees, and we can also look for the distinguishing features of this specific tree. How many branches does it have? How large is it? What is the color of its leaves? What is the shape of the trunk? What is the texture of the bark?

Most of the time, classifying our perceptions of reality into types based on similarities helps us to quickly understand our current circumstances. Once we establish the classification, we can note the differences between the general characteristics and the uniqueness of any object in question. But sometimes this system doesn't work well. We may observe our reality with the presumption of knowing what to expect. This presumption can give us a biased view of reality. When a preconceived concept of reality is imposed on reality, observation ends and stereotyping begins.

People who have strong beliefs in a conceptual framework of reality often interpret reality to fit their biases. Those who have strong political views often interpret reality to reinforce their political explanation of the world. To the communist, reality divides itself into the "people" and the "exploiters of the people." This is a concept of class struggle. There is a built-in bias, so the communist must assume that whoever is in power, as long as it isn't another communist, is trying to exploit those who are not in power. A strong identity class develops, with one group considered "good" and the other "bad." The good must defeat the bad, and this becomes a quest for justice. Any altruism the people in power may display must be overlooked. Any opportunism the people who are oppressed may have must also be overlooked. Moreover, the inadequacies of one group must be exaggerated if they happen not to be bad enough, and the strengths of the other group must be glorified if they are not good enough.

When conceptual views of reality bias reality, it is difficult to discover what is going on. Skeptics, fundamentalists, romantics, extremists, racists, idealists, and so on, may misread or misinterpret facts to reinforce their viewpoint of the world. This makes it difficult to include in their perception facts that contradict their theory.

When you examine reality with a preconceived idea of what you will find, you particularly notice those facts that reinforce your concept.

Some people have extreme concepts about reality; others have subtler concepts. When it is subtle, it is harder to see that a concept is being imposed on reality. Seeing the principle enacted in the extreme helps to identify the subtleties.

About fifteen years ago I attended a party at a friend's house. One of the guests was a middle-aged woman who was wearing a pin that resembled the planet Saturn. I asked her why she was wearing a symbol of Saturn.

"Oh, this isn't Saturn," she said as she looked around the room to make sure no one else was listening. "This is a spaceship."

"Okay," I began again, "why are you wearing a spaceship pin?" She looked around the room some more and whispered, "You see, in three years spaceships are going to land and set up a world government."

"I see," I said, as if this were the obvious explanation, "and who are these space people?" Her eyes became serious now. "These are the ascended masters."

Knowing my metaphysics concerning "ascended masters" and having a large degree of mischief in me, I asked, "If they are ascended masters, why don't they simply manifest themselves on the planet? Why do they need spaceships?"

"Well," she said with great sincerity, "they don't want to freak anybody out."

Our space friends are a little late. I, for one, would be glad if they came. Let them organize garbage collection and road building and, of course, the space program. But, alas, I fear we must still do it ourselves for the present. I wonder what the space-pin lady is saying now about their arrival. Maybe we blew it? Perhaps we were not evolved enough to deserve the attention of the space folk? Or maybe their more advanced civilizations didn't have the benefits of a Casio computer watch, so they just don't know what time it is?

Being a "true believer" can be comforting in our day and age. The skill of accurately observing reality can be developed over time and with practice, but this is difficult to do when you are ready to impose belief, theory, conjecture, presupposition, assumption, and concepts about reality on reality.

When you begin to observe reality, begin freshly with the notion that you know nothing. Separate the ideas you have from your observations. You might find this hard to do. But if you truly want to know how reality is, your observations must not be burdened by your own biases. It takes practice to put preconceived concepts aside and observe what is truly going on. When you master this practice, you will have a powerful tool you can use to create what matters most to you in life.

Part Two

The Creative Process

The Creative Cycle

Three Stages of Creation

There are three major stages in the growth and life-building process: *germination*, *assimilation*, and *completion*. Every complete creative process moves through this cycle and always in the same sequence.

The cycles of creating are as natural and organic as the human birth cycle and have the same three stages.

Germination occurs at conception. This is the prime initiating act from which the entire process emanates.

Assimilation, the second distinct stage, is akin to gestation, during which the fetus develops and grows.

Completion, the final stage, occurs when the birth of this new human being takes place.

Germination

In creating the results you want, germination has a very special energy—the energy characteristic of any beginning. You tend to feel this burst of energy when you initiate projects: when you first begin a new diet, when you start a new job, when your organization decides to create a new line of products, when you tackle a new legal case, when you begin to research and design a new technical tool, when your management team sets a new goal, when you first bring home a new piece of stereo equipment, when you meet someone with whom you hit it off well, when you start a new class or workshop, when you first start to write a major research paper, when you first buy a house.

Composer Roger Sessions described germination as "the impulse which sets creation in movement."

The great joy for filmmaker Alfred Hitchcock was in conceiving and planning his films. For months before he worked with cameramen, actors, scenery, costumes, or other details he thrived on germinational energy by sketching the entire film, frame by frame, on long sheets of yellow paper. He was fond of saying that filming the movie itself was much less exciting to him than conceiving, writing, and planning it. Hitchcock was not alone in taking particular delight in the germinational stage of the creative process. Many people love the thrill of germination.

During the initial stages excitement, keen interest, and freshness abound. It is a time for generating action. Great insight, realization, enthusiasm, change, and a sense of power often occur. As everyone knows, however, these experiences of germinational energy dissipate over time, often after a brief time.

Unfortunately, most approaches to human growth and potential focus exclusively on germination. While this stage is an important and powerful one in the creative process, by itself it is not sufficient to produce real and lasting results, for it is only the first step. If you had a wonderful germinational experience, but did not follow it with the other stages of the creative process, the experience would not lead to much. It might make a nice memory, but you could not build your life on it. One reason some people become "workshop junkies" is that they love the experience of germinational energy. However, they do not know how to bring that energy to its next stage. So they seek more germinational experiences, hoping that this time it will last. But it never does, and it never can. Germination is only a beginning. It cannot be substituted for the entire creative cycle. Those who become hooked on germinational experiences are like people who have had only shipboard romances. As soon as the boat reaches port, the romance is over.

Even though Alfred Hitchcock loved the germination stage of creating, he was a master of the other stages as well. Had he been the filmmaking equivalent of a workshop junkie, he would never have made a single film.

For creators, germination leads to the next step in the cycle. Even before the germination stage is over, creators begin to anticipate and often move into the assimilation stage.

Assimilation

Assimilation is a crucial step of creating. Like the gestation period of the human birth cycle, assimilation is the least obvious stage of growth, particularly in its beginning phases.

During this internalizing stage, the result being created is growing organically, developing from within, and calling forth inner resources, while you are taking inner and outer action.

A senior vice president in a major financial institution began to write a proposal for a new project that involved several million dollars. She was not sure just how to organize her material. She had all of the information she needed, but she had not yet found a way of expressing it clearly and insightfully. She jotted down everything she wanted to express in the proposal, but in no special order. Then, on the top of the page, she wrote a note to herself describing the result she wanted in the report.

Next she went for a walk to distract her conscious mind. When she came back to her desk, she read over the notes she had made and put them to the side of her desk. She turned to a new sheet of paper and began organizing her material by establishing a series of categories, ones she had not thought of before. She then turned to her word processor and began to write a draft of her proposal. One section began to take shape. Soon another section fell into place. Momentum began to build and, almost faster than she could type, the rest of the proposal came together in a completed whole. This was a first draft, and of course she had some editing and adjusting to do, but her desired result was enhanced by her ability to move from the germinational stage into the assimilation stage.

A similar assimilation stage, of shorter or longer duration, occurs when you are learning a new dance, a new management technique, a new computer program, a new foreign language, or a new skill.

Germinational energy occurs when you are conceiving your vision. During the assimilation stage, you are teaching this vision to yourself. You are internalizing the vision, making it part of yourself. Your vision is no longer a new acquaintance but an old friend. In a sense the vision becomes one with you. Your creation begins to grow and develop both consciously and nonconsciously. Much of this development is not at all obvious. Assimilation has a hidden quality to it. You begin to have insights, ideas, connections, and added momentum. Your creation begins to take shape. It becomes more and more tangible. You begin to experience your creation as a concrete entity. The creation begins to take on a life of its own.

Although artists have difficulty describing assimilation, they are aware of it and of its essential contribution to the creative process. They are naturally in touch with the inner, hidden quality of their activities at this stage.

Roger Sessions describes this second stage as the composer experiences it, calling assimilation execution.

> The process of execution is first of all that of listening inwardly to the music as it shapes itself; of allowing the music to grow; of following both inspiration and conception wherever they may lead. A phrase, a motif, a rhythm, even a chord, may contain within itself, in the composer's imagination, the energy which produces movement. It will lead the composer on, through the force of its own momentum or tension, to other phrases, other motifs, other chords.

In a letter to a friend about how a composition forms itself, Mozart underlined the hidden quality of assimilation, the musical idea forming itself somewhere within, appearing when it is ready, not able to be forced out before its time.

> When I am, as it were, completely myself, entirely alone, and of good cheer—say, travelling in a carriage, or walking after a good meal, or during the night when I cannot sleep; it is on such occasions that my ideas flow best and most abundantly. *Whence* and *how* they come, I know not; nor can I force them. Those ideas that please me I retain

in memory, and am accustomed, as I have been told, to hum them to myself. If I continue in this way, it soon occurs to me how I may turn this or that morsel to account, so as to make a good dish of it, that is to say, agreeably to the rules of counterpoint, to the peculiarities of the various instruments, etc.

Gertrude Stein, talking to artists, graphically described assimilation:

> You cannot go into the womb to form the child; it is there and makes itself and comes forth whole— and there it is and you have made it and have felt it, but it has come itself.

The stage of assimilation generates momentum, so that as you move through the creative cycle the path of least resistance, emanating from structural tension, is toward the result taking shape, forming itself, becoming an entity.

The mathematician and physicist Jules Henri Poincaré viewed assimilation as work done at an invisible level. For him the result produced was "a manifest sign of long, subconscious prior work." In his writing on mathematical creation, Poincaré described how important this inner work was and how its momentum eventually moved it into conscious form.

> The role of this subconscious work in mathematical invention appears to me incontestable, and traces of it would be found in other cases where it is less evident. Often when one works at a hard question, nothing good is accomplished at the first attack. Then one takes a rest, long or short, and sits down anew to the work. During the first half-hour, as before, nothing is found, and then all of a sudden the decisive idea presents itself to the mind.
>
> It might be said that the conscious work has been more fruitful because it has been interrupted and the rest has given back to the mind its force and freshness. But it is more probable that this rest has been filled out with subconscious work and that the result of this work has afterward re-

> vealed itself to the geometer just as in the cases I
> have cited. Only the revelation, instead of coming
> during a walk or a journey, has happened during
> a period of conscious work, but independently of
> this work; the conscious work plays at most a role
> of excitant, as if it were the good stimulating the
> results already reached during rest, but remain-
> ing subconscious, to assume the conscious form.

Poincaré described a personal example of a time when the
assimilation process helped him make a connection between
two apparently unconnected fields of mathematics. It followed
a period of intense work "apparently without success."

> Disgusted with my failure, I went to spend a few
> days at the seaside, and thought of something else.
> One morning, walking on the bluff, the idea came
> to me, with just the same characteristics of brev-
> ity, suddenness and immediate certainty, that the
> arithmetic transformations of indeterminate ter-
> nary quadratic forms were identical with those of
> non-Euclidean geometry.

The profound result produced by this connection turned out
to be the opening of a door into new areas of research in the
field of mathematics.

Completion

The third distinct stage of creation is completion, which includes bringing to fruition, manifesting the whole, finishing,
following through, and learning to live with your creation.

Bringing to fulfillment that which you are creating is obviously important. Few people have mastered this stage.

All of us know people who do not bring their creative activity
to completion: graduate students who need only to write their
theses to receive their doctoral degrees, but never finish writing; entrepreneurs who begin businesses, yet somehow never
make them financially viable; engineers who need only to make
a few final decisions to get a project out the door, but get bogged
down in endless details; salespeople who need merely to iron

out a few arrangements to complete an important contract, but flounder and lose the sale; amateur boatbuilders whose home-made sailboats in the garage just need the final caulking, but they never quite make their craft seaworthy; people who start classes in karate but discontinue them just when they are beginning to acquire a degree of mastery in the art.

Such people are able to snatch defeat out of the very jaws of victory.

Some people feel uncomfortable having what they want. Receiving, or learning to live with your creation, is an essential phase of completion and hence of the creative process. It is the ability to receive the fruits of your endeavors.

Just as a composer releases a new composition to the public, so people who create in other realms "release" their work to the world. The created result is set free from its creator; it can then be received by its creator.

Cole Porter commonly experienced these two steps of releasing and receiving whenever one of his musicals opened. After the opening he thought of the work as something outside and entirely separate from himself. For him the completed result possessed an autonomy beyond the intention of the creator. For most artists, creating a work is like giving birth to a child, which, when born, assumes a life and identity uniquely its own.

When the television broadcaster and award-winning film-maker Phyllis Haynes completes a film project, she experiences the film as if she were just another member of the audience:

> When I am engaged in a project, I am totally involved in the elements of the work as they are revealed from one step to the next, and as these steps relate to the vision of the film.
>
> After a project is in the can, I watch it as if someone else had made it. I can laugh at punch lines as if I had never heard them before. I can be moved by it as if I was viewing the film for the first time. I can become involved with it because I am able to separate myself as an artist from myself as an audience. This is useful, because when I am ready for my next project, I have had the advantage of being part of the audience of my last project.

Moving Forward

In each of the three stages of the creative cycle, you generate a certain unique energy. That energy helps you move from the stage you are in to the next stage.

The energy of germination helps you move to assimilation, the energy of assimilation helps you move to completion, and the energy of completion helps you move to a new germination.

Cole Porter's completion of one musical inspired him to begin writing another. Poincaré's mathematical discoveries at the seashore sent him back home to create new mathematical connections and discoveries. The painter's finished canvas leads him or her to germinate new ideas for future paintings.

Last year I released two new albums of music. I wrote and produced the first, *Rainy Night on the Highway*, over a five-month period. Just when I was finishing this album, I began another, *Air Signs*. I wrote and produced this second album in only one week. I had developed so much momentum in creating the first album that this energy spilled over to the second. Had I not spent the five months it took for *Rainy Night*, I could never have completed *Air Signs* in such a brief time.

The nature of creative energy is not to run down but to increase and multiply itself.

After creating a successful gourmet meal, it is easier for you to create another one. After you once grow a successful garden, it is easier for you to plant and grow a garden the next year.

Completion urges you forward.

Special energy is present in each of the three stages of the creative cycle. Next we will more fully explore each stage in turn.

Germination and Choice

Making Choices

Germination does not consist merely of conceiving what you want and establishing a direction in which you want to go, but most importantly in activating the seeds of your creation.

The way you activate the seeds of your creation is by *making choices about results you want to create.*

When you make a choice, you mobilize vast energies and resources that otherwise often go untapped.

All too often people fail to focus their choices upon results, and therefore their choices are ineffective.

Learning to Choose

I often had lunch with a colleague of mine. I would open the menu and within fifteen to twenty seconds close the menu, ready to order. My friend would seriously study the menu with the intensity of a scholarly Jesuit. Usually the waitress would have to make two trips to our table just to get our order. One day my friend asked me how I decided what I wanted to eat so quickly. I told him my secret.

Years before, I had practiced making decisions in restaurants.

I would open the menu and quickly select an item. During this first experimental stage, I was sometimes delighted, sometimes disappointed. Over time I learned to let my eyes be drawn to just the right items and to make my choice immediately. After the choice was made, I would study the menu and check out the decision. I was almost always right. Somehow I had learned to be quickly drawn directly to what I wanted and to order it with confidence that I would enjoy the result of my choice.

I asked my friend how he made his choice.

He told me he carefully studied each offering and compared every one with every other one. If the menu offered many choices, he had quite a job. He had to read everything in the menu to make sure he did not miss something he might want.

As we talked, he noticed that this was a common way he made many other choices in his life. Rather than looking directly for what he wanted, he weighed all the available options.

When you attempt to avoid missing some possibility that might be a good one, you learn to be *indecisive.*

My friend was fascinated with the way I approached the complexities of choosing food in a restaurant. He experimented with it and found this method worked exceptionally well for him, too. He found that his eye would quickly be drawn to just what he wanted to eat. When he read the rest of the menu to test his choice, he found he was successful. He told me later he saved himself and the people waiting on him much time. And he now had more time to eat.

A small victory, yes. But small victories help prepare you for larger ones.

Making the Right Choices

The great twentieth-century composer Karlheinz Stockhausen once made this comment on the nature of composing: "The marvelous thing about composing is that you make thousands of arbitrary choices, how big to make the notehead, how large to draw the clef, how long to draw the stem of a note. None of these decisions changes the sound of the music, but by making those choices, you learn to be decisive."

As you practice making choices, you begin to develop an instinct for making the *right* choices, the ones that lead to the most successful realization of what you want to create. Who do you think has the higher probability of success, the person who has avoided making choices or the person who has made tens of thousands of choices and who has had a chance to learn the feel of right and wrong choices?

Choice takes practice. It is a developed ability. The more you choose, the better you will choose.

I recommend that you practice making small, quick choices whose outcomes have a low risk factor. The next time you are in a restaurant, quickly decide what you will order. The worst thing that may happen is you will end up with string beans when you really wanted peas.

Choice and Creating What You Want

Learning to make choices is one of the most overlooked and underestimated aspects of our traditional education. Educators suspect that if students were allowed choices, they may not choose what their parents and teachers would choose for them. Would students choose to be in school? Would they choose to do homework? Would they choose to be told how to behave and how to spend their time?

Some teachers think they are preparing their students for life by teaching them that the choices they have are limited. Thus the real lesson they teach is *compromise*: Learn to live with what you don't really like, because you will have plenty of that.

This assumes, of course, that you cannot create what you truly want.

Making choices is a vital part of the creative process. Not only do you choose what you want to create, but you also make a series of strategic choices along the way, choices about actions, experiments, values, priorities, hierarchies, and how further to support all your efforts.

Because creating is an art, it deals in approximation. There are no formulas to follow, no hard rules to apply. Creating is, at its roots, improvisational. You make it up as you go along. You learn to break ground. You learn to learn from your failures as well as your successes. Over time, your own unique creative process develops, and your instinct for making choices that are in your own best interest increases.

As we consider how little attention is given in school or at home to the skill of making choices, is it any wonder that our children are plagued by drug abuse, teen pregnancy, suicide, alienation from society, and confusion and ambivalence about their futures? When one has had such limited experience in making choices, desired results will always give way to immediate demands. It is easier to watch television than to do homework. It is easier to take drugs than to experience the complexities life often offers. It is even easier to engage in unsafe sex and respond to the heat of the moment than to consider the goal of a long and healthy life.

Some choices are better than others. When the subject of choice becomes a centerpiece of education, we will begin to prepare our children to create their own futures, rather than futures that grow out of how they react or respond to circumstances.

It is never too late to learn. Even if you have spent your life randomly making choices, you can learn now to orchestrate your choices strategically. After all, you make choices anyway, and it's hard to make a good argument in favor of being less effective than you can be.

Avoiding Effective Choice

In the reactive-responsive orientation, there are eight common ways in which people avoid or undermine effective choice and by which they lose the potential power of choice.

1. Choice by limitation—choosing only what seems possible or reasonable.

George wanted to be a doctor. His parents, however, continually dissuaded him from that career because of the financial difficulties involved. Although he had the intellectual ability to pursue a career in medicine, it seemed impossible for him to support himself financially through medical school, so he eliminated the possibility of becoming a doctor from his aspirations. He considered only career paths that seemed "reasonable." He became a pharmacist as a compromise.

If you limit your choices only to what seems possible or reasonable, as George did, you disconnect yourself from what you truly want, and all you have left is a compromise. George never had the same enthusiasm for pharmacy as he had for medicine.

Why? Because the human spirit will not invest itself in a compromise.

In organizations, the ranks of engineering, management, sales, marketing, and manufacturing personnel are sprinkled with unenthusiastic and uninspired people who are there because of a choice by limitation. They know they are living a daily compromise, but they are trying to be "reasonable" in the life they have created. They experience their choice as the best they can expect from the limitation their lives seem to offer.

2. *Choice by indirectness—choosing the process instead of the result.*

Some people choose "to go to college" rather than choose "to be educated," or choose "to eat health foods" rather than choose "to be healthy." Because this kind of choice invests undue power in the process, the result is inextricably tied to the process, and the ways in which the desired result can come about are limited.

Harriet was convinced that her interpersonal problems stemmed from her bad relationship with her father. Over the years she read many books designed to help her release her unexpressed anger toward him. She attended several workshops that focused on that process and pursued various therapeutic approaches. During these sessions she would sometimes find herself screaming at the top of her lungs, crying her eyes out, making lists of grievances toward her father, conducting imaginary dialogues with him, and sharing with groups the story of her relationship with her father.

What Harriet actually wanted was to be a whole person.

The processes she chose were not the result she wanted. She chose them hoping they would bring her what she wanted. Through her pursuit of process, Harriet never chose to create the wholeness she sought, although she attempted to convince herself she was making choices that would lead to the wholeness for which she longed.

When company profits are sliding, worried high-level executives may find themselves investing their hopes in new processes. "Let's put all the sales force through this workshop on excellence and see if it helps."

Often people become so involved in processes that the results they truly want to create are obscured or entirely forgotten. Without a clear vision of the result, they have little chance of creating what they desire. In many cases they are not even aware of the result they are after.

3. Choice by elimination—eliminating all other possibilities so that only one choice remains.

This typically occurs when a person escalates the conflict in a situation by polarizing differences to a point where they are irreconcilable and the person is "forced" to take the only obvious alternative left.

People often leave one life situation and move to another by choice by elimination. Most of us have had the experience of making matters worse and worse until we feel we must leave because the situation is intolerable. For some people this is a way of life. Most situations they leave come from the intensity of an escalated conflict.

For example, after Jerry exacerbated a disagreement with his wife into a full-scale fight, he told his friends at the tavern, "Things got so bad, I had to walk out on her. I had no choice." By the time Jerry left his marriage, the situation was similar to a cold war, with skirmishes breaking out every two or three days. Jerry overlooked any pleasant times and made the bad times seem worse than they were. In his mind the conflict grew and grew until it seemed critical. To him it seemed there was no choice except to leave.

This is how many people leave their jobs. Through self-propaganda, their relationships with colleagues and senior management become strained and misunderstandings increase. They interpret little remarks as criticism. Even the walls begin to seem conspiratorial. Every day looks blacker than the one before. It becomes harder to wake up in the morning and face the turmoil. These people complain to their friends, who advise them to look for another job. They develop resentment toward colleagues who seem to like the organization. They begin to question the organization's integrity, adding fuel to the fire. Typically they become more preoccupied with the conflict than they are with their job. When someone leaves a job this way, it seems like a noble act in a moral cause. "I had no choice. I had to leave. What would you have done?!"

One of the tendencies in modern times is to polarize the political left and right, so that all that remains are two undesirable extremes: tyranny from the right or tyranny from the left. People then see themselves as controlled by circumstances, faced with two undesirable choices, and forced to settle for choosing the lesser of two evils. Certainly choice by elimination is what we see happening with tragic consequences in Central America, Northern Ireland, the Middle East, and Africa.

4. *Choice by default—the "choice" not to make a choice, so that whatever results happen seem to occur without choice.*

The deadline is missed. The contract goes unsigned. The "go-ahead" is never given. The vote is not cast in the election.

Because of an inability or unwillingness to choose, the person in this mode assigns the power to the situation and abdicates his or her own power. Such refusal to choose cripples any effective action in its earliest stages. All that is left is reaction.

5. *Conditional choice—imposing preconditions on choices.*

Conditional choice follows the typical formulas: "I will choose this when . . ." and "I will choose this if . . ."

"I'll begin this new project when I get my raise." "I'll design the new approach when Jan and Carl are assigned to my team." "I'll invest in a new home after my mother-in-law moves out."

Rather than choose the result they want directly, some people impose certain conditions or circumstances upon the result. "I'll be happy when I find the perfect relationship." The implication here is that they will not be happy until they have the perfect relationship, and their choice to be happy is dependent on whether or not they have a perfect relationship. Such people place the power to organize their lives in certain arbitrary external conditions, and these conditions are then somehow supposed to have the mystical ability to set up an environment that brings satisfaction.

6. *Choice by reaction—choices designed to overcome a conflict.*

This occurs when people make choices not to initiate a creative process but to reduce discomfort or eliminate pressure.

A computer executive announces at a staff meeting, "Let's

build a lap-top computer as soon as possible, because our major competitor already has one on line."

After having a heated conversation with a boss who is no longer enchanted with the engineering team, the head engineer suggests to his team, "Let's design an auto body just like the foreign designers are doing so that we can recapture our loss of market share."

As soon as circumstantial stimuli reach a critical level of discomfort, the person in this mode makes a choice designed to relieve the discomfort. The power here lies in whatever produces discomfort, and the choice is made solely to eliminate that discomfort.

Society trusts that most people make choices by reaction, so when society does not want people to act in certain ways, it threatens to make life uncomfortable if they do—fines, imprisonment, eviction, humiliation, ostracism, and even capital punishment. Choice by reaction is often a knee-jerk reaction, as when some drivers automatically slow down when they see the state police.

7. Choice by consensus—choosing by finding out what everyone else is willing to recommend and following the results of that poll.

Because a person in this mode often achieves consensus by using successful preliminary public relations, the vote at the poll usually turns out to be consistent with what the person actually wants to do. Because others are giving the advice, however, the person chooses not according to his or her own desires but as dictated by the will of the group polled.

A woman described her choice to find a new job in the following way:

> My boss is hard to talk to, and I've been extremely bored lately in my job. I don't feel any support from the rest of the staff. In fact, they all seem to care about things that are completely superficial and unimportant. Meantime, I've just had this new job offer in an exciting organization. The new job seems challenging, involving, and important. And the people with whom I'd be working share my real caring for organizational transformation.

What do you think I ought to do? Do you think I
ought to quit my job and take the new one?

It is difficult to imagine anyone advising her to stay in the
old job. In this example her public-relations activity was quite
overt. Usually it is more subtle, but the general strategy remains the same.

Once I knew a corporate executive who practiced a variation
of choice by consensus. When faced with a company decision,
he would collect advice and opinions from several people he
knew. Then he would follow the advice of those who agreed
with what he wanted to do. If it turned out that this choice was
not successful, he would go back to the people whose advice he
appeared to take and blame them for his failure.

8. *Choice by adverse possession—choice based on a hazy
metaphysical notion about the nature of the universe.*
The theory is that whatever you possess in current reality
you have somehow chosen, if not in this lifetime, then in another: "I have hemorrhoids, therefore I must have chosen
them."

If you accept this notion as true, you are forced to conclude
that some "part of you" outside your awareness has chosen all
of the circumstances operating in your life, including those situations you do not consciously want. The power in your life
then lies in some unknown part of you and therefore beyond
your reach.

Actually the life experiences you now have are, *in part*, a
natural outcome of the structures you have previously established in your life. If the path of least resistance produces outcomes you do not like, you may find their causes in the
structural makeup you established, rather than in some per-
verse or unwitting choice you may have made. Often the situation is not at all what you chose or what you wanted.

Choice and Power

The way people choose reveals where they see the power in
a situation residing and how that power is activated and used.
In each of the foregoing eight ineffective ways of choosing characteristic of the reactive-responsive orientation, the power in

the situation is abdicated or handed over to something or someone outside the person.

When you create, power is not situational. That is to say, your power to create does not come from the circumstances, but from yourself. Nothing forces you to make the choice to create what you want to create, and nothing can take this power from you.

Choice in the Creative Orientation

In the creative orientation, you consciously choose results you want to see manifested.

Choosing is deceptively simple, yet it does take practice to do it correctly. As I have mentioned, one way of making a choice incorrectly is to commit yourself to a process rather than to the result you want. Many people engaged in processes designed to bring them specific results have never actually chosen those results, either formally or informally. Some people who eat special health foods, take large doses of vitamin supplements, exercise assiduously, and avoid alcohol, coffee, tobacco, chocolate, bleached flour, red meat, and refined sugar have never made the choice to be healthy. Many people take healthful actions and still do not make the choice to be healthy.

Some upper-management people attend business seminars and learn new techniques for marketing, management, production, and so on, convinced these will be "good for the company." They then launch their employees on a sea of trainings, hoping the training will make a positive difference in their organization. This type of manager puts blind faith in the processes adopted, but the adopted actions fail to focus the creative process. This is simply another example of searching for the correct response.

In many instances, both the managers and the health food eaters have chosen a process of doing what is "good for them." It is as if they are investing all their energies in the process, hoping that the process will bring them to a desirable result. Often they are committed to the process but not necessarily to the result.

Formally making the choice to be healthy can mobilize the inner resources of the body, mind, and spirit. By choosing to be healthy, you set up one of the components of structural tension, the vision. Through this choice you focus and release energy and you then tend to gravitate toward those processes that will be most healthful and helpful to you.

When an organization chooses a result, the members can more easily mobilize the resources of the organization. The processes that will aid in the direct creation of that result are more easily found or invented and executed.

When you merely choose a process, you do not establish structural tension, and you do not make energy available to complete the creative process.

Choosing Negative Results

Instead of choosing to *create what they want*, some people choose to *avoid what they don't want*. Instead of choosing health, some people choose the absence of sickness.

When you choose merely to avoid what you do not want, you do not establish structural tension. Instead, what you set up is a conflict structure.

Some people who engage in strict diet and exercise regimes are not clearly in favor of health, but are clearly against getting sick. The focus of their fear is not merely the common cold, but illnesses such as heart attack, cancer, ulcers, hypertension, diabetes, and other threatening diseases. They follow a strategy of avoidance, emphasizing what they do not want (serious illness or death) rather than what they do want (vitality and life).

Their behavior arises out of a structural conflict in which the path of least resistance is to take action designed to attempt to resolve an unresolvable conflict.

This structural conflict, revolving around feelings of discomfort, is a life-versus-death conflict. Because they want to make sure they survive, which is to say, that they do not get seriously ill or die, they keep in mind a negative vision—the vision of themselves succumbing at any moment (getting cancer or having a heart attack). They have thus exacerbated the conflict. They maintain a high level of pressure on themselves at all times because they cannot afford to slide back into illness.

Their strategy is to keep themselves in a state of conflict. They may think, "If I eat sugar and white flour, I'll get cancer and won't live, so I'd better make sure I don't eat food like that. I must remain vigilant." The actions they take, such as eating organically grown foods and exercising, are not focused toward health, but are actually designed to restore the experience of emotional comfort—to reduce the fear and worry they have generated in themselves.

Over a period of time they reinforce the belief that they are powerless; that the power over their lives lies in the food or exercise, not in themselves; that their life is threatened by eating certain foods and not exercising. Left to their own devices, they believe they would be irresponsible, so they need to control themselves by maintaining awareness of both the potential danger of slacking off in their practices and their irresponsibility about persevering in these practices.

I am not saying there is anything inherently wrong with eating healthy foods and getting plenty of physical exercise. In the orientation of the creative, once you have consciously made the choice to be healthy and you are attracted to eating certain foods and following certain forms of exercise, you are involved in an organic process. The structural tendency of this organic process is for you to be attracted to those processes that will be particularly beneficial to your health. Those processes might include the usual, expected ones, such as health food and exercise, as well as unexpected ones.

When you try to impose processes on yourself, you may lose touch with your own natural life rhythms, which may call for you to be engaged in very different types of activities as these rhythms change.

For example, you may have a policy of eating a fixed diet each day; however, your life rhythm may call for more protein on one day than on another. Because of your imposed diet, you might disregard your life rhythm and miss the foods or nutrition your body requires on a particular day to enhance your state of health.

What You Don't Want

Many people in corporations throughout the world spend a major portion of their time and effort avoiding what they don't want: an uncooperative staff, inadequate management, excessive inventory, losses, returns, product defects, credit refusals, lawsuits, overdrafts, bankruptcy, hostile takeovers, and so forth.

In the creative process you do not make choices about what you *do not* want. You make choices about what you *do* want.

Knowing what you now have that you do not want can, of course, be useful information, because often the opposite of what you do not want is what you do want.

If you do not want your car to keep breaking down, what you probably want is a car that consistently runs well. If you do not want to work under boring conditions, what you might want is an interesting and challenging job. If you do not want to work with an uncommitted and indecisive staff, perhaps what you do want is a dedicated and decisive one. If you do not want to argue and fight all the time with your mate, what you might want is its opposite, a loving, supportive, and harmonious relationship.

When you focus large amounts of energy on the problems in your life, it is easy to remain fixated on those problems. At certain times the only thing that seems important to you is to get the problem to stop being a problem or to have it go away.

The more entrenched the problem seems, the harder it may be to separate what you want from what you do not want or from what you think is possible.

Quite often I have spent fifteen minutes or longer simply asking someone the question, What do you want to create? only to have the person continue to reply, "I don't want this" or "I don't want that" or "I don't want to have to deal with this" or "I'd like to be rid of that."

Imagine composer Béla Bartók trying to create his third string quartet by using only a list of things he did not want it to be. "I don't want it to be orchestral music. I don't want it to be a piano piece. I don't want it to be like other compositions I've written. I don't want it to be expressionless," and so on. As you can see, focusing on what you do not want does not create much of a vision, nor does it generate any germinational energy.

When choices about what you do not want hold the dominant power, what you do want is lost in the shuffle.

Formally Choosing

When you make a choice, take two steps:

First, conceive of the results you want, that is, have a clear vision of what you want to create.

Second, formalize the choice by actually saying the words, "I choose to have . . ."

It is not important that you say the words aloud, but certainly say them to yourself and inwardly: truly make the choice to have that result. Saying the words of your choice is not the same as muttering an incantation with mysterious magical powers, nor is it a type of repeated affirmation. Rather, you are simply concretizing the choice into a verbal form to give your vision a bit more focus.

When you make a formal choice, you activate the seeds of germination. You align all the energies at your disposal and set them in motion toward your choice. You initiate the first stage of the creative cycle.

For many, making such a formal choice seems to be a momentary leap into the unknown, especially if the choice they are making involves something important they have never chosen before. After that moment of uncertainty, however, they often experience clarity, energy, and physical lightness. Whether or not you have unusual experiences, when you make a choice in the orientation of the creative, you actively set energy in motion in your chosen direction. Choices about results have power.

Primary, Secondary, and Fundamental Choice

Three distinct kinds of choices operate as strategic elements in the creative process: *primary choice*, *secondary choice*, and *fundamental choice*.

Primary Choice

Primary choices are choices about major results.

You may make primary choices in almost any area of your life. At work, you may choose to be one of the most effective managers in your company, to harness superconductivity for practical applications, to develop a safe method of transporting hazardous materials, to integrate artificial intelligence and sophisticated retrieval systems, to open a manufacturing plant in Singapore. Personally, you may make primary choices to have a superb relationship, a meaningful job, a house in which you really feel at home, or a wonderful vacation. You may make a primary choice to create a work of art, to cook a fantastic meal, or to conduct a brilliant workshop or meeting. *A primary choice is about some result you want in itself and for itself.* It is not something you want because it will lead you to something else—even though it may. A primary choice does not function mainly as a step in a series of steps. It functions as the ultimate goal.

While a primary choice may also bring other results into being or serve as a foundation for future results, its major purpose as a choice is to achieve what is being chosen. When an artist paints a painting, the primary choice is for the completed painting itself to exist, rather than for the painting to be a stepping-stone in the artist's career, or a way of bringing the artist emotional satisfaction, or a way of earning money. An inventor creates an invention not primarily to patent it, but to see the invention exist.

Since inventing the first tunable dye laser in 1966, Mary Dietrich Spaeth has been active in developing the process of laser isotope separation. Like most inventors, her primary goal is in seeing that her inventions work, not in the financial rewards they bring or in owning patents for them.

She once described how Hughes Aircraft Company, her employer at the time, had been trying unsuccessfully to build a ruby range finder using a component she had invented. She was sure it could work, but Hughes had assigned her other tasks:

> I had been given a direct order not to work on it, but I worked on it anyway and saved them a lot of money over the years. Most of the concepts I've worked on over the years, however, aren't patentable. In fact, I was never much interested in patents. I was much more interested in getting things to work together. It's a struggle to get a patent. I was much more interested in something that works, rather than a piece of paper.

If you have doubts about whether what you want is a result unto itself or part of a process aimed at attaining some other result, ask yourself, "What is this choice designed to do?"

If it is designed to help achieve something beyond itself, it is part of a process. It is, therefore, not a primary choice but at best a secondary one.

If it is not designed to bring you some further result, it is a result in and of itself and therefore is a primary choice.

When I asked a friend why she plays the piano, she said, "Because I love to play the piano." This is an example of primary choice.

The primary choice for artists may simply be the joy of creating. As twentieth-century sculptor Henry Moore once remarked, "I sometimes draw just for its own enjoyment."

A friend who is a gourmet cook said to me while preparing dinner for us, "What I like to do is get involved in improvising in the kitchen. Often, like tonight, I don't know exactly what I have in mind for dinner. I like to see what will turn up when I enjoy playing around with the ingredients."

My friend had indeed made a primary choice, which had at least two results. The first was an excellent meal. Earlier that evening he may not have known exactly how this particular meal would end up looking or tasting, but he knew the qualities of the dinner he was after. He could be sure that the first result he created—a superb dinner—would successfully match the aesthetic and gustatory criteria of great food.

The second result he had in mind was the sheer joy of cooking. This result was like my pianist friend's joy at playing the piano, or like a mountain climber's excitement in scaling a mountain, or like a vacationer's delight in lying on a sunny beach. For him the experience of cooking was an end in itself, independent of the dinner it would produce.

For people in the reactive-responsive orientation, it is often difficult to make a primary choice, because they emphasize process (how to get where they want to go) rather than the result (where they finally want to be).

I have met people so totally involved in process they could not conceive of the results they wanted. Instead, all they could conceive of were process steps, which led to other process steps.

"What do you want?" I asked a man during a workshop.

"I want to get in touch with myself," he said.

"What will you have once you are in touch with yourself?" I asked, trying to help him focus on the result he wanted.

"Then I can see what holds me back," he replied.

"What will happen once you can see what holds you back?"

"Then I can overcome the way I sabotage myself."

"Once you know that," I asked again, "then what?"

"Then I can stop doing it."

"What will happen when you stop doing it?"

"Well, I don't know," was his reply.

When people who are focused on process are asked where

their process is taking them, they often do not see where it might lead, even five or six steps down the line.

An Exercise in Primary Choice

There is tremendous power in knowing what results you designate as primary. Once you make primary choices to create those results, you may effectively and naturally rearrange and reorganize your life in ways that help bring those primary choices into reality.

When you formally make a primary choice, you generate germinational energy, and new strategic secondary choices—choices that support a primary choice—become clear and apparent. When you make these strategic secondary choices, you match your actions to the result you want to create, so that each step you take creates a foundation for and builds momentum toward the full realization of the primary choice. Here's a good way to begin:

Step 1. Make a list of everything you want, from now through the rest of your life. Include both personal and professional wants. Also include what you want for the world in general. Be honest about what you want. Do not consider whether it is possible or probable while formulating this list.

Include the *qualities* you want in your relationships with others. Do not include ways specific people should behave. To say, "I want Harry to do such and such," is an attempt to impose your will on Harry. Rather, focus on the nature and quality of the relationship you want. Write, "I want a relationship that has the following qualities . . ." The relationship you ultimately create may or may not be with Harry.

Be sure to list only those items you *do* want. Do not include items you *do not* want, such as "no more war," "no more arguments with my manager," or "no more ulcers."

Also do not include items you think you *should* want because you think they are expected of you or because you think you would be selfish not to include them.

Treat this list as a first draft.

Step 2. Reread your list to make sure it includes all of the major components you want in your life. Add anything you may have forgotten in your original list and cross off any item you do not really want.

Step 3. Test each item on your list with this question: "If I could have that, would I take it?"

If the answer is no, then either cross the item off your list or adjust it so that it is something you want. Sometimes you may discover that you really don't want a result you thought you really cared about.

If the answer to the test question is yes, formally choose the item by saying to yourself: "I choose this result: (fill in what you want)."

Step 4. Continue the process until you have chosen every item you truly want on your list.

By making these choices, you have taken the first step in the creative process. Conceiving and choosing what you want is an act of germination. As you choose what you want, you release germinational energy, which enables you to move in the direction you want to go.

Secondary Choice

A choice that helps you take a step toward your primary result is called a secondary choice.

Thus you might choose to go shopping (secondary choice) in order to have the ingredients for the meal you want to serve (primary choice). Or you might purchase a word processing program that alphabetizes bibliographical references (secondary choice) in order to complete a reference book you want to write (primary choice).

Secondary choices support a primary choice.

Some months ago I decided to have a well-toned body. That was my primary choice. One of my major secondary choices was a three-month Nautilus exercise program. I made many other secondary choices, even daily, to support my primary choice.

Often during the program I would wake up in the morning and the thought would occur, "I could stay in bed this morning. After all, I've exercised the last few days. I am doing a good job. I don't really need to exercise this morning!"

I would then get out of bed and go downstairs in my robe and slippers.

Downstairs the thought would occur to me, "Now that I'm

awake, I can just go to the bathroom and then right back to bed. After all, I don't really need the exercise!"

I would then put on my sweatsuit and sneakers.

Once dressed for my workout, the thought would occur, "Now that I'm awake and dressed, I could lounge around and read some more of that book I like so well and have a very pleasant morning!"

By this time I would have put on my jacket and walked out my front door.

As soon as I was in the car, the thought would occur, "Now that I am in the car—This is great!—I can drive down to get some croissants!"

I would then drive to the Nautilus gym.

Usually by this time, thoughts of avoiding exercise would have temporarily disappeared. About two or three exercise routines before the end of the series, however, the thought would occur, "I've done a good job! I've certainly done enough for the day! I don't have to finish all the exercises in the series!"

I would then proceed to finish the last few exercises.

This is an example of making a series of secondary choices to support the primary choice. I was able to choose to get out of bed when it would have been more convenient to have stayed in bed; to get dressed, when it would have been more convenient to go back to bed; to leave the house, when it would have been more convenient to have stayed at home; to drive to the gym, when it would have been more convenient to drive to the bakery; and to complete the entire series of exercises, when it would have been more convenient to cut them short.

Each step along the way, I was easily able to make these secondary choices, because I had clearly made my primary choice. At no point along the way did I experience a sense of loss or think I was giving up anything. Most of the thoughts that occurred were descriptions of possible alternative behaviors. It is true, I could have stayed in bed, could have stayed home reading, could have gone for croissants, and could have cut the exercises short. All of those were choices I *could* have made.

At each point of decision, however, I was able to see clearly what mattered more to me. At no point did I need to argue with myself, and at no point did I argue with myself. What mattered to me more at each point along the way was my primary choice to have a well-toned body. Each of the secondary choices I made—to get up, to go to the gym, to complete the exercises—was made easily and without hesitation because each directly supported my primary choice.

Not all secondary choices are as easily accomplished as getting out of bed or getting dressed. For persons who have chosen to be professional musicians or athletes, secondary choices may involve years of practice.

In the creative orientation, once you know your primary choice, whatever secondary choices you need to make in order to achieve the primary choice become clear along the way and easier to make. They become the most obvious course of action to take.

Secondary choices are always subordinate to a primary choice. Often there is no reason to make such choices outside the context of the primary choice that calls for them.

Athletes and musicians may not enjoy practicing long hours, but they do so just the same: not out of duty, obligation, or any other form of self-manipulation, but because they are making secondary choices consistent with their primary choice to be able to perform music or excel in sports. They may even come to love the secondary choices, because these choices so support their final vision.

The great jazz saxophonist Jerry Bergonzi said this about his process of making record albums:

> Vision is my vehicle for creating the records I make, secondary choices are the engine, and it's all a labor of love.

Leaders Making Primary and Secondary Choices

In organizations, the leader as creator understands the relationship between choices that are *primary*—such as results, objectives, and goals—and choices that are *secondary*—those strategic choices of employee teams, hours of work, timing, training, scheduling, researching, meeting, and so on.

Organizational leaders are frequently called upon to designate a heirarchy of values and functions. Often they must schedule results to be created. While, to others, these different results may seem to be of equal value, the leader will need to designate one as more important than the others.

Once the work team knows which choices are primary, it will always be clear how to make secondary choices: They are the ones that support the primary choice.

A simple primary choice might be to develop a certain product. Secondary choices may include engaging in various types of research and development, making managerial time available, committing financial resources, and organizing engineers in a project team.

Mutually Exclusive Wants

If you wake up tired one workday morning and want to stay in bed but your job requires you to be at work at a particular time, how do you make the choice of staying in bed or getting up and going to work?

In such a situation you want two things, but having one of them prohibits having the other. You cannot both remain in bed and be at work on time.

Once you know what your primary choice is, you will easily know what to do.

If your job is your primary choice, then the secondary choice will be the choice that supports the primary one, which is to get out of bed, get dressed, and go to work.

Some people are confused when two things they want are mutually exclusive. They may feel stuck, unable to choose. As a consequence they often do not make a real choice. Instead they may get up and go to work as automatons or out of guilt, fear of punishment, or loss.

Unless they make a real choice in such situations, they will always feel leftover reluctance and perhaps even resentment, no matter which alternative they end up deciding. They may physically go to work, but they may spend some or all of their time there mentally still in bed, resenting the imposition of their work schedule.

In the reactive-responsive orientation, a conflict of this kind is usually experienced as an unresolvable dilemma. The two alternatives are seen as being of equal value and importance.

In choosing one or the other, reactive-responsive people always experience loss and a degree of powerlessness. In their view, circumstances are forcing them to give up something they want.

In the orientation of the creative, you as creator determine the hierarchy of importance among results. Then you choose what is primary. This enables you always to be in the powerful position of inventing along the way the course of action that most effectively supports the result you value more (your primary choice). Instead of experiencing a sense of loss and powerlessness about the things you want but can't have, you are always choosing the things you want most. The things you want less become subordinate to your more important wants.

Furthermore, as you make secondary choices in order to support your primary choice, the primary choice becomes even more clearly defined as an important result and therefore can be even more easily created.

It became easier for me to create a well-toned body by making the various secondary choices I did along the way, for with each additional secondary choice I clearly defined a well-toned body as primary for me.

In making such secondary choices, it never seems as though you are giving up anything. When you make secondary choices—when you actually make the choice supporting what is primary—the experience you have is of doing what you truly want. Making strategic secondary choices is very empowering.

Long-Term Goals and Short-Term Demands

Some of your primary choices are long-term goals. Often while you are pursuing these goals, short-term demands—situations that seem to demand immediate attention—intervene.

Long-term goals and short-term demands play very different roles, because they each lead to different places and produce different results.

Everyone has some long-term goals: to educate all their children, to write a book on the wildflowers of Long Island, to be president of the company they work for, to become a licensed clinical psychologist, to travel around the world. Your list will be specific to you.

Everyone has many short-term demands, many of them familiar to all of us: "I'm hungry." "I'm bored." "I want to watch the late movie." "I don't want to study." "I can't live without that dress." "I have to make this deadline." "I need a break."

Short-term demands will always seek action. The action they seek most often is relief. These actions are usually designed to help people feel better. They eat. They drink. They take drugs. They go on shopping sprees. They watch television for hours. They look for distractions.

When relief becomes the driving force, people often take actions that are not in their own best interest. Such actions, however, do not help them feel better for very long, not only because most of these actions do not help them create their long-term goals but also because the conflict causing the short-term demand does not go away. In fact, some people seem to move from one short-term demand to another, and then another.

When you stay in touch with your long-term goals by asking yourself, "What results do I want to create in my life?" it is easier to take needed actions toward these goals. Secondary choices become clear. Even intervening temporary conflicts do not distract you from your life direction.

As you define your primary choices and form secondary choices that support your primary choices, you will be able to develop the ability to distinguish between your long-term goal and the short-term demands that can distract you from them.

Gregory was a carpenter. Whenever he was hired for a particular job, he would be asked to estimate how long it would take. Of course, he would estimate the time based on how many hours of carpentry were needed. But once he started the project he would allow himself to be distracted—a news story on the radio, people having a conversation outside, a phone call from home. Because of the distractions, he found that the job often took twice as long as he had originally estimated, much to the annoyance of his employers. After taking the TECHNOLOGIES FOR CREATING® course, he developed a habit of making choices in favor of his long-term goals, rather than in favor of the short-term demands that always seemed to complicate his work schedule. Instead of engaging in a conversation or thinking about problems at home, he would focus on his carpentry project. This way he was able to complete any task in the time he estimated. Whenever he found himself about to be distracted, he made a strategic secondary choice to continue to work on the project.

Fundamental Choice as a Foundation

It seems that ultimate success is not directly related to early success. Many of the most successful people in history did not give clear evidence of such promise in their youth.

Pablo Picasso needed a tutor to help him prepare for entrance into secondary school, and the tutor gave up in despair when he could not teach the boy.

Einstein's teachers considered young Albert "an idle and dull boy." His speech was always hesitant, learning languages was difficult for him, and he did not do well in school. When pressured, his relatives agreed to subsidize Albert's studies at the Polytechnic Institute in Zurich, but he failed to pass his entrance exam and had to return to secondary school to remedy his deficiencies.

As a child, the great humanitarian Eleanor Roosevelt looked as though she would never amount to much in life. Her mother felt that Eleanor's daydreaming habits made her an "impossible child." Her relatives said that she lied, stole sweets, and was poor in arithmetic, spelling, and grammar. She bit her nails; she had a great fear of burglars and the dark; she was shy and awkward.

The teachers of young Marcel Proust complained that his compositions were disorganized. Stephen Crane, Eugene O'Neill, William Faulkner, and F. Scott Fitzgerald experienced failure in college. The composer Giacomo Puccini consistently failed examinations.

Yet each of these young people grew up to become successful and prominent creators in the world. Why?

In the early days of DMA, when I first began working in the area of human endeavor and creativity, I was struck by the fact that some people, after taking my TECHNOLOGIES FOR CREATING® classes, would easily create the results they wanted, while certain participants in the same classes found it more difficult.

For months I wondered what made the essential difference. It puzzled me, since often those who were the most successful creators were not the ones who originally seemed most likely to succeed.

Then I discovered fundamental choice. A fundamental choice is a choice that has to do with a state of being, or basic life orientation, whereas a primary choice concerns itself with specific results and a secondary choice supports those results.

A fundamental choice is a choice in which you commit yourself to a basic life orientation or a basic state of being.

Many accomplished men and women, such as the people listed above, made such a fundamental choice in their lives. Because of this, their early experiences did not set the direction of their life. Once they had made fundamental choices, they could change the direction of their lives toward creating what mattered to them.

A fundamental choice is a foundation upon which primary and secondary choices rest.

If you have never made the fundamental choice to be a nonsmoker, then no matter what system you try to help you quit smoking, it will not succeed. You may try hypnosis, aversion therapy, smoke-ending programs, gradual elimination, or cold turkey. None of these processes will help you become a nonsmoker if you have not fundamentally chosen to be a nonsmoker.

On the other hand, if you have made the fundamental choice to be a nonsmoker, just about any system to stop smoking will work for you. Furthermore, after making the fundamental choice, you will tend to be particularly attracted to those systems that will work best for you, because by using them you will most easily get the job done.

Being a nonsmoker is a basic state of being, very different from the state of being of a smoker who is trying to quit smoking.

In the early days of TECHNOLOGIES FOR CREATING® those who had made a fundamental choice to create what they wanted to create were the most successful students.

Those who had not made that fundamental choice had a very different orientation toward their own growth and development. Rather than making it *their* business to see that they succeeded in having the life they wanted, they passively let circumstances dictate what happened. They hoped somehow that the circumstances of the courses they were taking or the approach they were following would transform them.

Those who had made the fundamental choice to have the life they wanted, on the other hand, were not at all passive about their success. They actively sought out and put into practice whatever might be useful to them.

Since my discovery of fundamental choice, every TECHNOLO-GIES FOR CREATING® student is taught the importance of fundamental choices and how to work with these choices. Because of this, almost all of the students in these classes are able to accelerate their progress greatly at mastering their own creative process.

One such student was a woman who had suffered from claustrophobia since the age of eight, when she accidentally shut herself in an old trunk and was not found for two days. Because of this, she avoided traveling by trains and planes. During the TECHNOLOGIES FOR CREATING® class, she decided she wanted to travel to Spain for a vacation. This was an unlikely choice, because she had never flown in her life. In the past, just the thought of being in a plane made her nervous. Then she made a fundamental choice to be the predominant creative force in her life. Her choice to travel to Spain by plane might conflict with her claustrophobia. But because she had made this fundamental choice, she suddenly found that her fears were gone. She booked her ticket and went on the trip. Because she had made a fundamental choice to be the power in her own life, she was able to move to a new orientation, one in which her choices about her life had more influence than her past circumstances. Almost miraculously her claustrophobia disappeared and never troubled her again.

This is a typical example of the orientation change that can happen once you make a fundamental choice. You are able to reorganize your primary and secondary choices so that they are consistent with your fundamental choices. When people make a fundamental choice to be true to what is highest in them, or when they make a choice to fulfill a purpose in their life, they can easily accomplish many changes that seemed impossible or improbable in the past.

As time and circumstances change, you may lose touch with what you most deeply care about. But since the truth is that you do deeply care about these choices, you will easily be able to remake them.

A Choice of Soul and Direction

The operatic composer Giacomo Puccini said, "The conscious purposeful appropriation of one's own soul-forces is the supreme secret. . . . Then I feel the burning desire and intense resolve to create something worthwhile."

Martin Buber describes the force of a fundamental choice as "direction." In his book *Daniel: Conversations About Realizations*, Buber explains,

> Direction is that primal tension of the human soul
> which moves it at times out of the infinity of the
> possible to choose this and nothing else, and to
> realize it through action.

In his concern for the future of civilization, Buber advises us to be conscious of our fundamental choices. In Buber's terminology, to make fundamental choices would be "to act with direction."

The fundamental choices for most people are the choices to be free, to be healthy, and to be true to oneself.

Freedom finds both inner and outer expression. Outer freedom includes the ability to choose and create the circumstances of your life. Inner freedom includes the experience of limitlessness.

Health includes physical, mental, emotional, and spiritual aspects, separately and collectively.

Being true to oneself is the choice to live in accordance with one's essential nature and morality, with the individual and unique purpose of one's life.

Qualities of a Fundamental Choice

Fundamental choices are not subject to changes in internal or external circumstances. If you make the fundamental choice to be true to yourself, then you will act in ways that are true to yourself whether you feel inspired or depressed, whether you feel fulfilled or frustrated, whether you are at home, at work, with your friends, or with your enemies.

If, on the other hand, one day you decide that it is all right not to be true to yourself because it is inconvenient or might make you feel uncomfortable in a particular situation, you have probably never made the fundamental choice to be true to yourself to begin with. You are basing your commitment on the conditions or the circumstances in which you happen to find yourself at any particular time. When you make a fundamental choice, convenience and comfort are not ever at issue, for you always take action based on what is consistent with your fundamental choice.

Once you make a fundamental choice, an entirely new basis for dealing with reality becomes available. The meaning of circumstances often shifts because of a fundamental choice. You begin to see how circumstances, no matter what they may be, can work toward the fulfillment of your fundamental choice.

If your fundamental choice is to be true to yourself, you look at the circumstances and use that information to make any adjustments of the circumstances that you need to make in order to be true to yourself.

One stockbroker I know worked for a large investment firm. He often complained about the difficult circumstances of his job and of his company. Once he had made the fundamental choice to be true to himself, however, he was able to change his relationship to the circumstances at work from acting as if he were a victim of them to using them as necessary feedback.

One of his most common complaints had been about his boss, whom he often criticized as being unhelpful to him. After my friend had made his fundamental choice, he committed himself to supporting his boss as best as could. As a result, his entire experience at work changed. He personally became a much more effective stockbroker for his clients, and he went from being unsatisfied with his job to being deeply satisfied. Instead of looking to his work to satisfy him, he brought his own satisfaction to his work.

In the reactive-responsive orientation, people look to the circumstances to provide them with satisfaction. They are inevitably disappointed, because circumstances themselves do not provide satisfaction.

In the orientation of the creative, you create your own satisfaction, independent of the circumstances. Then you bring satisfaction to those circumstances in which you are involved.

You need never look to the various projects in which you are involved to bring you satisfaction. Therefore you never have to guess or speculate which projects will bring you satisfaction. You need only consider whether or not you care enough about those projects to be involved with them, knowing that whatever you do, you will bring to it your own level of satisfaction. When you choose to be involved with a project, you have no ulterior motive—you are not analyzing what you can get out of it. You have only your enthusiasm and commitment—to see the results of the project fulfilled.

Once you have made any fundamental choice, say, to be true to yourself, you create a new structure in your life, and the path of least resistance in that structure leads toward the fulfillment of your fundamental choice. In this new structure you might find yourself suddenly easily able to give up unwanted compromises. You might suddenly stop old habits, such as gossiping, being petty, complaining, blaming others, or looking for sympathy. These old habits would cease based on the strength and power of your commitment to your fundamental choice and not because you tried to manipulate yourself into giving them up.

One of the approaches in which I train psychotherapists is in the use of choice. I encourage them to have their clients first know what they want out of therapy (primary choice). I also recommend that they explain to their clients the dynamics of secondary choices. A major step is to have the therapists then encourage their clients to make the fundamental choices to be whole, healthy, free, and true to themselves. For most, making these fundamental choices creates a new orientation toward life. Until they choose such an orientation, they will experience little effective or lasting therapeutic work.

Primary Choice and Fundamental Choice

A primary choice is about concrete results, whereas a fundamental choice is about life orientation or a state of being.

You can make a primary choice to be a symphony musician and make all the secondary choices to successfully achieve that primary choice, without making a fundamental choice to live up to your highest potential.

You can make primary choices to have a well-painted house, an organized closet, or an interesting career, without making the fundamental choice to be the predominant creative force in your own life.

There are many people who have chosen the religious path (primary choice), without making the fundamental choice to live in accordance with their highest spiritual truths.

There are many people who have chosen to be married (primary choice), without making the fundamental choice to live from within a committed relationship.

Fundamental Choice and the Reactive-Responsive Orientation

People in the reactive-responsive orientation have never made an authentic fundamental choice about their own lives.

It is important to note that a fundamental life choice does not have to be formally made. Some people are true to themselves even though they have never made a formal choice to be so. But by the way they live their lives they have made, in essence, a de facto fundamental choice to be true to themselves. By formalizing that choice, however, they can expand the power of that choice.

A fundamental choice can provide the crucial difference in successfully making the shift from the reactive-responsive orientation to the orientation of the creative. Without making the fundamental choice to be the predominant creative force in your life, no matter what you do to attempt to benefit yourself or enhance your life, you will merely be finding more sophisticated ways of responding to circumstances. This will, in turn, reinforce your reactive-responsive orientation. Furthermore, the things you do within the reactive-responsive orientation to attempt to better yourself can give you the impression of change and movement, but it is not likely that any significant change will take place. Even if your attempts seem to work temporarily, they will not fulfill your truest desires.

On the other hand, once you make the fundamental choice to be the predominant creative force in your life, any approach you choose to take for your own growth and development can work, and you will be especially attracted to those approaches that will work particularly well for you.

·   ·   ·

The Predominant Creative Force in Your Own Life

This one fundamental choice—to be the predominant creative force in your life—is a foundation for the entire orientation of the creative. Once you have made this choice, the meaning of current reality changes for you, from one of circumstances externally imposed to a view of life in which you see current reality as relevant and necessary feedback in the creative process. The choice to be the predominant creative force in your own life does not mean forcing yourself into a different view of reality, nor is it a form of self-manipulation through willpower, a change of "attitude," a motto to recite, an affirmation to make, or a posture to assume. It is a choice. It comes from a desire to be the predominant creative force in your own life, not out of need, or out of conflict, nor even out of the circumstances, but because that is what you want.

From this choice the meaning of the word *desire* changes for you, from "idle wishes and hopes" to "true vision of that which is highest in human aspiration and vision." The meaning of *human endeavor* changes from "actions taken in an attempt to regain emotional stability" to "actions taken to bring into the world the full realization of the vision you hold."

Moreover, the entire quality of your life changes dramatically, from the tragedy, drudgery, pain, tolerance, struggle, sameness, and boredom so often characteristic of life in the reactive-responsive orientation to the excitement and adventure characteristic of life in the orientation of the creative. Because of this fundamental choice, every moment holds the potential for true expression of the human spirit, where anything good and wonderful may happen. But this choice is not made with the motive of relief from pain or struggle. In fact, when you have made this choice, you are more able to be involved with all of life, the bad times as well as the good.

Emotions, Attitudes, and Behavior

Many of your attitudes may remain unchanged when you make a shift of orientation to the creative. You may still dislike certain people, you may still get angry at pettiness in the office, you may still get discouraged at your financial situation. You may still hold the same political or religious beliefs. You may still prefer to live in certain cities and areas in the world. You may still be the negative, critical, cranky person you have always been. A fundamental shift in orientation is not primarily about a change in attitudes, style, or manner of living.

You will, however, experience change. This change will accommodate whatever is necessary to support your life as a creator—one who spends his or her life bringing into being the creations that personally matter.

Many of the changes will lead to a complete rearrangement of your life. Several people, after having made the fundamental choice to be true to themselves, have changed their job situations, their relationships, their actions, and the ability to move consistently in the direction that matters to them. These people often stop taking any actions that are not consistent with being true to themselves.

Many examples of this principle from TFC graduates fill our files. A senior vice president of a *Fortune* 500 company discovered that he had spent his whole corporate life trying to become the CEO. When he made the fundamental choice to be true to himself, he realized he had never really cared about the CEO position. He did, however, care about the company he worked for. When he reviewed what really mattered to him, he saw that he really wanted to be leading the division he was already in charge of. He decided to continue in his present job. His fundamental choice led to a new enthusiasm and excitement about his relationship with his company. When he was offered the position of CEO, he declined the offer. He is now more effective than ever, loves his work, and is no longer burdened with an empty quest for "higher position."

Once she had made a fundamental choice to be true to herself, a successful consultant decided to change her career. She had enjoyed being a consultant, but she discovered that her real love was working with individuals rather than how they interact in narrow business settings. She realized her consulting practice was only a means to accomplish what she really wanted. At the age of thirty-six she began to study psychology at a major university and today is a successful clinical psychologist.

After years of heavy cigarette smoking, a man in his early forties made the fundamental choice to be healthy. He had tried to quit smoking several times without success. Once he had made the fundamental choice to be healthy, he was able to quit smoking for good, change his diet, and begin to exercise regularly. He could have taken all of these actions without having made the fundamental choice for health, but his tendency for success would not have been as great. In the past he had tried to take these actions, but he had never been able to make them a way of life.

When you make a fundamental choice, you bring into play the qualities of your character, so that they can become more fully expressed in your life. Each of them becomes an element in your current reality and thus part of your creative process.

Furthermore, this shift in orientation is not primarily about behavior but about the underlying structure now in play. Your behavior will, of course, change. But it will change as a natural outcome of a change in structure, for the path of least resistance in the creative orientation leads toward behavior consistent with creating what you want to create.

So, what can this change be that I am describing, if it is not a change in behavior, emotions, attitudes, or style of living?

It is a change in the very structure of your being, which determines your ability to manifest on the planet that which is highest in you.

How to Make This Fundamental Choice

The way to make a fundamental choice is essentially the same as the way to make a primary choice.

First of all, you must *truly want* whatever it is you are choosing. This step is essential. If you do not really want to be the predominant creative force in your life, you cannot make that fundamental choice.

If you do not clearly desire it for its own sake, the choice you make does not qualify as a fundamental choice. You may choose to be free, for example, only because you feel unfree. In this case, you are choosing out of reaction to being unfree. You are not making the fundamental choice to be free, because you are not yet in touch with wanting to be free, but only with not wanting to be unfree. Under these circumstances, if you then "choose to be free," it would be meaningless as a fundamental choice, for structurally it has no chance of having any significant impact on your freedom.

To truly make the fundamental choice to be free, first you must recognize what freedom really is and be aware that freedom is what you want. "If you could have it, would you take it?" If the answer is yes, then freedom is what you want. In making this fundamental choice, if you know that you want freedom, independent of past, present, or future circumstances, you can easily and clearly make the fundamental choice to be free.

The fundamental choice to be free is one of the choices integral to a complete shift from the reactive-responsive orientation to the orientation of the creative. Here are the steps to take to make the full and complete shift.

Step 1 is to know what you want. To do this, consider whether you want each of the following items. Do not assume that you automatically want them. In fact, make no assumptions. Start without any preconceived notions. My suggestion is that you spend at least two minutes, but no more than five, considering each item:

Do you want . . .
1. To be the predominant creative force in your life?
2. To be true to yourself?
3. Health (physical, emotional, mental, spiritual)?
4. Freedom?

Step 2 is to choose what you want.

If you want freedom, health, to be true to yourself, and to be the predominant creative force in your life, then inwardly formally choose each of them in turn. Say to yourself:

1. I choose to be the predominant creative force in my life.
2. I choose to be true to myself.
3. I choose to be healthy.
4. I choose to be free.

•　　•　　•

The Effects of Fundamental Choices

If you have made these choices, over time you may begin to observe natural changes and shifts in the way you live your life. You may notice changes in how free you are, how healthy you are, how true you are to yourself, and how fully and effectively you create the results you want. These changes develop from within your new orientation and its structure. Your natural tendency will be to gravitate toward reorganizing your life in ways that are consistent with these four fundamental choices. Circumstances may change slowly or quickly. But once you have made these choices, time is on your side, for the structural tendencies of your life are now designed to fulfill those choices.

Your natural temptation at this point would probably be to ask for an example of how this shift might look in a person's life. But in the creative orientation, we cannot predict what the shift will look like, for it will be unique in each case. In fact, it is probably more useful not to have a model or picture of how it might look, because then your temptation would be to try to match your reality to the picture in the example.

Though Beethoven and Mozart were both great composers, Beethoven's long, tedious creative process was very different from Mozart's quick, brilliant creative process. Your way of creating the life you want will unfold differently from anyone else's.

If you have read this far without making the four fundamental choices, I recommend that you go back and consider those four items. And if you want them, choose them.

I could describe the taste of vanilla ice cream to you, but until you have tasted vanilla ice cream for yourself, you would not know what I was describing. Actually making those four fundamental choices is quite different from just reading about them. The best way to experience the power of fundamental choices is to make them.

Assimilation

A Natural and Normal Stage

Assimilation, the stage that follows germination, is one of the most natural and normal phenomena of growth and development.

We are all familiar with assimilation. As children learning to walk, we experience it as we incorporate the skills of balance, coordination, and movement. When learning to talk, we assimilate and incorporate the vocabulary and syntax of our native language. When learning to write, we assimilate the shapes of letters and words and the muscle movements required to make them with a pencil or pen. And when learning to ride a bicycle, we assimilate the skill of keeping ourselves balanced while we pedal the bicycle forward.

We continue to use assimilation throughout our adult lives—in sports, professions, relationships, and daily life.

Assimilation is an important stage of growth and development because it is the period during which we incorporate intricate physical and mental skills in such a way that they become a natural part of ourselves.

Yet assimilation remains poorly understood.

The Beginnings of Assimilation

One reason the assimilation stage is so little understood is that during this stage, progress in growth and development remains invisible for a time. For long periods it may look as if nothing of significance is happening or being learned. A common experience during the early steps of assimilation is for no change whatever to take place.

At the point when the first excitement of the germinational stage is over and the creation's new development is not yet obvious, people often give up the pursuit of their desired result.

This is the point when beginning music students give up studying their musical instruments. This is the time when most people who enter exercise or fitness programs stop going to the gym. This is the time when many adults who want to learn a foreign language lose interest or become "too busy to continue."

The emotional experiences common to this crucial stage in the creative cycle are discomfort, frustration, and disappointment. "Nothing seems to be happening." "I don't seem to be making any headway." "I see no signs of progress."

In the reactive-responsive orientation, the path of least resistance at this stage leads you to give up. Giving up is an attempt to avoid emotional frustration, disappointment, and wasting time.

In the orientation of the creative, the crucial moment at the beginning of the assimilation stage where nothing seems to be happening is not a threat, for two major reasons.

The first reason is this: People in the creative orientation understand there will be periods in the creative process during which nothing seems to be happening. They understand further that these periods do not inhibit the development of the result being created but, in fact, enhance it. This understanding comes from experience.

Learning to ride a bicycle includes a period of time—maybe a day, maybe a week—during which the learner frequently loses balance and falls. Many beginners find that during their first attempts at sailboarding, they are more often in the water than on the sailboard. When learning to use a computer, it may take longer to make a calculation or write a memo than to do the same task by hand.

This period of assimilation naturally includes much trial, error, and experimentation. But the outcomes of such experiments teach you what you need to learn in order to have the result you want. Losing your balance and falling off the bicycle or sailboard is not a failure, but a moment of learning. You absorb and internalize such learning into yourself as part of what will become your automatic knowledge and ability.

Assimilation is a step beyond mere learning, for in assimilation you incorporate the learning into yourself. The creative process is a realm of continual learning. Moreover, you not only learn the specific skill you are practicing, you also learn that

1. You can learn.
2. You can assimilate whatever you need to know in any creative process.

Whenever you assimilate a learning, you deepen your base of experience of assimilation. You can internalize future learnings. Professional actors become quicker and quicker at memorizing their parts. Musicians become more facile at performing difficult passages. Cab drivers learn new routes more easily. Auto mechanics learn to spot the trouble more immediately and learn the new engine designs more quickly.

Assimilation and Structural Tension

There is a second reason the early moments of assimilation are not experienced as a threat in the orientation of the creative. Even if it seems to you as though nothing has changed or you have made no real progress toward achieving your desired result, that very observation becomes part of the description of your current reality. As such, you may use it to reinforce structural tension by highlighting the discrepancy between what you now have and the result you want.

Deepening Assimilation

Assimilation deepens as you move toward the realization of your vision.

When I first attended the Boston Conservatory of Music, the clarinetist Attilio Poto was one of my teachers. The first lesson he assigned me was a bit more difficult than I was technically ready for. After a week of diligent practice I still couldn't play it well. When I went for my second lesson, I expected Mr. Poto would have me spend at least another week practicing the same exercise. Instead, he assigned the next exercise in the book, which was even more difficult than the one with which I had struggled for the past week.

I spent the week attempting to play the new exercise, and when the time came for my lesson, I could not play it very well. I suggested to Mr. Poto that it was time to perfect my technique by focusing on that exercise for another week. Mr. Poto only smiled as he turned the page to the next, and more difficult, exercise in the book.

For three more weeks I was assigned progressively more difficult exercises to play, each of which I was unable to play well after a week of practice.

At the sixth lesson Mr. Poto turned back to the very first exercise he had assigned me—my exercise for the first week— and asked me to play it. Although I had not even looked at that exercise for the past five weeks, I was able to play it well. He then turned to the second week's exercise and, again, I was able to play it well.

Had I spent six weeks attempting to perfect those first two exercises, I would not have been able to play them as well as I did that day.

Mr. Poto knew something about assimilation I was only beginning to learn: *One powerful way to assimilate your present step is to move on to your next step*, even if you feel inadequately prepared for it. When you move to your next step, you are somehow able to incorporate more than you now know about your present step.

Assimilation as an Inner Process

When you begin to assimilate your vision, the inner part of the creative process forms internal shifts, alignments, connections, and relationships. Your entire being becomes an automatic process of focus. You begin to breathe with your vision, move with your vision, and live in alignment with your vision. At this stage of the creative process, there is often an interplay between your conscious thought process and your internal automatic thought processes. The creation begins to take on a life of its own. It begins to have its own identity, its own instincts, its own rules of development, its own rhythm, its own energy, its own spirit.

The American poet Dan Shanahan described this part of the creative process, when creator and creation begin to interact:

> After writing poems for twenty years I've had the time to see changes in my process and approach. When first beginning in my late teens, words were of primary importance. Often one word would excite me enough to build a poem around it.
>
> Then in my early twenties I began to see that language itself was moving and living all around me. The stones, the sky, the intensity in people's eyes: everything was speaking, singing, flowing. Everything one needed for the poem seemed to hang in the air like fruit to be picked. This was a major shift for me.
>
> Now there is the inner voice that calls out or moves awareness to a place or a cluster of images. I try to marry the interior languages of memory and reflection with the world around me. I am more trusting of these works now and less dependent on how I think the poem should be. The traditional structures of sound and sense are still present, but over the years life with the poem has been a continual discovery and creation of heretofore unknown expressions.
>
> In the past few years I have used a large flip chart to write my poems. The large surface allows me to treat the images as if they were a painting. I can move toward and away from the poem as if it were a landscape. The poem is expanded and stands more on its own, less dependent on me. It is alive and we speak back and forth to each other, asking and answering questions.

As a newly planted seed begins to establish itself in the soil by sending out roots, so the vision you have germinated is also taking root within the structural tension you form.

Once the plant's basic root system is established, the path of least resistance in that structure is for the plant to sprout through the ground and become visible. The growth then is both more deeply inward and more expressly outward.

As your vision becomes rooted during the assimilation stage, the movement is progressively deeper and more and more obvious as the creation unfolds.

Assimilation as Organic

In 1970–71, I spent much of my time in the woods making observations about changes and cycles in nature. As a composer, I was interested in isolating principles of structure I could use in my music, and the environment of the woods was a series of lessons in natural order and organic forces in play with each other.

During that period I began to appreciate more deeply the principle that new forms emerge from the disintegration of old forms—moss growing upon dead tree trunks, seedlings sprouting through dead leaves. These changes of growth and decay had a rightness to them that permeated the entire woods as an organic system.

In the creative process a similar kind of rightness exists, particularly in the assimilation stage of the creative cycle. As an organic process, assimilation generates actions, some of which naturally build new and useful structures and some of which naturally discard outmoded and less useful structures.

New England has one of the most beautiful fall foliage seasons in the world. The colors are combinations of rich reds, soft yellows, royal purples, bright oranges, all mixed with the deep greens, silvers, and grays of evergreens and leaves that have not yet changed color. The leaves become translucent, and the sunlight pouring through them can take your breath away. Soon the color spreads to the ground, and the countryside becomes color above and color below. Throughout late September, most of October, and a week into November, New England is alive with transformation.

And then the trees lose their last leaves. The leaves on the ground turn brown, gray, and dull. The autumn rains come. The land is barren and the air is cold. The tourists are gone, and New Englanders turn inward. Somehow they are preparing themselves for the long, hard winter that can seem more like an endless night than merely a season. It would never occur to a New Englander to try to hold on to the foliage season. The leaves are not saved for their color; instead they are collected and burned in small bonfires. No one climbs a ladder and staples the leaves back on the branches.

Yet we do not always translate this same wisdom and respect for the forces of nature into the rest of our lives. We have the human trait of holding on, past the seasons and cycles of our lives. We can miss the preciousness of the beauty of the moment and hold on, often when it is too late to hold on. We fear endings. We resent change. We ignore the seasons and cycles of our lives.

These cycles do not disappear simply because they are ignored. The forces in play follow the path of least resistance. Sometimes the forces are in the forming stage of growth, sometimes they are in the maturity stage of growth, and sometimes they are in the decay stage of growth. If you attempt to hold on to the status quo when it is time for decay, you will not succeed. If you try to hold on to the status quo when it is time for new formation, you will not succeed.

There are times when things come together, and there are times when things fall apart. This is an organic process. If you attempt synthetic manipulations of organic process, not only will you fail, but you will develop an insensitivity to the organic nature of life. You will not know the movement of the cycle. You will not know what the times are.

Perhaps you are holding on to a relationship that wants to fall apart. If the movement is toward falling apart, all you are doing is postponing the day when it will be over. If you are holding it together and it wants to fall apart, it will fall apart with more force and intensity than before. This is because the structure is compensating for your synthetic intervention.

Perhaps you are in a relationship that wants to come together even more than it has. By trying to hold on to how things are, you will prevent the relationship from coming together as much as it could.

Perhaps you are in a job situation that wants to fall apart, or in a family situation that wants to fall apart. If you ignore the natural movement of the cycle you are in, you will make the changes more difficult to include in your life. You will be less able to assimilate these changes.

In the creative process, change is the norm. Old life gives way to new life. Old forms give way to new forms. Old ideas and values give way to new ideas and values. Life moves, changes, grows old and young. Nothing is fossilized. The creative process is an endless series of phoenixes. New life emerges from the ashes and dust of what is past and over.

This principle is captured in an exquisite poem, based on a true story, entitled "Story of the Woman of Aniak," by Dan Shanahan, from his series, *The Alaska Poems.*

Each year when the berries were ripe she would leave
the village. She went out onto the tundra alone to
renew her spirit with a fast of silence and berries.
She would return in about seven days.
None worried, for she was a wise
old Eskimo woman who knew how to take care of herself.

One year everyone in Aniak knew she would not return.
The old woman was beaming as always with the light
of the long years of silence in her eyes. The people in
the village felt her leaving and her footsteps walked
through them with sadness and resignation.

After the seventh day someone
followed the trail
for two days and found her. She appeared to be
sleeping.
A peaceful sky moved across her face. She had carried her
tired old body as far as she could, and then left
it behind on the tundra.

To have the wisdom to move on when the times move is unusual. But this is a human wisdom that confronts a human tendency to try to hold on beyond the time of holding on. This is beautifully expressed in the Robert Frost poem "Reluctance":

Ah, when to the heart of man
   Was it ever less than a treason
To go with the drift of things,
   To yield with a grace to reason,
And bow and accept the end
   Of a love or a season?

When you establish structural tension, the path of least resistance may include new forms generated out of old forms. Some of the ideas, events, arrangements, associations, and forms of expression may change. This change, however, is part of the organic nature of the creative process.

How different is this understanding from our societal notions. We hope for permanence in a universe that can only change and then change again.

Nowhere does this principle become more obvious than in American business. Throughout the sixties, American business fell on good times. Many people in corporations thought that the only challenge they would face was increasing the size of the ever-expanding profit margin. This was a period of a stable economy, steady growth, and overall expansion. American business thought it had "made it." Although this was a time for great innovation, business became complacent. But the times were changing. The world was moving ahead. Is it any wonder that the growing industrial competence from Asia would have such impact on the American consumer? All that American auto manufacturers were left with was making an appeal to buy inferior, more expensive cars out of a flimsy notion of patriotism.

Suddenly panic set in. In reaction to the new circumstances, terms such as *reindustrialization* became the catchwords of the day. American business began adopting Japanese management practices. Quality circles, management-union cooperation, and worker ownership spread like wildfire. But American business was playing the game of catch-up. Robotics threatened job security. Innovation slowed down. New experts roamed corporate America the way hired guns roamed the old West. The corporate personality changed. Forsaking secure, stable, formal, and "old-boy network" manners in the boardrooms, fiery, savvy, dynamic, hip, and young managers established themselves. Loose and creative became the style. First in high tech, then in finance and Wall Street, old jeans and designer jeans became the new corporate status symbol. A company that had groups of employees who looked like hippies from the late sixties couldn't be all bad. Street-wise and street-smart managers rose to senior levels in organizations, pushing the old guards right out the door.

But the point has been missed. If American business follows the fads rather than becoming sensitive to the times as they change, all we will develop are senior executives who think progress is a management team that wears an earring, listens to rock, and is fluent in the latest fashion trends. If you follow the fads, you will always be behind the times, because by the time something is a fad, the innovation is over. You cannot hold on to the past; you cannot even hold on to the present.

Can American business learn the lesson? Yes. One marvelous quality of America and American life is a natural industriousness and enthusiasm. Americans instinctively hate bureaucracies. America is a large nation that includes the human drive to achieve. Is this mindless ambition, as it is often thought of in a Europe where innovation is at a standstill? Is the West spiritually bankrupt, as proclaimed by Aleksandr Solzhenitsyn?

Hardly. But the times will change and change again. One of the best events that has happened to America is the challenge from Japan. This is because the American spirit and tradition is one of revolution. And this revolution is not simply revolution for the sake of defeating the old order, it is revolution in the service of higher values.

I am well aware of the history of the United States. I am just as critical of our mistakes and misdeeds as anyone. I do not think that America is pure, or righteous, or brave, clean, and reverent. Some of the strangest and weirdest behavior fills the landscape from sea to shining sea. But America has one major saving grace. It can learn. The emerging power of the Asian economic force is a wonderful teacher.

Embodiment: The Key to Assimilation

What you embody tends to be created. This principle provides the key to assimilation.

Embodiment is distinct from behavior. To embody love is not the same as behaving in a loving style. To embody peace is not the same as acting serenely. In business, diplomacy, religion, politics, and personal relationships, some people manage to commit acts of hatred and violence quite serenely.

Those who "fight for peace" do not embody peace, but rather embody fighting. Those who worry about their health do not embody health, but rather fear. Those who lust for power and affluence embody neither.

One of the moral giants of our century was Dr. Martin Luther King, Jr. Although his was a brilliant mind, his leadership did not come from his intelligence. Although he was one of most eloquent orators in the twentieth century, his leadership did not come from speech making. Although he was one of the most courageous human beings in history, his leadership did not come from his courage. Although he was one of the most original spirits on the social landscape, his leadership did not come from his originality. He could have had all these qualities and not had the impact he had on the world. It was King's ability to embody the values he championed that left an ongoing mark on the history of freedom and justice.

King did not only preach peace, he was one with peace. He did not only preach understanding, he had understanding—even for those who made themselves his enemies. He did not only preach compassion, he was the embodiment of compassion. He did not only preach freedom, he was free.

King was also a master of structural tension. In his most famous speech, the "I Have a Dream" speech, he described the current reality that existed in 1963, as well as a vision of freedom and justice. The power of those images has entered into the world consciousness. From that time on, all people have had available to them the image of hope. As the current reality changes, we still have a dream. We can compare our vision of freedom and justice with our current world situation. It is in us to want to move toward that ideal. This dream does not go away, but becomes stronger over time. This is a legacy for our future generations. While confronted with reality as it is, we are also confronted with the dream as it is. We may get closer or further away at times, but there is still a call to the dream.

At a refugee camp for Salvadorans in Honduras, one young refugee woman expressed her desire for embodiment when she stood up and offered this spontaneous prayer:

> In spite of being oppressed, I promise not to oppress.
> In spite of being exploited by others, I promise not to exploit.
> In spite of experiencing much suffering, I promise not to cause suffering.

> In spite of living in a world of lies, I promise
> not to lie.
> O Father, help me to live this promise and re-
> move the oppressor mentality from my heart, and
> to practice justice and truth, so that I may be able
> to recognize your presence in my life.

If you embody the creative process, life, as it moves and changes, becomes your ally. It is as if you were to align yourself with life rather than be its enemy, as in the ancient Ch'an saying, "I lift my finger and the whole universe comes along with it."

This embodiment is not simply adopting the right behaviors or finding a new response. It is an embodiment of structural tension. The embodiment of your vision and the embodiment of your current reality.

Cathleen Black, former associate editor at *Ms.* and *New York* magazines and now publisher of the revolutionary newspaper *USA Today*, describes embodiment simply. "I only work for publishing I believe in. I *was Ms.* to the people I dealt with in that job, and I *am USA Today* now."

What you embody speaks louder than your behavior, to the same degree that your actions speak louder than your words.

Furthermore, you assimilate what you embody. As you internalize what you embody, inner development occurs that is consistent with what you embody. All aspects of your consciousness realign themselves in accordance with what you embody.

Two Phases of Assimilation

Assimilation, like embodiment, has two phases—an internalizing phase and an externalizing phase. What you create grows within you and eventually expresses itself outwardly as you give birth to that which you are creating.

During the assimilation process, you mobilize inner and outer actions. This energy builds on itself, so that the path of least resistance leads from internal to external expression.

When you truly learn a new language, you use both phases of assimilation. At first, the language is "foreign" to you. Little by little, you take it in as you practice it. The more you embrace it, the more it becomes part of you. This is the internalizing phase of assimilation. As you internalize the new language, you become more fluent. You are able to construct sentences and learn vocabulary and syntax that are more and more conceptually sophisticated. Eventually the language becomes fully internalized, so that you can think in that language, imagine in that language, and even dream in that language.

The externalizing phase of assimilation occurs when you begin to speak and communicate with others spontaneously in that language. You retain new vocabulary easily, you use it naturally. In fact, with this new language you are able to speak, write, and create things you were never taught.

Using Assimilation in Your Life

What you assimilate internally tends to be manifested externally. Internal changes often tend to be manifested outwardly.

You will not be able to create change in all your external circumstances, but you can certainly create change in your internal realm. You do not need anyone's permission or agreement. You do not have to wait for outside resources to empower you. As you begin to gain experience in your own creative process, you can assimilate each new creation, and this makes each future creation more and more probable. You can create momentum by embodying your own creative process.

Momentum

How Assimilation Builds Momentum

Assimilation is a graduated process. Its steps build upon one another. As they build organically, the process generates energy. This energy builds on itself, and the process gains momentum.

The more you assimilate the early steps of a growth or learning process—as in learning mathematics, management, sports, cooking, sewing, accounting, computer science, or a foreign language—the more able you are to assimilate the next steps. And once those steps are assimilated, momentum builds and you will be able to assimilate steps that are even more advanced. In fact, assimilation will become easier and easier.

It is easier to learn a new foreign language if you already speak a foreign language. By learning a foreign language, not only do you assimilate that language, but you also assimilate your ability to learn other languages. If you speak two foreign languages, it is even easier to learn a third.

Assimilation may yield exponential growth: assimilating one thing makes it easier to assimilate more and more things. In fact, in the orientation of the creative, once you have assimilated your own creative process, your life mastery in general increases, so that you are enabled more naturally and easily to create what most matters to you.

There are moments in this process of growth when you achieve a level of competence in which you finally know for sure that you can create. This does not happen by faith, or affirmation, or self-hypnosis, but by the actual experience of accomplishment. Not only do your creations speak for themselves, they also speak to you. They will tell you, "You can create." After several experiences of the completed creative cycle— germination-assimilation-completion—you know that you are a creator. Until that time no amount of self-propaganda will work to convince you of what is not yet a fact. If anything, proclamations that "I can do it!" or "I can be anything I want to be!" create an air of hype in which nothing seems real and relevant. Trying to produce self-confidence based on such distortions makes it hard for you to assess reality accurately.

Whether you can create what you want in every case will always be a matter of reality *after the fact*. It is only when you have done it that you can say with complete accuracy that it can be done. All else remains to be seen.

As the electronics inventor Stanford Ovshinsky, who holds over one hundred patents relating to high-speed ovonic devices, said in an interview after his center-drive machine was being used all over the world:

> It gave me the confidence that I was an inventor and that what I could do could be totally different from anything that had even been considered before.
>
> It was a self-confirmation, a positive reinforcement. Once you're off and running and have a success like that, you think, Okay, I can invent . . . this is right . . . I love it . . . this is exciting . . . it's what I want to do. So, it's a commitment that you make, and it's also, in a sense, a calling that you answer.

The assimilation process is one that builds. This building process takes place over a period of time. Therefore, in assimilation, change is not instantaneous but rather developmental.

In Japan it takes seven years to master the art of sushi making. It often takes over twenty years to master the cello. It usually takes ten years or more to become a master cabinetmaker.

Mastering your life-building process in the orientation of the creative is not an instantaneous transformation either, because one inextricable part of the creative process is assimilation, which can occur only over a period of time.

Often the well-meaning people who seek to develop their "human potential" hope for instantaneous transformation. Much of the jargon in the human potential movement panders to this hope—"getting it," as if there is something to get, which, once gotten, changes your life forever; "change of context," which, once changed, will show the true nature of reality; "enlightenment," which, once experienced, will give you ultimate understanding of the universe. Maybe it will take you years to get to the point of instantaneous revelation, but the theory is that, once experienced, you have "made it."

The notion of "breakthroughs" is such a theory. First you must invent an imaginary barrier to break through, then you must come up against this barrier, then you must overpower the "resistance" of this barrier, then you come to the "other side" of the barrier, where the sun always shines and the sky is not cloudy all day. Some people imagine that their life is one breakthrough after another after another. The experience they report is probably true. If you do not experiment, learn from the experiment, apply the learning, and assimilate the entire process, what else can you do except spend your life banging your head against the imaginary barriers of your own incompetence?

The notion of "making it" is a version of the dream of retirement. For many people life is just a series of unpleasant chores you perform until that day when you no longer have to work for a living. Then you can relax and die. Maybe you will win the sweepstakes so that you can quit your job and then relax and die. Creators hardly ever retire.

The other day Rosalind and I had two charming people over for some refreshments and conversation. Both of them are professional creators. She makes amazing weavings, he is a world-class potter. It was natural for all of us to talk about the arts. I asked them if they ever knew or heard of any artist retiring.

"Never," he said.

"Not one," she agreed.

Nor, in fact, have I. Maybe in some corner of the universe there is one, but this surely is the rare exception. Even God once took a day off, but that was so rare a point had to be made of it.

How different it is in our society. Retirement is a goal for many people. Often their retirement dream is to buy a recreational vehicle and head for the Sun Belt in the winter and the Snow Belt in the summer. That might be fun for two or three minutes, but then how much sightseeing can anyone do?

In the old TV program *Route 66*, two young men traveled throughout America to find adventure, experience, and truth. This was the proper fantasy—engaging life as it came to pass; knowing people you otherwise never got to know; loving and leaving, collecting memories so vivid that even in reruns twenty-five years later, it can seem fresh and relevant. But even Buzz and Todd worked as they traveled, and in reality they were actors who perfected their craft and their art. And they were also aided by some of the most creative people then working in television.

What is the essential difference between creating and most other realms? Why is it so rare to see a creator quietly steal into the night and never lift pen or brush again?

Because there is in the creator a deep longing to create. This is not ego in the popular sense, but purpose in the higher sense. For a creator there is always a next step, always a new place to go, never just marking time, waiting for it all to end.

Creators seem to be intuitively aligned with what life is at its roots: *a creation*. How can there be an end to purpose in a world in which there is so much to create?

Occasionally I talk to people who think that life is a form of prison—that we have "heavy karma" to pay, and that when we learn our lessons and undo the great wrongs we have unleashed on the world, we can finally leave. After all, is it not all suffering and struggle? This sad view too often permeates notions of the "spiritual" life. Teachers come and teachers go who promise the way out. Nirvana itself becomes spiritual retirement.

I would like to see these great enlightened souls stick around for a while and make music or paint or write poetry. Perhaps if they did, they might like it here a little better.

When we think about Robert Frost and Georgia O'Keeffe, or Michelangelo, Voltaire, Goethe, Tennyson, Hugo, Verdi, Tolstoy,

Shaw, Haydn, Churchill, or Picasso, all of whom lived until their eighties and nineties and still made the Muse their intimate companion, we find not a way out, *but a way in*, the way in to a world that has in it the mystery of life, always giving, always fresh, always new.

The seventies' notion of "finding it," or "getting it," is over. What ended it was people "finding it." This experience did not often lead to the kind of retirement many people hoped for— that of no longer aspiring, no longer learning, no longer striving. They had not found the one simple answer that would deliver them from the complexities and ironies of life.

The tradition of creating is not the tradition of instant enlightenment, but of steady progress; not of finding relief from life, but living life; not of desperate hopelessness, but of living a life filled with the purpose of bringing new creations into being.

When I first created the TECHNOLOGIES FOR CREATING® curriculum, workshops promoting instant enlightenment were just becoming popular. I had set up the basic course as a five-week program with one class a week. This format allowed the students to learn principles of the creative process during the classes and practice and experiment with these principles during the week. A few of my friends who thought they were experts in what people are willing to do told me that hardly anyone would stay in a course for as long as five weeks. (They changed their minds when they themselves did the TECHNOLOGIES FOR CREATING® course, and after tens of thousands of people had signed up for the courses.)

To me the five weeks were just the beginning of a much longer practice of the creative process. If you took a five-week foreign-language course and did not practice the new language, you would not be able to speak, read, or write it. It is only when you practice and assimilate your new skill into your life that you can become fluent.

Learning the creative process is not the most difficult skill to learn. It is easier than mastering the cello, carpentry, or even sushi making. This is because creating is more natural to human beings than these more complicated skills. But it still takes time and experience. Each creation adds to each future creation, and new levels of mastery become next logical steps. You never finally "make it" in the pop notion of instant stardom or fortune.

Every creator is engaged in a progression of works that enhance more and more mastery. Beethoven composed nine great symphonies; each one embodied a new step in his development; each work added creative power to the next. Had Beethoven lived longer, he would have written a tenth symphony, and then an eleventh. Each one would have pushed his art further, not as a breakthrough but as an evolution.

When you consider your own life, do you hope for the key to instant salvation, either through riches, fame, retirement, or death, or do you see the time you have available as a resource for what you can bring into being? To a creator the time we have in life is precious. Not only as a place to create but as a place to appreciate and experience. Poetry, probably more than any other art form, can capture the specialness of the moment, especially the little moments that would otherwise go unnoticed and unseen. Even the moments of pain and conflict can be appreciated and loved. (I have a theory that if it isn't written about in a pop song, it probably isn't true.)

Each life event can build momentum in your creative process.

Assimilation as Generative

Not only is assimilation an organic process itself, but it tends to generate other organic processes. *The steps by which you move from where you are in your life to where you want to be cannot be put into a formula.*

The steps of that process develop organically, and what you are creating is unique, at least to your life. You may find yourself taking actions you have never taken before, thinking thoughts you have never thought before, being moved and inspired in ways you have never experienced before.

The Boston Symphony percussionist Frank Epstein is also the founder of Collage New Music Ensemble. Begun over fifteen years ago, this group is one of the country's most important ensembles dedicated to the performance of new music. Epstein's involvement in this project has led him to new desires, experiences, and directions:

Collage was a vision born from a desire I had over twenty years ago, beginning with my internship at the Berkshire Music Center (summer home of the Boston Symphony Orchestra), under the guidance of its director Gunther Schuller. The desire was to perform new chamber music. This was a whole new direction for me. I was challenged with new technical and musical skills to develop, new concepts of music to perform, and the opportunity to work with composers to bring their musical visions to life. This led to new musical and artistic goals. The formation of Collage became a vehicle of that development. Since its inception, Collage has commissioned and performed over 150 new works. Perhaps from these new and creative impulses will come the future classics. Perhaps we are making history.

Assimilation and the
Reactive-Responsive Orientation

If you try to control synthetically the process by which you will move from where you are to where you want to be, you will inhibit true assimilation. Trying to control the process limits the possibilities of what can happen in your life.

If you are in the reactive-responsive orientation, you tend to inhibit the process of assimilation for a number of reasons.

First, in this orientation, the actions you take do not generate further actions; each step you take toward your goal will be taken by itself, without benefit of the momentum that comes from learning and assimilating what you have learned.

Second, each new step you take will remain at the same level of potential difficulty as previous steps, since the previous steps do not add to your learning, experience, and increasing capacity. With each step you may feel like you're starting over again from the beginning. All the steps you take will be driven by the prevailing circumstances and are therefore subject to the circumstances.

Third, many of the steps that would be crucial to creating the result you want will not even occur to you if they represent a departure from preconceived processes.

Most of our education is based on identifying and comparing:

This looks like that, that looks like this. This belongs here, that belongs there. This is a diagnostic approach to life. Identify the circumstances, compare the circumstances with what you know, and then execute the proper response. This training inhibits original thought.

Because of this method of thinking, people try to learn more and more to have a larger basis for comparison. But this collection of facts and theories does not help us create nor understand what may be occurring in reality. When people think this way, they find themselves collecting endless information, which in the end is not terribly useful. This is one reason people do not easily create momentum in their lives. Once a student at Stanford University said to me, very proudly, "The more I learn, the less I know."

"Stop learning," I said. "It isn't working."

His notion of learning was collecting more and more facts and theories. His sense of "knowing less" came from the realization that there is so much information available, he would never even make a dent in comparing and categorizing it all, even if he spent his whole life doing it. Not only was he not able to create momentum, he was losing ground.

Because the creative process includes many events that are unpredictable, unforeseen, unusual, and sometimes illogical from a linear point of view, preparing yourself with more theory and facts doesn't help you and may even hinder you. Often steps in the creative process seem to have "no right" to occur as they do, but they happen anyway. As you increase your ability to create, these kinds of nonsequential events become predictable, reliable, and useful as you develop an economy of means. Too often people make the unusualness of the process seem important. It is not. What is important is that you have more easily created the result you wanted to create.

In the files of TECHNOLOGIES FOR CREATING® there are thousands of examples of people for whom nonsequential events were part of the process of a creation. Many of these were neither planned nor expected. But they were welcomed for their usefulness.

A travel agent whose vision was to double the size of his agency went to a party he hadn't planned to attend and met there a "silent partner" who was willing to invest fifty thousand dollars in his project.

A young editor, who was not wealthy, envisioned traveling

around the world, staying in the finest hotels, and eating in the best restaurants. She was offered a job by a travel publisher that would allow her to travel around the world to review restaurants and hotels for travel books.

A Chicago-based graphics designer had always wanted to create television graphics for a New York network program. She won an award for the best television-image designer in Chicago, her award was noticed by a New York producer, and she was invited to accept the job she had envisioned—creating graphics for *The MacNeil-Lehrer News Hour.*

A woman from the Boston area wanted to create a career in catering. She started working with a well-known caterer as a dishwasher. Because the caterer was often short-staffed, the woman was trained to do other jobs as well. One job she had not been allowed to do, however, was cooking. She had taken the job to learn, so she was still grateful to be around the kind of business she eventually wanted to run herself. On the weekend of a very important wedding banquet, the second chef became ill. Again they were short-staffed, and the caterers asked her to take the place of the second chef. Since she had been studying the chef's techniques, she found that she could fill in successfully. One of the values she received from her TFC course was the importance of learning from mistakes as well as successes, so she didn't allow the first mistakes she made to stop her. Instead she developed a practical competence on the job that weekend. Within the next ten days the caterer she was working for offered her a partnership.

A Los Angeles guitar player worked in an ad agency as a copywriter. He decided that he wanted to write jingles, not copy for ads. His agency loved his copy, but would not let him write jingles. He made a decision to leave, even though there wasn't a new job in sight. The very next day he got a phone call from the husband of a former guitar student he hadn't heard from in seven months. The man worked for a radio station and offered him a contract to compose and record a jingle for one of the stations clients. He wrote a jungle that is still being used around the country today. This was the beginning of his successful jingle business.

A professor of aerospace engineering worked in a very staid and repressive research environment. He spent much of his creative energy making witty complaints and sarcastic comments to his coworkers. During the TFC course he decided that he was wasting his talents. On the fourth week of his course he created a major breakthrough in his field: a new material for use in helicopters. He was awarded a patent and went on a worldwide tour to explain his work. When he returned, his university offered him a new department, a new budget, and all the freedom to research what he wanted.

When you utilize assimilation, each step you take teaches you about the next steps. The energy you apply toward what you are creating regenerates and builds. The resources you need somehow begin to gather themselves. The organic process of assimilation may include unusual "coincidences" that lead you directly to where you want to be.

Momentum and the
Reactive-Responsive Orientation

For people in the reactive-responsive orientation, momentum is one of the most difficult and elusive properties of growth and development to understand and use. When you are in that orientation, you do not build momentum toward achieving the results you want. You experience only shifts of conflict that create momentary bursts of energy as you take action designed to avoid or reduce the discomfort associated with the conflict.

Furthermore, each step taken remains a single isolated action—like a reflex knee-jerk reaction—unrelated to any other actions and designed only to resolve the specific conflict at hand. For every conflict there is a reaction. In the reactive-responsive orientation, each action-reaction situation is an isolated event, leading nowhere in particular and certainly not beyond the confines of the conflict.

In the orientation of the creative, you are naturally and easily able to build momentum. Every action you take, whether it is directly successful or not, adds additional energy to your path. Because of this, everything you do works toward creating eventual success, including those things that are not immediately successful. Over a period of time, creating the results you want will get easier and easier.

A riverbed is structured in such a way that the water flows along a path of least resistance. As more water is added, the flow gains momentum, and the general force of all the water moving through that structure increases.

Learning to Build Momentum

All successful entrepreneurs have learned to build momentum.

One way is to create a pattern of success by deliberately structuring a series of small successes on the way to your final goal. Each success adds to momentum, is easily assimilated, and helps build credibility and mastery.

A carpenter and general handyman I know wanted to become one of the city's major general contractors. At first, while he worked for another contractor, he bought a rundown home in an area of the city that was attracting young, middle-class people, and during the evenings and on weekends he refurbished the property. When he sold it, he had enough money to buy two more rundown units and pay some of his friends to help him refurbish these properties.

Soon he was working only for himself. After four years he had reached a point where he had twenty employees, and his contracting business was viable and successful. He then shifted his interest to larger-sized properties and began buying and refurbishing older apartment buildings.

Naturally he began a second business, apartment rentals and management. That was shortly followed by a third major business, real estate development. This time, as he built on his experience, skills, and business contacts from contracting and renting, the new real estate agency became viable and successful in less than two years in a market that was overcrowded with real estate agencies. His friends affectionately called him "the condo King Kong" because they told him he was climbing all over the city's buildings.

As he built momentum, he also expanded his capacity to produce successful businesses. Four or five years after his first building project, he had much more capacity for success, including financial resources, relationships with banks, human resources, know-how, and contact with a growing number of people who could help him. Through momentum, he developed his capacity to attract to himself the kinds of people who could manage his organizations.

He has more time for himself now than he had five years ago, even though he now owns several companies. He loves his work, loves his team of employees, and loves his life. He has said, "It isn't the money. The money is nice, but it really doesn't matter except for convenience. What does matter is I am bringing beauty into the world. I am bringing people and places together, I am changing the face of the city."

When you assimilate the actions that you take, you build energy toward new actions. What the entrepreneur was able to do was to let each action he took become a part of him. With all of these steps incorporated as part of his development, every step he took was both a step toward his goal and, even more importantly, a step in learning to use such movement to build momentum toward attaining any future goals.

Momentum is more than self-consciously learning from your actions, whether they happen to be successes or mistakes. For the successful contractor, momentum meant building his entrepreneurial muscles. He was able to incorporate into himself the additive power provided by each business step he took, in the same way that bodybuilders incorporate within their muscles the increased strength and endurance that comes from regular exercise.

How to Use Momentum

How did this entrepreneur achieve results?

First of all, he was building momentum rather than problem solving. Each step of the way he was able to use whatever happened as a learning experience that taught him how to build momentum more effectively.

Second, he looked for new ways to build momentum. He experimented and sought out challenges. At first, in real estate, he tried selling properties that were beyond his present ability. He sought, for example, to broker a large commercial tract. He learned from his lack of success that he was reaching too far prematurely. He shifted his attention to a simpler approach, selling private homes, smaller apartment buildings, and condos, and chose real estate projects that were more easily accomplished. Then he began looking for, and being attracted to, projects that were within his range yet still offered him a challenge. Challenge helped build momentum. As time went on, he kept expanding.

Third, he learned that experience helps build momentum. Every project he undertook taught him many lessons about being an entrepreneur. Even when projects were not successful, he learned new techniques. He learned to coordinate administration, finances, and timing. Not only did he learn, but he helped his staff learn also. During his early years he kept his risks low so that he would not go out of business while he was learning what he needed to learn. Each decision he made taught him how to make decisions: The ones that worked taught him about the qualities of successful decisions, the ones that did not work taught him about the qualities of ineffective decisions. All the time he was gaining perspective about his entire area of business.

As he incorporated the learning into himself, he could step back and see the broader sweep of his business with greater and greater perspective. From this perspective he was able to anticipate developments in his field and make decisions based on his foresight. More and more, the path of least resistance led him toward increasing success, and each success supported and built momentum toward still greater success.

The Place of Standard Formulas

Because this contractor assimilated the actions he took, he became the expert on his own individual creative process. While conventional wisdom was also available for his use, he was never confined or limited to it. What he was doing, in fact, was inventing his own steps along the way and developing his own unique method of creating what he wanted. If he had relied only on standard formulas prescribing how to run a successful business, he would never have been able to build the momentum he did or to assimilate the steps he took. He was able to build momentum and assimilate the steps only because he made them his own.

There was no business school in the country that could have taught this contractor everything he needed to know, for some of what he needed to know was specifically tailored to his own unique situation. The creative process is a matter of invention, not mindless convention.

"The human tendency toward the fossilizing of form is shocking, even tragic," wrote painter Wassily Kandinsky in a letter to composer Arnold Schoenberg. "Yesterday the man who exhibited a new form was condemned. Today the same form has become immovable law for all time. This is tragic because it shows over and over again that human beings depend mostly on externals."

Pioneers like Kandinsky and Schoenberg invented new forms of expression along the way. They did this not for the sake of the forms themselves or to create an artistic school or movement, but to express their artistic visions.

As Schoenberg put it in a letter to Kandinsky, "I have long felt that our period—which is, after all, a great one—will bring forth not one, but many possibilities."

Schoenberg was embarrassed by those who called themselves atonalists and claimed to be his followers. "Damn it all," he told Kandinsky, "I did my composing without any isms in mind. What has it got to do with me? Personally, I haven't much taste for all these movements, but at least I don't have to worry that they'll imitate me for long. Nothing comes to a standstill sooner than movements that are brought about by so many people."

In the orientation of the creative, you are on your own. Even if you find a book or a course that provides you with helpful information, you still need to assimilate this information by making it your own and applying it to your particular situation to create momentum.

In the creative orientation, when you are able to assimilate the steps along the way, the underlying structure reorganizes itself, so that the path of least resistance leads directly toward what you want to create. And the increasing momentum helps move you along that path more and more effectively.

Assimilating Structural Tension

When you first begin to learn any skill, you must become conscious of the steps you are learning.

When you begin to learn to drive, you need to think consciously what pedal your foot is touching and how much pressure to apply. You must consciously think about how to turn the steering wheel, when to shift, how to use the rearview mirror, how to gauge distance, how to back up, how to parallel-park, and so on.

Once you assimilate these abilities, you no longer need to consider consciously how much pressure you need to apply to the brake pedal in order to stop the car smoothly and safely. When you want to stop or slow down, you automatically carry out the necessary movements.

When you first begin to use structural tension in creating a specific result, you must consciously hold in mind both your vision (the result you want to create) and current reality (your present circumstances).

As you consciously practice simultaneously focusing on your vision and observing current reality, you will begin to be able to assimilate this action, and eventually it will become an automatic habit. You will also naturally incorporate structural tension itself as a major force in your underlying structural makeup.

Many years ago I moved to Los Angeles. When I first arrived, I was surprised to hear the local people tell me that they had snow. Having never heard of snow in Los Angeles before, I asked, "When do you have snow?"

"When we drive to the mountains two hours away," they answered.

Because I grew up in New England, my concept of "having snow" was quite different. For me, snow wasn't something you went to visit. Snow visited you. You lived with it.

When you first begin to work with structural tension, you will have a tendency only to "visit" it. It will not be part of your normal way of life. But as you work with structural tension more and more, it will become assimilated into your life. You will find that it becomes part of your reality. When that happens, you will automatically be aware at any moment of what you want to create and what truly matters to you and you will observe the prevailing circumstances of your current reality.

Assimilation itself will also become natural and automatic to you. As you begin to achieve the results you want, new or more far-reaching results will become easier because you have assimilated structural tension and the orientation of the creative. Through your assimilation of structural tension, you will begin to master your own creative process.

Chapter 16

Strategic Moments

Apparent Lack of Progress

In the creative process there are certain strategic moments in which it seems as if you are either standing still or even going backward. These moments of apparent lack of progress are strategic because the actions you take at such moments will largely determine whether or not you are ultimately successful.

A novice hiker backpacking on the Appalachian Trail was standing on top of one mountain. The peak of a neighboring mountain seemed only half a mile away. He set out in the direction of the second mountain, only to find himself in a valley much deeper than he had expected. He had already walked at least two miles. From his vantage point in the valley it appeared that he was now farther away from the second mountaintop than when he had first seen it.

Often you assume you are closer to your desired result than you actually are. When the novice backpacker was in the valley, it seemed to him that he was farther from his destination than he had been when he started, but actually he was closer. He had not moved away from the second mountaintop, losing ground, but was actually moving toward it. In the same way there are moments in the creative process when it seems that you are farther away from your result than when you began, but in fact you are closer to it.

The backpacker was at a strategic moment in his quest. He could have made either of two assumptions. He could have assumed that the path that seemed to lead toward the mountain was actually leading him away from the mountain. Or he could have assumed that the second peak was farther away than he had at first thought.

Of course he realized that the second assumption was true and the first one false. However, the situation in the creative process is not always as clear as it was for the backpacker.

When you attempt to move in the direction of results you want, there are times when you discover that the route to those results is more involved or longer than you originally thought. The difference between our mountain example and the creative process is that the backpacker knew that if he continued walking, he would eventually reach the second mountaintop. At such a strategic moment in the creative process, it is not always clear that you will reach the result you have in mind.

Time Delay

When you first begin to make changes in your life, there is often a delay between the time you initiate the change and the time you begin to see the results of the change.

If you train assembly-line employees in an automotive plant, there will be a time delay before the improvement in quality is realized in the manufacture of the vehicles. There will be another time delay between the increase in manufacturing quality and the market's perception of it, as reflected in increased sales.

Often a result does not immediately follow the action you take to bring about the result. Therefore it is possible to initiate effective changes but not know, for a period of time, that they are effective.

If you go on a diet, you expect to lose weight. But if you eat a very big meal just before going on the diet, you might actually gain weight on the first day of your diet.

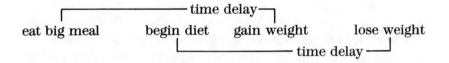

eat big meal   begin diet   gain weight   lose weight

At this point your immediate temptation would be to conclude that dieting causes weight gain or that this diet does not work for you. What is really going on, however, is that the result of the diet has not yet had a chance to appear. There is a time delay between action and result.

The way you define results is a crucial part of the creative process. If you had defined gaining weight, which is the result of eating a big meal, as if it had been the result of beginning your diet, you would probably have stopped the diet.

Because of time delay, people often give up taking actions that are, in fact, effective, but the result of those actions has not yet had a chance to appear. The meaning you give to the actions you take can contribute either to building or to reducing momentum. Considering the factor of time delay can help you describe current reality more accurately. If you inaccurately assess the effectiveness of the actions that might ultimately work, you will tend to stop taking that action.

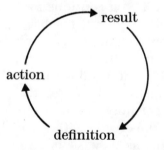

Action produces a result; a result gives rise to a definition or meaning. How you define the relation between the action you take and the result you observe affects your future action. It also affects your momentum.

In the creative orientation, when you move toward the full accomplishment of the result you choose, there may be delays along the way. For some people these cause great frustration and trepidation. But as you continue to move forward toward your result, these moments often become strategic, for they present important opportunities to catalyze the creative process.

Over time and with experience, the actions you have taken that are useful will begin to produce the results you desire. You will learn how to take better actions and correct your course by working with the actions you are taking that are not so useful.

Resenting Current Reality

One of the more difficult lessons in the creative process is to learn to *recognize current reality as it now is*, which is often different from what you think it is supposed to be or how you want it to be.

If you find yourself continually resenting the fact that your present circumstances are not what you expected, you hinder your ability to use the power of current reality fully in creating structural tension.

If you are on a white-water rafting trip, you need to be able to recognize current reality as it presently exists. When you reach the rapids, no amount of resentment that "the water used to be calm and it should still be calm" will help you negotiate through the rough waters and rocks. In fact, based on your inability to recognize reality immediately, as it presently exists, you might find yourself in the water or on the rocks.

On the other hand, if you continue to paddle as if you were still in the rapids when the raft reaches calm water, not only do you waste enormous amounts of energy but again you may end up in the water or on the rocks.

Often current reality will be different from what you had expected. If you continually build up resentment at the disparity, then you are no longer fully in touch with current reality. An important ability in the creative process is the ability to recognize changes in reality as they occur.

Unwanted Situations

A corporate executive scheduled an important meeting to improve overseas distribution of the company's electronic products. Two of the five company representatives from European countries were unable to attend the scheduled meeting because of a sudden snowstorm in Europe that curtailed flights. The executive decided to hold the meeting without them. But he spent the entire time resenting the fact that the two representatives were not present. He even seemed to take out some of his resentment on the three who were there. He refused to recognize and accept current reality fully for what it was, which was that he was meeting with the three European representatives who could attend the meeting.

Because current reality often includes unwanted or unplanned-for situations, you may have a tendency to avoid accepting reality as it is. This nonacceptance disempowers you, for you cannot create the result you want based on a misrepresentation of current circumstances.

Analyzing Current Reality

Some people avoid an accurate recognition of current reality by continually analyzing how current reality got to be the way it is. The question How did things get to be the way they are? is a different question from What is presently going on? Many people confuse the two questions, and so spend time futilely theorizing or explaining to themselves how they got to be where they are.

A middle-aged married couple was driving to the Grand Canyon. That morning at the motel they were told that the canyon was four hours away. After four hours of driving, the Grand Canyon was nowhere in sight, and they were lost. Eventually they found a service station, where they got directions. But for the hour and a half it took them to drive to the canyon from the service station, they kept rehashing all the turns they had made, or not made, that had led them to the wrong place. And for the first half hour of their visit to the Grand Canyon, they continued to analyze how they had gotten lost.

In the reactive-responsive orientation this kind of unproductive analysis is usually accompanied by the rationale that it does some good to find out how you got where you are.

But the fact of the matter is that *you are exactly where you are.*

Furthermore, rehashing how you got to where you are paradoxically has the function of obscuring where you are. The conversation this couple had was useless, for it did not help them in moving from the place where they were lost to the Grand Canyon.

If you find yourself repeatedly reviewing how you got to be where you are in your life, you are obscuring a clear view of current reality.

A young woman took her first job away from a small Midwest farming community where she had been raised. When she arrived in New York, she was excited about her new life in the Big Apple. She soon discovered that many of the lessons she learned growing up were not particularly useful in Manhattan. Greeting strangers, helping people who seemed in trouble, and lending friends money and her personal possessions, actions she often took in her hometown, began to cause her problems. She soon felt unprepared for the realities of city life. She began to analyze her upbringing. She began to resent her parents and friends for their influence on her apparent naïveté. She began to feel that the city, and the world itself, was hostile and dangerous. She began to feel like "a stranger in a strange place." For months she continued to analyze how unprepared she was to deal with the new world she found. None of this analysis helped her improve her ability to deal with her life in the city. Had she recognized that current reality included that New York was not the same as her hometown and that she did not know how to live there, she would have saved herself many hours of resentment and anger about her situation. Because she knew how to live in her hometown, she assumed she would also know how to live anywhere else. This was not true. She reacted by attempting to learn how the situation got to be the way it was, rather than simply finding out what the new circumstances were.

Often, when people leave long-term relationships, the mix of emotions can make it very difficult to observe reality accurately. People might vilify each other, seek forms of revenge, and think of the other person as two-dimensional, so as to dehumanize him or her. Often, the reality is this: *One of the two people in the relationship wants out.* In a relationship, it takes two people to say yes, but only one to say no. When a relationship ends, at least one of the two has said no. All of the feelings of abandonment, injustice, betrayal, loss, unfairness, pain, bruised egos, forced changes of life-style, and an uncertain future make reality harder to see at first. In fact, it takes great wisdom to be able to be objective in light of such pain and confusion. But this is another aspect of learning what reality is and teaching it to yourself. Those who have become fluent in naming reality have the best chance of moving to their next step and creating what they want to create.

The more directly and faster you can recognize reality, as it now is, the better. This ability is especially important when current reality turns out to be different from what you had expected. Developing this ability may take a little practice. In the creative process, as you become more proficient in immediately recognizing shifts in current reality, you become better able to reorganize your approach spontaneously in ways consistent with the change in circumstances. You come to recognize even sudden and unexpected changes not as detrimental but rather as valuable and necessary feedback in the creative process. Current reality is always your new starting point.

Much successful psychotherapy is based on helping individuals have a greater acceptance of their current reality. Your mental health and emotional stability are directly affected by your recognition of your present state of affairs. This means telling yourself the truth about how reality *really* is without distortions from editorials and explanations about causality.

The Truth About How Things Are

Because avoiding discomfort is so highly valued in the reactive-responsive orientation, people often do not tell each other—or themselves—the full truth.

Beginning from childhood there is enormous pressure in society to collude in misrepresenting what is really occurring.

We tell children, "We don't have any more candy," when we know there is a drawer full of it but we do not want the kids to spoil their appetites. We misrepresent the truth when we tell children things like, "If you lie, your nose will grow," or "Aunt Sally isn't fat, she's just gained a few pounds," or "Dad and I aren't fighting, we're just having a—discussion."

Socially accepted misrepresentation is designed primarily to protect people from feeling bad. When the waiter finally comes to our table and asks, "How was your dinner?" we tend to say, "Fine," even when what we might really want to say is, "It was terrible. The liver was as tough as shoe leather. Are you *sure* it was *calf's* liver? The vegetables were overcooked, the potatoes were greasy, the dessert was stale, and the service was just as good as the meal."

Once, after I spent an uncomfortable night on a extremely lumpy mattress in a hotel at an English seaside village, the proprietress ask me how everything was. "Well," I said off-handedly, "your mattress is a little lumpy."

"It shouldn't be," she said, somewhat offended, "We just got that mattress last year!"

"Well, maybe you can still get your money back!" I replied. She didn't think it was funny.

Some people will give you an argument about how you *shouldn't* have experienced what you *have* experienced. If the mattress was less than a year old, I should not have found it lumpy; if the meat was just fresh from the market, the diner should not have found it spoiled; if the car was just fixed, the driver should not have still heard the loud knocking sound.

The attempt to shelter people from the truth assumes that people cannot handle the full truth of reality. The fact is that almost everyone—including you—is much stronger, more resilient, and more powerful than he or she is usually given credit for.

When you habitually misrepresent reality, the truth can seem dangerous to you.

The truth is *not* dangerous, it sets you free to create. It is only through your recognition of the facts of reality that you can engage the senior force of structural tension and move toward creating what really matters to you.

The Pivotal Technique

Those moments when circumstances are not the way you would like them to be are actually very powerful and pivotal moments in the creative process. *However wanted or unwanted your present circumstances may be, they function as needed feedback so that you can know the current status of the result you are creating.*

Furthermore, times in which the situation or circumstances are not the way you want them to be are strategic moments, because in those moments you are able to redefine what you want (your vision) and where you are (current reality) in such a way that both become clearer and you strengthen structural tension.

The pivotal technique in the creative orientation may help you use unwanted circumstances as a catalyst to help propel you toward where you want to be.

The technique is quite simple, yet profoundly powerful.

Step 1. Describe where you are.

In other words, know exactly what the current reality is. If you are lost on your way to the Grand Canyon, report your circumstances to yourself factually, avoiding interpretation, analysis, or editorial comment. "I am lost. I do not know in which direction the Grand Canyon lies. I am coming into a small town."

Step 2. Describe where you want to be.

Spell out the result that you want to create. "I want to be at the Grand Canyon." Remember to separate what you want from what you think is possible, so that you are clearly in touch with what you want. Do not limit yourself to only that which you think is possible under the circumstances.

Step 3. Once again, formally choose the result you want.

Inwardly say the words, "I choose . . . ," adding the result you want ("I choose to be at the Grand Canyon").

Step 4. Move on.

Once you have observed where you are (current reality) and where you want to be (vision) and have formally chosen the result you want to create (reestablished structural tension), change the focus of your conscious attention from being in an unwanted situation. Shift gears. Change the subject. You may look at the scenery, read a book, enjoy each other's company, or go back to what you were doing before you became focused on being lost or stuck.

Once, when the great mathematician Jules Henri Poincaré was stuck trying to solve a complex equation, he took a nap. When he awoke, he had his answer. A famous chemical engineer seemed unable to find a formula to explain what he had discovered in the laboratory. He decided to take a ride around town on a bus. As he was stepping onto the bus, the solution came to him.

Author John Hyde Preston once asked Gertrude Stein,

> But what if, when you tried to write, you felt stopped, suffocated, and no words came and if they came at all they were wooden and without meaning? What if you had the feeling you could never write another word?

Gertrude Stein replied, laughing,

> Preston the way to resume is to resume. It is the only way. To resume. If you feel this book deeply it will come as deep as your feeling is when it is running truest, and the book will never be truer or deeper than your feeling. But you do not yet know anything about your feeling because, though you may think it is all there, all crystallized, you have not let it run. So how can you know what it will be? What will be best in it is what you really do not know now. If you knew it all it would not be creation but dictation.

Applying the Pivotal Technique

How might the executive concerned about his overseas distribution have used the pivotal technique in the unwanted situation in which two of the five company representatives were snowbound in Europe?

Let us go through the four steps for him.

Step 1 is to describe current reality. The executive might have described his situation this way: "A meeting that was to involve five European representatives vital to my company's overseas distribution can be attended by only three of them."

This would seem to be an adequate description of his current reality. To create structural tension, it is necessary to have a clear representation only of the facts of current reality; theories, explanations, apologies, and other embellishments of the facts are not necessary. Particularly *unimportant* in the executive's description of current reality would be a statement of the reason why two representatives were not present.

However, as you will see below, in light of the result the executive truly wanted, this picture of current reality was quite inadequate.

Step 2 is to describe the result you want to create. The executive might have described the result he wanted to create as "a fully attended meeting, with all five representatives present."

Would this actually have described what he wanted?

Sometimes this step can be a little tricky. Upon reflection, it would become clear that the executive was actually describing not the result he wanted to create but the *process* he had originally designed to get what he wanted. If what he had set out to do was only to have a fully attended meeting, he would not have been able to establish an effective structural tension that would have led him to the ultimate result he wanted to create. Why? Because he failed to be clear about the result he really wanted.

What did he really want?

We might have discovered from questioning him that the result he actually wanted was "exceptional overseas distribution of his company's product." The meeting with his overseas representatives was only part of a process designed to help accomplish this result. The result he truly wanted was quite different from what he first thought. Now that he knew the result he wanted, his vision could be described as "exceptional overseas distribution."

His now-clarified vision of what he wanted to create, however, would modify what was relevant in his description of current reality. If exceptional overseas distribution was the vision, what was the current reality *about overseas distribution*? At this point he would need to revise step 1 of the pivotal technique.

Step 1 is to describe current reality. At the time of the meeting, the executive's current reality was that the overseas distribution of the company's products was inadequate. Shipments arrived at local distribution points after long delivery delays. Because of these delays, many of the local European outlets found it difficult to satisfy their customers. Adequate shipments of the product were being sent from the United States to Europe; the delays were happening after the shipments arrived in Europe.

Based on this more adequate picture of current reality, the executive would be able to clarify his vision.

Step 2 is to describe the result you want to create. In carrying out step 2 of the pivotal technique, the executive would describe the result he wanted as "an exceptional overseas distribution, which includes local European outlets receiving our products within thirty days of their orders."

At this point in the technique the executive would be careful to avoid getting involved in considerations of whether or not this result was possible. At this point he would simply not know whether or not his vision was possible. He would only know— and would only need to know—that this was the result he wanted. Furthermore, in his mind the result is clear enough that he would be able to recognize it if it occurred.

The final test to see whether or not this was a result he wanted would be his answer to the question: "If you could have exceptional overseas distribution with thirty-day delivery service, would you take it?" His answer would probably be yes. Therefore this was a result he wanted, and he would be ready to move to the next step.

Step 3 is formally to choose the result you want to create. Inwardly the executive might formally choose it by saying, "I choose to have exceptional overseas distribution of our company's product, with thirty-day delivery service."

Step 4 is to move on. The executive might do this by conducting his meeting with the three attending European representatives. By moving on in this way, he would allow structural tension to exist between where he was (inadequate distribution) and where he wanted to be (exceptional distribution). He would further allow an organic process to take place in which the path of least resistance would lead toward "exceptional distribution."

In this context, the meeting with the three representatives would take on an entirely new meaning for the executive.

First of all, the meeting's own highest potential as a step in the process toward the result he wanted to create would tend to be realized, whatever that might be.

Second, the meeting itself might or might not directly contribute to the result of exceptional distribution of the product. But it would not really matter, for the executive would be able to invent whatever processes were needed to accomplish the result. He would be able to do this organically, so that what would become available would be not only conventional methods but also new ones that had never before occurred to him.

How would you apply the pivotal technique to your own life? Perhaps you are typing an important report, but the project is not going well. To use the pivotal technique, you would first define your current reality (step 1):

> "My report is off track. Two of the three sections are leading to my conclusion, but the third section doesn't make my point."
>
> Then you would focus on what you want (step 2):
> "I want this report to be clear, concise, and conclusive, with the ideas expressed well."
>
> And then formally choose that result (step 3):
> "I choose to have this report be clear, concise, and conclusive, with the ideas expressed well."
>
> To carry out step 4, you may move on by doing something else or by resuming writing your report. Moving on may include resuming the activity you were engaged in before you began this pivotal technique.

As you move on, the structural tension you established in the first three steps will work organically to help you create the result.

Another example:

> *Step 1*: "The software we designed and shipped to our customers turns out to have a major flaw. It often freezes when the user is trying to save a file. We have had several complaints and returns. The software is beginning to acquire a bad reputation in the marketplace, even though it is fundamentally a real advance in technology. The bug is only on one of seven formats and is not difficult to fix."
>
> *Step 2*: "We want this software to work exceptionally well and satisfy our customers. We also want this software to have a reputation as the best software of its kind, reliable and easy to use."

Step 3: "We choose to have this software work exceptionally well, satisfy our customers, and have a reputation as the best and most reliable software of its kind."

Step 4: "We will move on by taking actions to support our vision, including quickly fixing the flaw, asking our sales force not to sell any of the flawed programs, and shipping our corrected version as soon as possible."

And another example:

Step 1: "The children demand more of my attention than I want to give them. I find I react negatively to them after a few hours. I feel trapped. I haven't had a good conversation with an adult for weeks. I love the children, but I am beginning to express hostility toward them rather than love."

Step 2: "I want to have a good relationship with my children. I want the children well cared for. I also want time for myself. I want a full, rich life filled with many types of experiences."

Step 3: "I choose to have a good relationship with my children. I choose to have the children well cared for. I choose to have time for myself. I choose to have a full, rich life filled with many types of experiences."

Step 4: Move on, perhaps by reading a book, calling a day-care center, playing with the children, or phoning a friend.

Mastering Structural Tension

Step 4 of the pivotal technique leaves the structural tension *unresolved*. This is very desirable, because then you are able to assimilate structural tension more easily. The tension will be particularly helpful in generating natural processes in which the path of least resistance leads you directly toward the result.

The natural structural tendency is for all the resources available to you, known and unknown, to reorganize themselves organically in ways that will resolve the tension you established by taking the first three steps.

One of the great secrets in the art of creating is mastering the force of structural tension. If you attempt to resolve the tension you have established prematurely, you weaken your ability to create the results you want. One way you might do this is to pretend that reality is not what it actually is: "We don't have a problem with that software. The users just don't know how to use it." Or you might pretend that your vision is not what it actually is: "Sure, we missed the Grand Canyon, but who wants to see a big old hole anyway!"

Years ago I was trying to use a handsaw to cut a piece of wood. A friend who was a skilled carpenter came by as I was struggling ineffectively with the saw. He smiled and said, "Let your tool do the job it was designed to do." He then showed me how to use the handsaw properly, and I was able to finish my project using only a fraction of my original effort.

In a similar way, instead of trying to force yourself to resolve the tension created by the discrepancy between current reality and your vision, let structural tension do the job it was designed to do. As a creator, even in an unwanted situation you can learn to establish tension and hold that tension until it is organically resolved.

The Ethics of the Creative Process

In the orientation of the creative, you are never in the position of violating your own moral, spiritual, or ethical standards, because one of the results you create in shifting to this orientation is "being true to that which is highest in you."

The executive in the earlier example would not only generate effective procedures for producing the exceptional overseas distribution he wanted, but he would do so within the framework of being true to himself. He would never find himself in the position of justifying wrong means to a right end, because right means—ones consistent with what is highest in the human spirit—are the most effective means. They are the ones organically generated from the structure, and they allow you to follow the path of least resistance to the desired result.

In fact, the only time people use processes that violate their moral or ethical standards is when they are in the reactive-responsive orientation, where the assumption of powerlessness permeates the structure. At times, such persons attempt to compensate for powerlessness by compromising themselves "because the circumstances require it."

Any moment always has the potential to bring forth the highest good. This potential is not at all a matter of attitude—for example, thinking positively—but rather a matter of the highest good being evoked by an act of creation.

Therefore all moments, but especially those moments that seem difficult, troublesome, problematic, or hopeless, are moments of great creative power in your life. The "difficult, problematic" moments are, in fact, strategic moments that can help you bring the creative process to completion.

C h a p t e r   1 7

Completion

The Third Stage of the Creative Cycle

Completion, the third and final stage of the creative cycle is the full and total accomplishment of the result you want to create. When this stage is finished, you have successfully created your vision.

"Prisoner Syndrome"

Shortly before prisoners are to be released, they often experience sleepless nights, anxiety, loss of appetite, and a host of other unpleasant feelings. This experience comes, paradoxically, after years of looking forward to the day when they will be released.

For many people, such anticipatory anxiety can occur on a much subtler level. For example, as we have seen from observing structural conflict in people who want a good relationship, the closer they get to having what they desire, the more pull there is in the opposite direction. Often the path of least resistance leads them away from the relationship they want. The structure leads to oscillation, and the greatest tendency is for them to move away from the result they desire.

The Experience of Completion

There are two common experiences people associate with having what they want or with any result coming to completion.

One experience is of fulfillment and satisfaction.

In her diary, novelist Virginia Woolf described her experience of bringing a book to completion:

> Here in the few minutes that remain, I must record, heaven be praised, the end of *The Waves*. I wrote the words O Death fifteen minutes ago, having reeled across the last ten pages with some moments of such intensity and intoxication that I seemed only to stumble after my own voice. . . . Anyhow, it is done; and I have been sitting these 15 minutes in a state of glory, and calm, and some tears. . . . How physical the sense of triumph and relief is! Whether it's good or bad, it's done; and as I certainly felt at the end, not merely finished, but rounded off, completed, the thing stated—how hastily, how fragmentarily I know.

The other common experience is of depression and loss. An example of depression after completion is reflected in the "postpartum blues" women sometimes experience after completing the process of childbirth.

Virginia Woolf also had moments of panic and despair upon completion, followed by satisfaction with her creation. In her diary she described the completion of another novel:

> Seldom have I been more completely miserable than I was about 6:30 last night, reading over the last part of *The Years*. Such feeble twaddle—such twilight gossip it seemed; such a show-up of my own decrepitude, and at such huge length. I could only plump it down on the table and rush upstairs with burning cheeks to Leonard [her husband]. He said: "This always happens." But I felt, No, it has never been so bad as this. I make this note should I be in the same state after another

> book. Now, this morning, dipping in it, it seems
> to me, on the contrary, a full, bustling live book.

Since many people associate uncomfortable emotional experiences with completion, and they have a tendency to avoid such emotional discomfort, they also often have a tendency to avoid successful completion itself.

In the creative cycle, completion is a unique and separate stage and has its own requirements to be mastered.

The Ability to Receive

One of the major abilities of creating is the ability to receive the full fruits of your labor.

Some years ago I became conscious of my own undeveloped ability to receive fully. I was beginning to accomplish the results I had been working on, in some cases for years. My relationships with people I cared about were deeply satisfying, the TECHNOLOGIES FOR CREATING® courses were becoming more and more successful, the DMA organization was beginning to flourish, the approaches to growth and development I was creating were directly useful to many people, and I was living in the town where I had dreamed of living ever since I was a teenager. Even though I was glad to see these creations existing, I also felt somewhat strange. The more results I was accomplishing, the stranger I felt.

I examined what was going on and realized something that surprised me greatly. I had not learned to receive. Somehow I had not completely allowed myself to have the results I had worked for so many years to create.

Once I realized that I was inadequately receiving those results, I quickly decided to learn to accept and fully receive them, for I saw clearly that receiving was an essential part of the creative process.

Receiving is a very simple process. When the United Parcel Service delivers a package to you, you receive the package by accepting it from the carrier. But until you accept it, you don't have the package.

If you are unable to receive what you are creating, you are stopping short of completion. Until you fully accept the results into your life, the results are not fully created. You don't have the package.

Many people with whom I work have a natural desire to serve. In a sense, they are experts at giving. However, they are often inept at receiving.

Many who spend much of their lives supporting others have not developed the ability to receive. If you are one of these, there is nothing altruistic about your inability to receive well, for no one is served any better by your inability to receive. If anything, it only teaches the people being served by you how *not* to receive the service you are giving them.

Reverse Alchemy

Alchemists of old sought to turn lead into gold. Many people have a talent for reverse alchemy: *turning gold into lead*. Turning a wonderful relationship into a difficult one, turning a pleasant dinner party into a cold war, turning success into failure. Some people can't take *yes* for an answer.

Once you have made the shift to the orientation of the creative, where the senior force of structural tension supersedes structural conflict, receiving what has been created becomes natural and familiar. At first it may be an unusual and unfamiliar experience to have what you want. In time, however, having what you want becomes relatively easy to live with.

People can develop tolerance for the most terrible circumstances: war, strife, hardship, cold, famine, pestilence. And people can develop tolerance for having what they want. You can learn to live with it.

Completion and Acknowledgment

According to the Judeo-Christian tradition, as expressed in the opening chapter of the book of Genesis, human beings are made in the image and likeness of God. Since the first description of God in the Bible is as a creator, it follows that humans made in the image and likeness of a creator are made to be creators.

Not only does Genesis imply that we are creators, but the story of Creation reveals the universal structure of the creative cycle.

The stages described in Genesis for each day of creation include germination, assimilation, and completion.

Germination is initiated in a sequence of choices made by God: "Let there be light," "Let the waters be gathered together," "Let the dry land appear," and so on.

Assimilation occurs as the parts of the cosmos form themselves into their full manifestation, as described in the text.

Completion occurs when God declares that the results created are good, for example, "And God saw that the light was good." The repeated declaration, "And God saw that it was good" is an act of acknowledgment.

Each day of creation had its own acknowledgment. In the creative process, acknowledging the steps you have taken toward your goal is an important act of completion. "And on the seventh day God rested" was an acknowledgment that the entire creative process was complete.

Acknowledging What You Have Created

Acknowledging the results you have created is a different act from receiving those results into your life.

Receiving is an incoming action: You accept into your life what you have created.

Acknowledging is an outgoing action: You bestow your judgment upon the results. You judge the results as being complete. When an artist signs a painting, he or she acknowledges the painting and judges it as being complete. The judgment is: *This painting is consistent with my vision of this painting.*

In light of structural tension, when you acknowledge results as being fully or partly created, you are recognizing an important aspect of your current reality: the fact that the current state of the creation is changing and moving in the direction of your vision of that creation.

Furthermore, acknowledging the results you have created establishes and reinforces the fact that you are in the stage of completion.

When you are in the reactive-responsive orientation, you may often neglect the step of acknowledgment. Your recognition that a desired result has been achieved means little, since you consider the result existing more from the good graces of the circumstances (good luck) than by your own creative process. You can hardly sign your name to something created by lucky circumstances.

When you are creating, you are the only one who is able to declare a result complete, for it is you alone who can determine when reality satisfies your vision.

Consider the controversy about the colorization of black and white films. Color changes the universe of the film. The outcry from the film community is little understood in Congress, which is considering legislation to prohibit colorization of films. The question of who owns what you create has become an important issue. If you create a work that satisfies your vision of the work, does anyone else have the right to change it?

Because judgment is such an essential part of the creative process, the judgment that a creation is finished can only be made by its creator.

If you are creating a painting, at what point is the painting complete? This is an important question, since it is always possible to add more details or to change the painting in other ways. You determine that it is finished by your recognition that it satisfies your vision. In other words, current reality matches your vision of the result.

Similarly, if you are writing a report, at what point is the report complete? Since it is always possible to add more details or to edit the report in other ways, it is up to you to determine when it is finished. You do this by your recognition that the report satisfies your vision of it.

In the creative orientation, judgment of this kind is essential.

A notion recently in vogue is that people should avoid being judgmental. However, making judgments about the status of results you are creating is a necessary part of creating them.

As Charles Krauthammer observed in an astute essay in *Time* magazine,

> Perhaps the deepest cause of moral confusion is the state of language itself, language that has been bleached of its moral distinctions, turned neutral, value-free, "non-judgmental." When that happens, moral discourse becomes difficult, moral distinctions impossible and moral debate incomprehensible. . . . The trouble with blurring moral distinctions, even for the best of causes, is that it

can become a habit. It is a habit we can ill afford, since the modern tolerance for such distinctions is already in decline. Some serious ideas are used so promiscuously in the service of so many causes that they have lost all their power. Genocide, for example, has been used to describe almost every kind of perceived injustice, from Vietnam to pornography to Third World birth control. A new word, holocaust, has to be brought in as a substitute. But its life before ultimate trivialization will not be long. Only last month a financial commentator on PBS, referring to a stock-market drop, spoke of the holocaust year of 1981. The host did not blink.

In the reactive-responsive orientation, the fashion of avoiding distinctions and judgments is designed to minimize the experience of conflict. In the creative orientation, making judgments is essential, and the ability to make significant distinctions is one of the prerequisites of the creative process.

The Judgment on Judgment

Sometimes I think George Orwell really had a point. Even though we don't have a real Big Brother or the thought police, or even two-way televisions monitoring our every conversation, we do have Newspeak. In Orwell's ominous vision, Newspeak was a way of controlling thought. Words make distinctions. If certain distinctions are not made, certain thoughts are not thought. The following is from Orwell's essay, written as an appendix to his novel *1984*:

> The purpose of Newspeak was not only to provide a medium of expression for the world-view and mental habits proper to the devotees of Ingsoc (English Socialism), but to make all other modes of thought impossible. It was intended that when Newspeak had been adopted once and for all and Oldspeak forgotten, a heretical thought—that is, a thought diverging from the principles of Ingsoc—should be literally unthinkable, at least so far as thought is dependent on words. Its vocabulary

> was so constructed as to give exact and often very subtle expression to every meaning that a Party member could properly wish to express, while excluding all other meanings and also the possibility of arriving at them by indirect methods. This was done partly by the invention of new words, chiefly by eliminating undesirable words and by stripping such words as remained of unorthodox meanings, and so far as possible of all secondary meanings whatever.

In Orwell's 1948 novel, one of the manipulations perpetrated on the oppressed populace was the invention of new words that obscured distinction, and the outlawing of certain words that formed distinctions.

Welcome to the present, where we have new words that are designed to obscure distinctions. Many of the words that crystalize clear distinctions have become virtually outlawed. This trend is occurring throughout society, as evidenced by techno-jargon, bureau-jargon, psycho-babble, socio-rap, and so on.

Edwin Newman, in his books *Strictly Speaking* and *A Civil Tongue*, points out the absurd lengths to which this trend is leading:

A corporate report told its shareholders that its new products included

> ... improved long-span and architectural panel configurations which enhance appearance and improve weatherability.

A bureaucrat, listing precautions that had been taken after city employees had been robbed after drawing their paychecks, concluded,

> These precautions appeared to be quite successful in dissuading potential individuals with larcenous intent.

But nowhere does this trend seem sillier than in "New Age thinking." After all, it is understandable that some bureaucrats would invent words and phrases that would make simple jobs seem complex. By doing this, they attempt to seem indispensable or seem important when they may be unimportant.

But what we see in the "New Age" is often mindlessness for the sake of mindlessness. Nouns are promiscuously turned into verbs (language becomes "languaging"), eliminating the real verbs, which define the action. Passivity takes on a new prominence ("I am angry" becomes "I *have* anger"). This defines people as being acted upon rather than acting.

Sometimes many of these people attempt to be "channels for their experiences." (Sounds important, doesn't it?) Whether the experience is spiritual, emotional, psychological, or psychic, channelers act as passive receiving stations, relating what is "coming through them" without the filter of individual personality or opinion.

One of the words outlawed by New Age Newspeak is *judgment*. It is correct New Age form to avoid judgment at all costs. It's not uncommon for people to say in an apologetic tone of voice, "I have judgments." Translation: The individual in question has created an opinion. The opinion is critical of something or someone else. It is not permissible to have a critical opinion, and so this person is being self-critical for being so unenlightened. Saying "I *have* judgments" (vs. "I have made a critical judgment") suggests that it is truly not the person's fault. These opinions simply showed up, in defiance of the person's real wishes, which is to have no judgments or no critical opinions.

This is reminiscent of a similar accusation heard in the late fifties and early sixties by what were then known as pseudointellectuals: "That is a value judgment!" Value judgment was the no-no of those times. Those guilty of such a transgression had committed an intellectual faux pas.

Individuals who uphold these mottoes can have no sense of humor, and certainly no sense of irony. Isn't it a value judgment that value judgments are no good? Isn't it a judgment that it is wrong to have an opinion, particularly if the opinion is unfavorable? And what about truth? If you have an opinion, you have an opinion. No amount of couching it in vagueness changes this simple fact. People have opinions, whether or not they want to have them.

Moreover, in New Age Newspeak, people indiscriminately mix meanings. For example, there is a profound difference between judgment and prejudgment. Many people use these words interchangeably. But to judge is to form opinions *after* observing reality. Prejudice is to form an opinion *before* observing reality. Prejudice is the kind of bias that makes real judgment difficult.

In an age in which critical judgment is not encouraged, critical judgment is not well thought out. People who are not fluent in forming their own opinions often substitute vague impressions for considered thought, further obscuring distinctions that can help in forming opinions.

In Dashiell Hammett's *The Maltese Falcon*, the antagonist Kasper Gutman (played by Sidney Greenstreet in the film version) asks the protagonist Sam Spade (played by Humphrey Bogart in the film version) if he is a close-mouthed man. Spade shakes his head. "I like to talk," Spade answers. Gutman is pleased. "I distrust a close-mouthed man. He generally picks the wrong time to talk and says the wrong things." Gutman observes, "Talking's something you can't do judiciously unless you keep in practice."

The same can be said of critical judgment. Good judgment takes practice. Judgment should be encouraged, not discouraged. When we see how little of this is taught to our children, can it be any wonder they can have such poor judgment in the area of drugs, sex, direction, values, and life purpose?

In the arts, critical judgment is a necessary prerequisite. Artists, whether in the visual arts, music, film, dance, or sculpture, must learn to make critical judgments: how large to draw the nose, how loud to make the chord, how high to leap through the air.

When you are creating, you need to make judgments about the current status of the creative process. How close are you to the result you are creating? Are the actions you are taking working or not working? Is the current state of your creation good or bad?

It is difficult to know where you stand in life, what matters to you, and what you live for when you do not make distinctions. When you avoid distinctions, everything takes on a glow of arbitrariness. Nothing seems to matter when everything has equal value.

One important basic lesson in drawing classes in art schools throughout the world is *value studies*. The art student creates a drawing in which some objects are darker than others. The difference in relative darkness or lightness defines the space of the objects that are drawn and creates a three-dimensional impression on a two-dimensional surface. The relationship of dark to light is called the value.

There is a lesson here for all of us. We decide what values in our lives will be more prominent or less prominent. We create the hierarchy. We determine how we will and will not direct our life energy.

Those who have adopted a policy of avoiding critical judgment, however, will find it hard to forge what they want into a specific direction. It's not that these people don't deeply care about what they want in their lives. It is only that they will have enormous trouble creating it.

A few years ago I gave a friend of mine several books containing interviews of artists. He was amazed at how opinionated these people were. He had come from an academic background in which one never had a strong opinion, or at least never expressed one's opinions as if they were strongly held. He had earned his Ph.D., in part, by learning never to come down definitively on any side of an issue. But here were artists from different historical periods freely expressing what they thought, never hedging their bets. Is this simply an occupational difference?

For artists to reach the heights of artistic expression, they cannot hedge their bets. In the tradition of the arts, not only do judgments need to be made, they must also be honestly expressed. Artists learn to be uncompromising with their vision and their view of reality. If they didn't, they would not be able to create real art.

When you practice and master critical judgment, you become more open to many viewpoints. In fact, when you have a firm foundation in forming your own opinions, it is useful to know how others consider an issue. Some people attempt to reject forming judgments with the misguided intention of being open to different points of view. But rather than openness, these people often impose a strict antijudgment dogma on others.

Seeking "Acknowledgment"

Many people in the reactive-responsive orientation seek "acknowledgment" or praise for the work that they do. They want validation to make them feel good about themselves and what they are doing. Their perception of success often depends on having other people approve of them. This is very different from the kind of acknowledgment we have been discussing. As Beethoven said,

> The world is a king, and, like a king, desires flattery in return for favor; but true art is selfish and perverse—it will not submit to the mold of flattery.

In the creative orientation what matters is not how you are doing but rather how close your vision—*what you want to create*—is to its final completion.

A thousand people could praise a result you had created, but if the result did not satisfy your vision, you would not be ready to acknowledge it as complete. On the other hand, a thousand people might condemn a result you had created, yet if you saw that it satisfied your vision, you would be fully ready to say, "It is done and complete."

Only you have the authority to recognize and confirm that a creation of yours is complete.

The Energy of Completion

When you bestow this acknowledgment on your creation, you enable the very special energy of completion to be released.

One function of this energy is to propel you toward the germination of a new creative cycle. Each time you complete an act of creation, you focus a life force. And since life begets life, this energy seeks to enlarge and expand its expression through new creation. In the stage of completion, your soul is ready for another act of creation.

Artist Laurie Zagon described her stage of completion this way:

> Excitement builds because my vision is appearing. At this point I accelerate the speed of my brushstrokes and assurances come over me, saying, "you've got it now!" The completion from there is easy. There may be minor adjustments,

but on the whole, I know in my gut that IT'S DONE.

In the past when a piece was done, I used to sit and look at it and take my time starting a new one. Over the past few years I have been painting more than ever, because at the moment of completion, I now grab the next blank canvas and scribble some brushstrokes on it to keep the momentum cooking. I have doubled my productivity over the past few years from this way of working.

Your life can be a series of creative acts that beget other creative acts.

Our Natural Instincts

Whenever I walk through any city, no matter what the crime rate or political corruption, no matter if overpopulation or environmental problems exist, I am struck by the fact that there is vastly more human energy being directed toward building our civilization than toward any other goal. Most of these creative acts and events do not make it to the news. Why? Because they are not news, any more than the trash being picked up properly is news, the electricity working as it should is news, or the newscast being broadcast when it is scheduled is news. But by watching TV news you can get a distorted view of reality. Mostly the news consists of reports about reactions, responses, and circumstances. For the newscaster's purpose, the more dramatic, the better.

We are creative beings. Our natural instincts, desires, and tendencies are toward creating. Our general aspirations as a species, including both Eastern and Western civilizations, are most naturally toward building, creating, constructing, inventing, forming, improving, structuring, and shaping that which we truly want. Our power to affect the world is now at its greatest point in the history of our planet. This power may be used in one of two ways. In the prophetic words of John F. Kennedy, from his inaugural address,

The times are different now, for man holds in his mortal hands the power to obliterate all forms of human misery and all forms of human life.

This power can neither be granted to us nor taken away. But we can take it from ourselves.

Human Destiny and Purpose

As an individual, only you can be the final authority on how you use—or fail to use—this power to create. Hence, your individual destiny is in your own hands.

No matter how difficult you may claim your circumstances are, there are individuals who have been in even more difficult circumstances and yet have created their lives in accordance with what truly mattered to them.

Christy Brown, a quadriplegic who could only move a few of his toes and his mouth, became a good painter and a great writer. Beethoven, perhaps the greatest composer, composed even after he was deaf. Leonardo da Vinci suffered all his life from dyslexia. Stephen Hawking, one of the twentieth century's foremost theoretical physicists, has had Lou Gehrig's disease for over twenty years. He weighs less than a hundred pounds, can barely move, and has lost the use of his vocal chords. Yet he is still doing some of the most important work ever done in his field. Earlier in this century, right-handed painter Daniel Urrabieta, known professionally as "La Vierge," suffered from severe cerebral apoplexy. He switched to painting with his left hand. He achieved such a high level of competence that he became a renowned illustrator of important French periodicals.

You are never the victim of your circumstances. These circumstances are simply part of the raw material of the creative process.

Learning to create is very natural. But since so little emphasis has been placed on creating as a way of life, few people in our society have mastered it. Even children have natural instincts and abilities to create, but these instincts are not often encouraged or developed.

When Mary Spaeth, the inventor of the tunable dye laser, was asked about her early creative process, she replied,

> People invent all the time. When I was a little kid,
> I used to re-cut cereal boxes. Whenever we bought
> cereal, I would carefully cut open the cereal box
> and cut little grooves, holes, and tucks so that I

could tuck the flap back in. Today, all cereal boxes come exactly that way. If I had only been smart enough when I was eight years old—I could have sold that idea to the cereal companies.

The instinct to create does not go away. It seeks expression. When you create, you align yourself with your most natural state of being. As a consequence, many of the difficulties of your life will either disappear or will no longer be important issues for you. This alignment with yourself will not come from attempting to "solve your problems" but from creating what most matters to you.

In the orientation of the creative, the physical, mental, emotional, and spiritual dimensions of your being realign themselves and work in harmony. Based on their realignment, the path of least resistance in your life will lead you toward fulfilling your deepest and most profound individual life purpose on this planet.

Transcendence

Signs of the Future, Signs of the Times

Many people nowadays think that the world is on the precipice of disaster. With nuclear weapons spreading to more and more countries, with ecological destabilization changing the balance of the planet, with growing extremism, with the AIDS epidemic, and with unsure world economy, they have a legitimate concern.

Somehow, though, I do not fear for our future. Maybe I am too naïve, or maybe I've acquired a degree of wisdom, or maybe both. I do not share the notion that we are on the verge of planetary self-destruction.

Haven't we been here before? The Dark Ages, the Black Plague, tyranny, oppression, slavery, exploitation, genocide, injustice, war, cruelty.

The difference between then and now is that *now* we can really do the planet in. One wrong finger on the button can send the world right down the tubes. It could happen, but I don't think it will.

One of the ironies about those who are most worried about the end of the world is that they still use the same type of reactive-responsive thinking that brought the world to this very situation. If *one* wrong finger can lead to doom, how can any action anyone takes lead to ultimate safety? Maybe it is a matter of statistical probability. The less potential danger, the less danger. This makes sense. But how did we get here? What kind of thinking and what kind of orientation led to this point in history? Can more of the same kind of orientation present less potential danger, no matter how many bombs there are or how many rain forests are demolished?

Two Streams

There are two direct streams in history. One is the story of a reactive-responsive world. Events that shaped the lives of people and civilization emanated from the existing circumstances. The other story is that of the builder, the explorer, and the creator. Events that shaped the times were based on a different aspect of humanity, that of the quest to build, create, and know what was around the next hill. This instinct has always been an important force.

These two streams have operated somewhat independently of each other. Sometimes they collide, and sometimes they collaborate. During times of war they have often done both.

In different ways these two streams have both been dominant. Even though there have been great wars, political shifts, intrigue, economic manipulation, and power wielding; building and creating have always been a dominant force in the development of civilization.

But perhaps, in spite of all our building, we are still in the Dark Ages. The majority of people are still raised to be reactive-responsive. Much of the political and educational thrust is still in support of reaction or response to prevailing circumstances.

After all, the people in the Dark Ages didn't know they were in the Dark Ages. They didn't say, "These are the Dark Ages. We will then have the Middle Ages, and then the Renaissance, and then the age of Enlightenment, and then the romantic period, and then the industrial age, and then the atomic age, the nuclear age, and the computer age." Instead they said to each other, "These are modern times. This is high tech!"

When we consider how much of the world still generates actions that are strategies of conflict manipulation, willpower manipulation, or staying within an area of tolerable conflict, we might even question the premise of progress itself. Do people make their most profound decisions any differently now than they did six centuries ago, or even twelve centuries ago? In spite of dramatic technological change, have we really advanced as human beings?

One Change

One change is in the relationship of power and the individual. There is a growing trend toward decentralization of power. More and more people have more and more resources available to them. This is not an age of great leaders. This is not even an age of groups, even though that had been the hope of many people in the sixties. The Age of Aquarius was thought to herald the loss of individual distinction and the emergence of a mass consciousness from the global village. But as the pendulum swung with historical oscillation, the group values of the idealistic sixties and early seventies gave way to the personal, self-centered values of the late seventies and early eighties. The hippies became yuppies. The left-leaning, politically conscious activists of the sixties became parents to a generation of conservative Republican children. Has the quest for democracy been lost in the shuffle of shifting party politics?

No, but democracy is not a political system, it is an ideal. The ideal, simply put, is the freedom of the individual. Once this ideal prevails, systems of government can then be designed and executed to organize society toward that end. When the individual is free, he or she might choose to join with other individuals for the common good, for amplification of common purpose, and for protection, development, and expansion of common desires. Out of freedom comes a natural desire for order.

The ideal of freedom had been seen as the province of government and politics. But this puts the focus on a system first. In this orientation, freedom must come *from* the system. Instead of a system created to support the ideal of freedom, the system must now generate the ideal of freedom. This is something a system can never be expected to do.

When a system (governmental, corporate, societal) loses its function to serve a result, it can only become self-serving. We elect legislators whose job it is to make laws. Every year more and more laws are created. Most of the old laws remain. This generates a need for more lawyers, "technocrats" of legality, but not champions of justice. The point of it all is lost when ideals such as freedom, justice, fairness, common good, and compassion can become only a matter for the bureaucrats to administer. Systems can run on automatic. Mindlessness sets in and fosters more mindlessness. The central seat of power has lost much of its credibility thanks to Vietnam, Watergate, and political hype. This change has been dramatic. We no longer look to government for a new deal, nor to explore new frontiers, nor to build the great societies. Most people no longer expect government or politicians to provide inspired leadership.

These days, with rare exception, politicians are often the last to catch up with the real leadership emerging from the grass roots. Politics has been left in the dust. This is one reason why there are so few truly exceptional people in politics and government. It simply isn't where the action is.

This is one reason that power has become decentralized. Decentralized power can create confusion in those who were used to centralized power, but not to their children.

Can there be freedom of the individual? When individuals are in structural conflict, their actions are governed by the tendencies of the structure. Are people really able to be free, no matter what the political opportunity?

Yes, if individuals have the ability to change the structure and if this change can come from their own hands. If people were simply mechanistic products of structure or conditioning or psychology, they could not be free. A small group of people are of this opinion, but they are not the artists of the world, who know the difference between choice, judgment, and consequence on the one hand, and predeterminism on the other.

Freedom of the individual can be supported by systems, but not created by systems. As Robert Frost said in the poem, "How Hard It Is to Keep From Being King When It's In You and In The Situation:"

> The reason artists show so little interest
> In public freedom is because the freedom
> They've come to feel the need of is a kind
> No one can give them—they can scarce attain—
> The freedom of their own material

The notion of freedom of choice, which is fundamental to the creative process, is a powerful democratizing force, particularly when democracy is considered more than simply a matter of politics. In fact, new forces of democracy are now on the scene, ones independent of politics in their origins, but that can have a profound impact on our political system.

What we are witness to is a real revolution.

The Real Revolution

At last the revolution has come, one in which more of the power ends up in the hands of "the people."

But this revolution has hardly been noticed by the politicos. They probably haven't been told yet. They still think that a change in governmental system or a change in political personalities will move the world and shake the foundation of the power structures. But they missed the action, because they were looking in the wrong place.

This revolution has come quietly and in the light of day. It has grown from a small seed to a mass civilizing force. It has changed the way people think, work, play, and relate. It has made resources available to more people than ever before. It has decentralized power. It has become a way of life for many people and will be a way of life for future generations.

This revolution is the personal computer.

The personal computer? A force of democracy?

Henry Ford foreshadowed this revolution in the first part of the century. Most of us can hardly imagine what the world was like before Ford. Ford made personal transportation available to the masses. Before that, only the rich were able to own automobiles. Ford changed first America and then the world. People suddenly had access to a much larger world than ever before in their lives. They could move out of the city. They could visit faraway places. They could be free from many of the previous limitations on their movements.

The present-day revolution was pioneered by Steven Jobs and the young men and women who worked with him to develop the Macintosh computer. They set out to invent a computer that would be easily accessible to a mass audience whose only exposure to computers was the dehumanizing experience of trying to straighten out inaccurate phone bills. Most of us come from an age in which the computer represented everything there was to despise in technology—an institutionalized bureaucratic mentality, amplified through the power of an anonymous machine that called the shots and turned people into numbers.

The Macintosh is more than just "user-friendly," it is a powerful creating machine. It communicates visually, leading to an ease in dimensional thinking, the ability to hold many types of information simultaneously. This computer helps people master the complex relationship of the parts to the whole. This is in sharp contrast to the typical IBM type of computer, which is a wonderful business machine, but linear in scope. The IBM is a magnificent adding machine that can handle repetitive tasks with tremendous efficiency. The Macintosh is an amplification and extension of the way people think during the creative process.

The Macintosh hardware begat software that was radically different from anything most people had access to before. These software programs enable the users to create animation, drafting, illustrations, music, typesetting, forms, reports, flight simulation, time management, project management, computer art, video games, and so on.

I was introduced to the "Mac" a few years ago. Until that time I had no experience in using a computer. A kind soul left a Mac and a music program in my hotel room where I was leading a workshop in Atlanta. He showed me a few of the basics and then left me and computer to fend for ourselves. At first I was intimidated. But the computer sensed my trepidations and put me at ease. After all, this was a computer of experience, practiced at dealing with the uninitiated. In about fifteen minutes I was composing four-part counterpoint on the little guy. And what do you know, it played back to me what I had written.

As soon as I got home from that trip, I went out and bought my first Macintosh. I later set up a complete electronic music MIDI (musical instrument digital interface) studio in my home. Years ago people thought of electronic music as limited to so many beeps and boops, and they were right. But the new technology has changed that too. Today most film scores are created on computers and electronic instruments that are as soulful and funky as the music on *Miami Vice*.

At DMA we have two kinds of computers, the IBM type, which are our business machines (accounting, mailing lists, and so on), and Macintosh, which are our creating machines (writing, artwork, course development, illustrations, video imaging, editing, and desk-top publishing). We are typical of companies, large and small, that have come to rely on computers, as we had relied on typewriters and copiers in the past. In the last few years more people have had more resources available to them as a result of the new technology.

Computers have become an important democratizing force. On a recent plane trip from Los Angeles to Boston, I sat next to a man who is one of the pioneers in pattern recognition, which is used in many of today's most advanced computer systems and is the basis of much of the research in artificial intelligence. We discussed the advancement of computer technology in the West and in the East. I had just seen a fascinating television program on computers in the Soviet Union, where there seems to be an official hesitation to the use of personal computers, even for students. Consequently, most of the Soviet people are computer-illiterate. "Why," I asked my fellow passenger, "do the Soviets lag behind in this important area?"

"They know the power of the computer," he said, "and they are not ready to make that power available to the masses. This would create a degree of freedom that would threaten their system to the core."

Ivan, my fourteen-year-old son, recently connected a modem to his Commodore 64 computer. By calling a local phone number, he can talk to people from all over the country. Suddenly his room transforms into a network for national communication. He plays games, has conversations, shares jokes, flirts with fifteen-year-old girls, meets pen pals, and develops relationships with people from all over America. His worldview is growing as the world opens up to him from the familiar comforts of his bedroom.

What does it all mean? The world is changing. Technology, which had once been viewed as disempowering, has another face—the face of a brilliant, energetic, and capable ally on the pioneering journey from aspiration to creation. What we have seen so far is just a glimpse of new sources of creativity that our children will have the privilege of taking for granted.

One of the benefits of the personal-computer trend is that you can do more with less. This is the height of an economy of means. Computers are coming down in price, growing in memory and computing power, more able to do complicated tasks, and more able to connect with other computers. The software is also able to connect with other computers. The software is also experiencing revolution and evolution as new generations of programs push the frontier even further.

One of the major differences between the technological age and the industrial age is the location of power. In the industrial age power was located in the hands of a few. Many people had to organize their lives to accommodate industry. People lived near where they worked. The local economy was fed from the work base, and complex, intricate relationships arose between the work force, the management, the local store keepers, the services from government, and national and international economic trends.

In the new technological age, power lies in more and more hands. This leads to more and more choice. Where to work, how to work, where to live, how to educate our children, how to organize our communities.

I do not see the computer as the savior of the ages, as it may seem from my enthusiasm. It could be a dead end or, in the last analysis, irrelevant. If this were the only factor in these times, we would have less reason to think of the computer as a civilizing force. But there are other forces that are in play.

Another Force

What might have had the power to change the People's Republic of China from one of the most oppressive communist states twenty short years ago into an interesting example of the growing trend toward more and more personal freedom? The success of Japan. As the Japanese have become a major economic force, they have proven to China the power of free enterprise. Free enterprise, by itself, is only an economic system. But free enterprise leads to a demand for other kinds of freedom. Experiments in degrees of free enterprise are beginning to be conducted all over the communist world, with a growing demand for freedom of speech, freedom of the press, freedom of religion, and freedom of thought. Even in countries that have a population that has known only communism its whole life, the instinctive desire for freedom remains. In Asia, Japan is now the dominant influence as other Asian countries, even behind what was once called the bamboo curtain, begin to experiment with free enterprise and other forms of freedom. This trend was not predicted or imagined by the architects of American foreign policy for most of the post-war period.

China has had a long tradition of free enterprise, a tradition personified by the astute and hard-working Chinese immigrants who have channeled their energies into business throughout the world. But the majority of the vast population of China today has known only communism and the communist system.

Mao Tse-tung was a master of political revolution. In 1949, the destiny of China seemed to be set for the conceivable future. The threat from China, as we were taught in school, was for all of Asia to succumb to Maoist doctrine. This was the famous domino theory. If China went communist, Indo-China would go communist. If Indo-China went communist (the rice bowl of Asia), India would go communist. Korea, then Laos, Vietnam, Cambodia, and Thailand would fall. Then the Philippines and India. Then maybe even Japan and Australia. This is a theory over which many innocent lives were lost. Lost in vain, it just might turn out. This makes the tragedy worse.

Although Mao knew how to throw a revolution, he did not know how to govern the world's largest population. He tried to instill the people with his political values, but he was losing ground. So he did an interesting thing. He held another revolution in the country he had won. The Cultural Revolution was vintage Mao: Rid the country of all the artists, teachers, thinkers, and intellectuals. Make them become peasants, so that they will understand the major difference between Marxism and Maoism, the values of the "workers" versus the values of the "peasants." In some ways, the Cultural Revolution was more dramatic and more frightening than the first Chinese revolution.

Before there were two sides. The Chiang Kai-shek dictatorship on the one hand and Mao on the other. For most Chinese, there wasn't much of a choice between the nationalists and the communists.

The Cultural Revolution did not have a Chiang Kai-shek type of villain to oppose. Chiang made a perfect symbol of what the first revolution was supposed to be about. Turning him out of power could be seen as some form of progress. But, less than twenty years later, in 1966, no one could serve as such a perfect symbol.

The new enemy became individualism, and individualism was made synonymous with decadence. The revolution rose to high pitch against anything defined as decadent, anything differing from so-called peasant values.

Compare then and now. Recently I saw a television program on modern China. Free enterprise is a growing trend, particularly among the "peasants." "Decadence" is everywhere in the form of stereos from Japan and blue jeans copied from America. The young people are listening to American and English rock 'n' roll. They wear their hair in Western fashion. They have small businesses and money to spend. Could this be the final result of the Cultural Revolution? Rock and jeans, entrepreneurs and stereos? Mao must be rolling in his grave.

One young Chinese interviewed on the program was talking about his new radio and his love of rock music. "What would Mao have thought of all of this?" he was asked. "Who?" he replied. "Mao Tse-tung," the interviewer said. "Oh," the young man said thoughtfully, "I wouldn't know."

Of course there are many factors that have led to the changes in China. But I think the Japanese example of the success of free enterprise has been the crucial factor. If Japan can create the degree of success they have, all of Asia, including China, must take particular notice.

A Legacy

When I was in my late teens, John Kennedy became president of the United States. It is easy to forget what was really going on from 1960 to 1963 in America. Much has happened to dull the memory and overlook the real legacy of Kennedy, which has been greatly misunderstood by most historians, journalists, and biographers. They focus on the events of that era and try to evaluate the political accomplishments in a narrow framework. They do not understand that Kennedy's true legacy was a spirit, that of reaching for what is highest in humanity. This spirit cannot be explained by events and accomplishments, just as it is impossible to explain the influence of Elvis Presley on the history of rock 'n' roll simply by listing his record and television appearances.

Kennedy told the nation,

> I believe the times demand invention, innovation, imagination, decision. I am asking each of you to be new pioneers of that New Frontier. My call is to the young in heart, regardless of age—to the stout in spirit, regardless of party—to all who respond to the scriptural call: "Be strong and of a good courage; be not afraid, neither be thou dismayed."

The assassination of JFK was one of the greatest shocks the country and the world had experienced in the post-war era. This bright flame of hope, purpose, and adventure had suddenly been snuffed out. In Madrid, in 1970, I was talking to an Italian filmmaker. "I miss Kennedy like I miss my own mother," he said. The pain of the assassination was too great for a world that loved him. As Lyndon Johnson led the country further into Vietnam, in the name of the Kennedy legacy, the youth of America knew that the world had reverted back to stupid men in positions of power. If anything could have had the ability to end the fresh new beginning of the Kennedy vision of exploration, building, and creating, it was the contrast between the two presidents, a contrast that created the deepest discouragement and led to the deepest disappointment imaginable in almost everyone I knew. But discouragement is also a force. It can take naïve and convenient idealism and re-form it into permanent resolution.

Kennedy has been trivialized, particularly by the media, as a man of style, a man of charisma, a handsome young pretender to power. Part of this trivialization is the result of politicians trying to imitate some of the style and mannerisms of Kennedy, and reporters more than happy to make the comparison. Many of the post-Kennedy politicians remind me of the difference between Elvis and Elvis impersonators. Many reporters, like many music critics, just don't seem to know the difference between the real thing and the imitation. They miss the substance. It was more than style and charisma and Camelot.

Kennedy told the world,

> So we are all idealists. We are all visionairies. Let it not be said of this Atlantic generation that we left ideals and visions to the past, nor purpose and determination to our adversaries. We have come too far, we have sacrificed too much, to disdain the future now. And we shall ever remember what Goethe told us, that the "highest wisdom, the best that mankind ever knew" was the realization that "he only earns his freedom and existence who daily conquers them anew."

When Kennedy expressed his hope for the world, young Americans were listening. He was able to capture the imagination of a deep latent altruism in the American psyche, that of the strongest country in the history of the world using its power to build, explore, and create. I remember going to school just after he had formed the Peace Corps. One of the biggest boys in the class, who had a well-deserved reputation for being the class clown, seemed completely changed. "What's going on with you?" we asked him. "I've just joined the Peace Corps," he said quietly.

First, after Kennedy's physical assassination, and then with his subsequent character assassinations, people have tried to find a way of dealing with disappointment, grief, pain, lost innocence, and lost hope. And yet, somewhere in our being, somewhere in that place that is highest in us, we have not forgotten a simple truth: that our destiny is in our own hands. That we want that which is highest in civilization. That we care about the planet and care about our children's future. Those who were inspired by these ideals are now moving into positions of power. These ideals are finding new expressions, purpose, and action.

The politics of the Kennedy era are over. The pain is growing dim. New generations have never had the experience, no matter how brief, of standing poised in the doorway of destiny. Public expressions of altruism are unpopular now. No one wants to "be had" or feel the pain that many people experienced from their involvement and subsequent loss of Kennedy. But the real legacy of the Kennedy era is a spark lying dormant that is still a profound force to be reckoned with.

Because Kennedy was a leader in the stream of history of explorers, builders, and creators, his legacy is not political. It is orientational. Even the intervening reactive-responsive stream of history since his death cannot defeat the power of his vision—a world that joins together in the business of creating a new civilization. Kennedy articulated the orientation of the creative when he said,

> When power leads man toward arrogance, poetry reminds him of his limitations. When power narrows the areas of man's concern, poetry reminds him of the richness and diversity of his experience. When power corrupts, poetry cleanses. For art establishes the basic human truths which must serve as the touchstone of our judgment. The artist, faithful to his personal vision of reality, becomes the last champion of the individual mind and sensibility against an intrusive society and an offensive state.

For a moment in time, government and the creative orientation were joined, and then it passed. But the effect has not been lost.

A Civilization of Creators

Just as the computer is a democratizing force, so is the technology of the creative process. In a similar way the creative process has vast implications for forming a new world. In the past centuries only a small percentage of the population knew how to create, and those who had mastered the creative process most often did not apply creating generally to all of their lives, but to only their field of focus. Usually this was music, painting, writing, dance, science, invention, architecture, and so on.

When you consider how inexperienced the world is in the creative process, it is amazing that we have done as well as we have.

Five hundred years ago, most people on this planet were illiterate. Today if you go on a job interview, it is assumed that you can read and write. Someday it will be just as common for people to be literate in the creative process. When you go on a job interview, you will not be asked, "Do you know how to create?" It will be assumed that you do. Creating can become as common as literacy, or fluency in using a computer.

The creative process, in the hands of more and more people, is an incredible civilizing force. What kind of world might it be when, as part of the normal educational process, students learn how to create what they want. This force can be more powerful than any bomb, more powerful than any political movement.

As we move toward the twenty-first century, great changes in the very nature of our civilization are taking place, with implications for every individual on the planet. With any turn of a century, it is common for new possibilities to emerge, new approaches to become common practice, new philosophies of living to become popular, and new qualities of leadership to help give birth to a new world.

We are already beginning to see signs of the twenty-first century arise as crocuses do in the spring, pushing their way through the hardened earth and up through layers upon layers of dead leaves. At first this growth seems small and insignificant compared with what appears to be a hostile and incompatible environment, and yet in a matter of weeks all of nature seems to have converted to the wonder of growth, change, and new life prophesied by the crocuses.

As we observe our times, radically new developments in support of that which is truly highest in the human spirit are beginning to sprout. At first they seem insignificant in light of a hard, bitter, and indifferent world entrenched in the ways of the past. And yet we can also observe the ground beginning to yield to the innate power and life-giving force of these new developments, which are both signs of the future and signs of the times.

The Power
of Transcendence

The Determining Factor

Many people feel trapped by their past. They think they are doomed by events that took place in the earliest stages of their childhood.

Some people imagine that the birth experience was so traumatic that it completely determined the course of their life; for them, the biggest problem they have is that they were born.

Some believe they are victims of their conditioning or how their parents treated them; they see this as the predominant determining factor in the life they now lead.

There are those who believe they are extensions of their genes and that what primarily determines their life experiences is their genetic code.

Others assign the determining factor of their lives to their astrological makeup or to their numerology.

Still others attribute the determining factor of their lives to their social, ethnic, or racial background.

Some say it is their gender that mostly determines their fate.

There are many theories, built primarily on the assumptions of the reactive-responsive orientation, that promote the idea that you are for the most part fixed in your life pattern and that you can only make changes—if changes are at all possible—by somehow dealing with the predetermined nature you carry within you.

Different theories suggest dealing with the determining factor by understanding it, overpowering it, denying it, manipulating it, experiencing it, accepting it, repressing it, surrendering to it, dialoguing with it, appeasing it, or integrating it.

Those in the reactive-responsive orientation find this notion of "determining factors" appealing, because it attributes causality to circumstances beyond their direct control.

When you shift to the orientation of the creative, you begin to move along the path of mastering causality. You become the predominant causal force in your life, which is a natural and desirable situation.

This shift is made by evoking senior forces, such as fundamental choice, primary and secondary choices, structural tension, aspiration to your true values, and being true to yourself.

These senior forces always take priority over lesser forces, such as willpower manipulation, conflict manipulation, and structural conflict.

There is another force inherent in the orientation of the creative that is senior even to mastering causality. This senior force I call *transcendence*.

Transcendence

Transcendence is the power to be born anew, to make a fresh start, to turn over a new leaf, to begin with a clean slate, to enter into a state of grace, to have a second chance.

Transcendence makes no reference to the past, whether your past has been overflowing with victories or filled with defeats. When you enter a state of transcendence, you are able to create a new life, unburdened by both the victories and the defeats of the past.

Transcendence is more than just the accurate realization that the past is over. *It is also a realignment of all dimensions of yourself with the very source of your life.*

The story of Charles Dickens's character Scrooge in *A Christmas Carol* epitomizes the power of transcendence. Guided by the Christmas Spirits, Scrooge was able to see his past, his present, and his probable future, and he was then given a second chance at life. When Scrooge awoke on Christmas morning, the very fact that he was still alive was the gift that provided new possibilities—including a new way of living that, up to that point in the story, had seemed improbable and even impossible.

Another major character in the story is Tiny Tim, the lame and sickly yet uncommonly wise child who symbolizes natural human goodness. Scrooge developed a special relationship with Tiny Tim during the night with the Spirits. When Scrooge asked the Spirit of Christmas Present whether Tiny Tim would survive, the Spirit replied, "If these shadows remain unaltered, I see a vacant chair beside the hearth and a crutch without an owner, carefully preserved."

Scrooge's reaching out to Tiny Tim and Tiny Tim's reaching out to Scrooge were catalysts in Scrooge's transcendence. In fact, by his transcendence, he was able to save Tiny Tim's life just as Tiny Tim was able to save Scrooge's life. Scrooge was able to redeem himself through his relationship to an innate love of the natural human goodness as symbolized by Tiny Tim.

When you reestablish your relationship to your natural goodness, you give a new life to what is highest in you.

From the moment he awoke on that Christmas morning through the rest of his life, Scrooge was truly changed. The change was not merely a superficial change in behavior. Rather it was a change in his entire life orientation. Scrooge realized the preciousness of each moment and his ability to aspire to the greatest good in each moment.

Had Scrooge merely had a "peak experience," he would have experienced no fundamental change in orientation. Although a peak experience might have temporarily changed his behavior, in time he would have reverted to his old, miserly ways.

Because Scrooge's change was orientational, he was fundamentally a new person, as if he had been born anew. From that point on, his past was irrelevant, and the nature of his change filled each subsequent day of his life.

Not all changes of orientation, even desirable ones, contain the power of transcendence. It is possible for you to have a change of orientation and still continue to exist in a linear, cause-and-effect system. Transcendence operates outside such a system. Transcendence evokes the power to start from scratch, outside the realm where previous causal actions are in play. Because transcendence is an ever-new state of being, once you enter into it, each new moment is alive with fresh possibilities—possibilities that may never have seemed possible before.

Transcendence and the Creative Act

Through the creative act you reach beyond yourself, beyond your identity, and beyond your own life, because you are working with two kinds of laws: the law of *cause and effect* and the law of *transcendence.*

First, when you create, you increase your ability to use causes to produce effects. (Cause and effect is sometimes called the "law of karma.") But this law is not the senior force in the creative process.

Second, beyond the time-space continuum and beyond its causal aspects, when you create, you are experiencing the law of transcendence. In this realm past causal factors are not in play. When you turn to a new canvas or initiate any act of creation, at that moment the past is literally over. As you stand poised before the blank sheet of music paper or the uncut piece of marble, the new moment yields new possibilities beyond anything you might ever have imagined before.

As a creator, past cause and effect are no longer dominant factors. You are in a state of transcendence, for in that moment *anything* can happen. You are not trapped by previous actions you have taken. You are not forced to extricate yourself from unwanted situations.

The past, of course, has its function in the orientation of the creative. It supports you in learning how to master cause and effect, which is an important aspect of the creative process, because what you are able to do with a period of transcendence is create new cause and effect. Your years spent in school or in other learning situations in no way limit the visions you can conceive and the results you can create. The past simply and only *helps* you.

In the creative orientation, mastering the law of cause and effect supports the experience of transcendence. It prepares you adequately to bring into reality the transcendent experience.

Through the creative act you bring into reality the play of your own *life force*.

To talk about transcendence by saying, "I am nothing but a channel" or "I am nothing but a tool of God's will," is a misunderstanding of the relationship between you and that special moment focused through you as creator. The notion that human action is inessential in the creative process distorts the power, beauty, and unique preciousness of the individuality of the human spirit.

Without human choice and action, many magnificent results would never have been produced. When Beethoven created his symphonies, he may have been influenced by his higher intuitive perception, *but it took Beethoven to compose this music. This was Beethoven's creation, and this music did not exist before Beethoven wrote it.*

By your presence on this planet, you make possible creations that would otherwise not be possible. They become possible because they come from your concept, from what you have learned, from your experiments, from your historical past, and from what you can aspire to.

I can't think of anything more divine than the creative act. All the myriad dimensions in which you exist converge in a single extended instant during the creative process.

The Prodigal Son

Another story that exquisitely illustrates the principle of transcendence is the parable of the prodigal son.

In this story there was a father who had two sons. One of his sons left home and went astray, while the other was a "good boy," who stayed at home and worked with his father.

One day the prodigal son remembered his home and decided to return to his father without any expectations of what might happen to him or how he would be received.

When he arrived home, his father, who had thought the boy was dead, was so overjoyed to discover his son alive that he celebrated the homecoming with great festivity. Not only did the father accept the prodigal back with all the rights of a full son, but he celebrated his love for his son far more than if he had never left at all.

The "good" son, who had remained at home all these years, was outraged at the father's acceptance and rejoicing over the prodigal. When the "good" son came to the father to protest what he was doing, the father tried to explain his actions by saying, "You see, I thought he was dead ... but he's alive. I thought he was dead, but he lives."

The father and his two sons represent three separate and distinct aspects of yourself. The father represents the source of your life; the good son is the part of you that has been aligned to that source; and the prodigal son is the part of you that has become misaligned with your source, the part of you that has gone astray from being true to yourself and true to what is highest in you.

There is a point at which the prodigal, reactive, and rebellious part of you remembers your source and desires to return to it, as did the prodigal son in the parable.

Furthermore, as in the story, your source longs to be reunited with all of you and reaches out to you, as the father reached out to receive the prodigal.

But the "good" part of you—the part of you that has tried through the years to respond appropriately, to be true to yourself, and to do the right things—rejects the reunion of all the parts of yourself.

It is not the prodigal aspects of yourself that deny your full integration, but the part of you that has been responsive, the part of you that has tried to be a good person.

Most people assume that it is their prodigal side—their indiscretions, failings, compromises, lies, dishonesty, opportunistic behavior, selfishness, hatreds, prejudices, jealousies, pettiness, greed, egotism, laziness, destructiveness, negativity, and rebelliousness—that keeps them from reuniting with what is highest in them, their source.

On the contrary, the immediate natural tendency of the prodigal part of yourself is to want to return "home" to your source and be realigned with it.

It is not your prodigal side that prevents you from forgiving yourself but the "good," responsive part of you that rejects your innately strong longing to be one with yourself.

When the prodigal son remembered that he could return home, he did so without any expectations—unconditionally.

When you awaken to your deepest longing to be whole, you

return to wholeness without making demands, without setting up expectations, without establishing any conditions. Similarly, as the father rejoiced over the return of his prodigal son, so your source welcomes you home without conditions, tests of sincerity, expectations of contrition, explanations, or repayment.

This unconditional love that the father (source) has and his great longing for your return is the very power that enables transcendence to occur. "I thought he was dead . . . and I find he's alive."

One-Way Bargains

In order to have the return of the prodigal complete and whole, the two sons needed to reconcile. However, there was a twist in the story. In the beginning of the parable the father and the son who stayed at home were aligned whereas the prodigal son was misaligned. When the prodigal returned home, however, he and his father became aligned, but the good son became misaligned. How did this change come about?

The good son had made what may be called a "one-way bargain" with the father. In a typically reactive-responsive way, he assumed that if he did all of the "right things" and adhered to the "right standards" and followed the "right precepts," he would be rewarded by his father. He was shocked to see his brother, who had not followed the "right path," being welcomed, honored, and celebrated.

Many people make similar one-way bargains. Typically in this unilateral bargain, one person assumes that if he or she follows certain practices, others (or perhaps even the universe itself) must reciprocate in some way.

In a one-way bargain the other party never really agrees to the bargain and often does not even know of it.

A classic example of a one-way bargain is found in the early stages of many relationships, when one person unilaterally decides not to date any other people, with the implicit demand that the other person in the relationship do likewise. This is a one-way bargain if the other person never makes that agreement.

There are those who attempt to live "good" lives as a one-way bargain with the universe. They decide that if they are "good," the universe must reciprocate and be good to them. The trouble is, the universe did not make that agreement with them.

In the parable of the prodigal son, the good son's actions were part of a one-way bargain, tied to the rewards he expected from his father. But that was not an agreement the father had made with him.

If the good son had been righteous because he wanted to be, rather than for the reward he expected from his father, his actions would have been their own reward. The parable implies, however, that the good son was good for an ulterior motive. *In a typically reactive-responsive way, the good son did what he thought he had to do, not what he truly wanted to do.*

The part of you that created one-way bargains with yourself is like the good son. If you find it difficult to forgive yourself for not having been true to yourself in the past, one reason might be because you have made such a bargain.

Being Perfect

Many people demand perfection of themselves and others. But we exist in an imperfect reality in which, ironically, the only perfection that can be found is in its imperfection.

Viktor Frankl points out in *Man's Search for Meaning* that the saints did not reach sainthood by trying to be perfect.

Many of the people I see in workshops begin with the notion that they have to be perfect. They then blame themselves for being imperfect and refuse to forgive themselves for their many "transgressions."

No one can forgive you but yourself—including forgiving the "good" part of you that has sought perfection and made it hard to forgive yourself until now.

When you come home to yourself without expectations, demands, ulterior motives, or one-way bargains, a fundamental change in the underlying structure of your life takes place. Its path of least resistance now leads you into a state of transcendence, in which total integration of your life cannot but occur.

While the goal of responsiveness in the reactive-responsive orientation is an impossible-to-reach perfection, the natural tendency in the orientation of the creative is transcendence.

The Power of the Source, the Power of the Primal Self

What enables transcendence to supersede the power of cause and effect is that in the structural play of forces, transcendence is a senior force and, like all senior forces, takes priority over lower forces.

Nothing is more powerful than the very source of life itself.

Your life source strives for expression through you. This is analogous to the great power of the unconditional love that the father had for both the prodigal son and the good son. The natural tendency of this power is to be fully expressed, so the longing of the father in the parable is the longing of unconditional love for its fullest expression. Since this love is unconditional, it demands nothing in return.

At the same time your primal self has the longing to be reunited with its source, as the prodigal longed to return home. "Primal," as I use the word, refers not to the needy, selfish, pained, angry, sexual, or infantile characteristics that are ascribed to it in some psychological systems; I use the word, rather, as the Kabbalists use it, to describe the "primal will to good." Primal, in this context, refers to the deepest longings of human nature to reunite with its life source.

Sometimes this longing is called the soul urge, because it exists at a level deeper than your psychological makeup, deeper than your conscious thoughts, deeper than your intuitive perceptions, and deeper even than the structures that are predominantly in play in your life. Saint Augustine referred to this longing when he observed, "Our hearts are restless until they rest in thee."

Transcendent Structure

The relationship of attraction between these two forces—the source and the primal self—is itself structural in nature and generates a path of least resistance that leads these two forces to reunite.

Since neither of these forces is time-dependent, their integration can happen at any moment, even at moments that, logically, would seem incongruous.

In the structure of cause and effect, which gives rise to events sequentially related to other events, it seems that the only possible step each new action can lead to is the next action in the cause-and-effect sequence. It therefore seems impossible for a change to occur that is unrelated to what already exists in the cause-and-effect chain.

And yet, as if miraculously and independently of normal causality, you can transcend your circumstances, your history, and the dominant structures that have been in play in your life, as well as every other aspect of your past and present.

You can come home to yourself.

Transcendence in Civilization

Transcendence is not merely a personal principle; it can occur in civilization as a whole.

When we consider the causal forces at work in history, we might conclude that at present our civilization has a probable future of destruction, decay, and disintegration. However, in each individual on this planet there is the deepest longing to reunite with what is highest in him or her. Thus, transcendence for the planet as a whole becomes more and more possible as the individuals who make up civilization shift from a reactive-responsive orientation to the orientation of the creative, in which transcendence becomes the norm.

During its history our planet has been characterized mostly by reactive-responsive people acting within the framework of structural conflict and being led through the path of least resistance from circumstance to circumstance, mostly driven by those circumstances and hardly ever having a real vision of what they truly wanted to create.

But at this moment in our history, a new door is opening into an era motivated by vision, energized by aspiration, rooted in current reality, forged by each creative act, and leading to a transcendence of civilization as a whole.

As people learn to master their own creative process, they have the potential to be the predominant creative forces in their own lives.

In organizations, as people become fluent in creating and put that fluency to use in the service of what they most deeply want and love, a new breed of leaders will begin to emerge, leaders as creators, transforming the meaning of the relationship of the individual to all of human endeavor and building a civilization unlike any before.

When historian Theodore White was asked what he thought was the force with the most power to shape history, he said, "The idea."

The idea that is currently in the air, the insight that is ripe, the principle that is the most powerful catalyst of our age is that each individual can be the predominant creative force in his or her own life.

Once you have discovered this principle for yourself, there is no turning back. Your life will be changed forever.

We hope you have enjoyed this book and have found the concepts and principles of value.

If you would like more information about the TECHNOLOGIES FOR CREATING® curriculum and the courses, programs, products, and consulting services offered by DMA, Inc., you may reach us at:

TECHNOLOGIES FOR CREATING®
DMA, Inc.
27 Congress Street
Salem, Massachusetts 01970
(508) 741-0780 or
1-800-722-1661 toll-free (outside Massachusetts)

Thank you for your interest.

About the Author

Robert Fritz is the founder of DMA and the developer of the TECHNOLOGIES FOR CREATING® curriculum. He lives in Pride's Crossing, Massachusetts.